To our Men

Who in this, as in all other units,
bore the full fury and sacrifice of War,
this book is dedicated.

The History
of the
33rd DIVISIONAL ARTILLERY
in the War
1914–1918.

By

J. MACARTNEY-FILGATE,
Late Major R.F.A. [S.R.]

With a Foreword by
GENERAL LORD HORNE
G.C.B., K.C.M.G., A.D.C.

The Naval & Military Press Ltd

published in association with

FIREPOWER
The Royal Artillery Museum
Woolwich

Published by
The Naval & Military Press Ltd
Unit 10 Ridgewood Industrial Park,
Uckfield, East Sussex,
TN22 5QE England
Tel: +44 (0) 1825 749494
Fax: +44 (0) 1825 765701
www.naval–military-press.com

in association with

FIREPOWER
The Royal Artillery Museum, Woolwich
www.firepower.org.uk

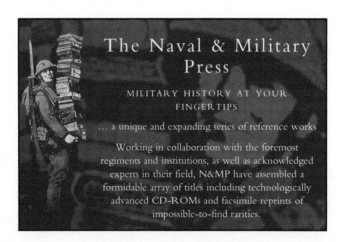

*In reprinting in facsimile from the original, any imperfections are inevitably reproduced
and the quality may fall short of modern type and cartographic standards.*

Printed and bound by Antony Rowe Ltd, Eastbourne

FOREWORD.

"YET the record of their actions is their best memorial." Field-Marshal Earl Haig wrote the above words in his foreword to the Royal Artillery War Commemoration Book. When it is recalled that during the Great War some three-quarters of a million of men fought guns of all calibres in every quarter of the globe, it may be realised that to write the history of the part taken by the Royal Regiment of Artillery as a whole must prove an impossible task.

All the more important therefore that each unit should take steps to place on record its own doings.

The 33rd Divisional Artillery fought in many important battles and engagements, and always fought with distinction and with the devotion worthy of the tradition of the Royal Regiment. This record bears witness of the high stage of efficiency attained by the Brigades and Batteries of the New Army, and we may say with our great Commander-in-Chief " The record of their actions is their best memorial."

HORNE OF STIRKOKE,
General.

H.Q., EASTERN COMMAND.
   May 31st, 1921.

CONTENTS.

LIST OF MAPS.

INTRODUCTION.

To write the history of a unit in the war must, even to the most able pen, prove a mighty task, for it is not given to many to be able in words to describe deeds greater almost than human intellect can grasp. But when the task falls to the lot of one who, himself neither author nor historian, can claim as a sole reason the fact that it was his humble privilege to serve with the unit in question, the work becomes doubly and trebly difficult. In a book of this nature it is probably desirable that personal experience should have preference to powers of rhetoric, and a knowledge of facts to fluency with the pen, and for this reason, after much hesitation, the work was undertaken. No skilful framing of words can portray in any way adequately a war history ; far better is it that in simple language should be recounted the story of the batteries, so that each man may judge of it according to his lights.

This History has been written primarily as a permanent record for all those who served with the 33rd Divisional Artillery, a record which they may keep for the benefit of themselves and their descendants when, in years to come, the intervening space becomes blurred by the mist of forgetfulness, and the story of those mighty days in France lies in danger of being relegated to the shadowy past. Secondly, it has been published in order that all those who were in any way connected with the gunners of this Division may learn something of their doings in France, may gain a little insight into the daily lives of those whose deeds they can but dimly comprehend. Moreover, although many regimental histories have already been published, this is one of the first to devote itself to the doings of a Divisional Artillery, and, throwing much light as it does upon the daily life of a field gunner in France, it must be of considerable interest to all those who wish to know something of the work of an artillery unit in the war. Lastly, since it deals in detail with every battle in which the 33rd Divisional Artillery was concerned, it will be found to contain records of minor incidents and operations into which the wider histories of the war cannot enter, but which were of vital importance to the actual troops concerned.

The expense of publishing the History has been borne entirely by old members of the 33rd Divisional Artillery, and in this respect I must express my deep gratitude to Captain Leonard Vestey, Major

D. M. Coffin and Colonel Sir Frederick Hall, by whose generosity, combined with that of several others, the publication of this book has been rendered possible. For personal help in collecting information and facts, checking dates and generally verifying the accuracy of the work I am also indebted to Brigadier-General C. G. Stewart, Lieut.-Col. O. M. Harris, Lieut.-Col. E. J. Skinner, Major M. A. Studd, Major D. M. Coffin, Major R. D. Russell and Major S. G. Taylor.

Finally, I wish to acknowledge the courtesy of the War Office in permitting the reproduction in this volume of the official maps used in France during the war.

JOHN MACARTNEY-FILGATE.

London,
May, 1921.

CHAPTER I.

August 1914 and its succeeding months will ever recall to the minds of that generation which was privileged to live through those epic days memories of a great turmoil, a chaos, a shattering of that normal—and in many cases humdrum—existence which to the majority represented Life. The outstanding impression will depend upon the character of the person who looks back—to some it will be a sense of overwhelming surprise, to some a rending and shattering of all their dreams of a long-awaited happy future, while to some it will be the promise of Great Adventure, the chance of seeing Life face to face and stripped of all its petty adornments and falsities, a sight vouchsafed to few and one which of necessity brings with it the presence of that companion Death, so closely allied to Life in its fierce and primitive state. Yet whatever the recollection and whatever may be the impressions retained, to one and all remains that proud memory of the wild enthusiasm which greeted the call to arms, the readiness to fight, to leave comfortable homes, to give up everything because the Country called for men ; because the Country, whatever the cause of the war might be, was in peril.

The 33rd Divisional Artillery, as its number implies, was not one of the first to be formed. So great was the early rush to the recruiting stations that the machinery to deal with the enlistment of men was unable to cope with it, and it was not until January 14th, 1915, that a War Office letter addressed to the Mayor of Camberwell authorised the recruiting of the 156th Brigade, Royal Field Artillery, by Major Frederick Hall M.P. in the Borough of Camberwell. So prompt was the response to this call that in March further authority was granted for the recruitment of the 162nd Brigade R.F.A. in the same neighbourhood, the formation of this Brigade being completed by the middle of May, when it was placed under the command of Major Duncan. It was then brought to the attention of the authorities that there still remained masses of excellent material

B

in Camberwell, that the district was overflowing with would-be recruits not yet enlisted, and that the whole of the 33rd Divisional Artillery might well be raised from there—a scheme which was received by the Borough with the greatest enthusiasm. The required authority was obtained ; the 166th and 167th Brigades R.F.A., the 126th Battery of Heavy Artillery and the attendant Ammunition Column were formed, and on June 1st 1915 the 33rd Divisional Artillery, as such, was complete, manned to its full strength, and manned by the men of Camberwell and Dulwich.

Meantime, from the day on which the first recruits had arrived, training was carried on with the utmost vigour. N.C.O. instructors were scarce, very few officers had been posted to the Division, and any kind of uniform was noticeable by its absence. The early training of recruits in those days was not calculated to enhance in their minds the glamour of war ; clad in the roughest and, in many cases, most tattered of civilian clothes, shod in the boots which they had brought with them, they were taught—day in, day out—that there were many accomplishments which they must learn before they would be fit for service in the field ; that personal gallantry, a feeling of complete superiority over the enemy, and a fixed intention of " sticking it with the best " would not alone take them to France. They must learn to indulge in that strange form of recreation known as " knees bending with arms raising," and all its accompanying acrobatics; they must be initiated into the mysteries of knotting and lashing, of horse management, of dismounted drill and a hundred and one other matters which go to form the training of a soldier. And then, when their knees ached with bending and stretching, when their brains whirled in trying to fashion some especially important and therefore, to their minds, difficult knot, when some of the most tender portions of their anatomy felt as though one more minute in the saddle would cut right through to the bone, Gunnery descended upon them. Gunnery, with its drill and its intricate and complicated mechanism, opened out a completely new item of training, a hitherto untrodden part of the long and tedious road which led from Camberwell and Dulwich to the battlefields of France. Yet to the weary mind of the recruit there was one great consolation. Here at last was something tangible ; here was something which spoke of War, which brought him much nearer to the goal of his endeavours. " Physical jerks " and the lurid remarks of riding masters were all very well in their way, but the average recruit had no intention of lying on his back outside a trench in France and of solemnly raising his feet in the air to let them have a look, as it were, at fresh surroundings ; he had no desire to trot along a road behind the Line without stirrups or reins, although he was quite prepared to recognise that it was a useful feat to be able to perform. No, he wanted to fling shells at the enemy, to be able to inflict upon the " other side " all that extreme discomfort which artillery is capable of administering ; he wanted, in short, a gun, and at last he saw one before him.

It was this shortage of guns for drill and instructional purposes which of necessity delayed the training of the batteries. During the time the brigades were at Dulwich there were only dummy loaders and three 15-pounders available, nor was it until July that four 18-pounders arrived to be divided up amongst the whole Division. Training, however, in other essentials was briskly carried on in and around Dulwich. Cold shoers were sent to Herold's Institute at Bermondsey, cooks to St. John's Wood, artificers to Woolwich, while every officer on joining was sent on a course of instruction to either Larkhill or Shoeburyness. Map-reading classes were conducted by Army-Schoolmaster Wilmot, and Lady Bathurst, with the assistance of ladies of the district, gave lessons in French and German twice a week. As far as billeting was concerned, the men of the 156th Brigade and the Divisional Ammunition Column were allowed to live at their own homes ; the 162nd Brigade was housed at Gordon's Brewery, the 166th Brigade at the Tramway Depôt, Peckham, while the 167th Brigade was partly billeted at home and partly at the East Dulwich Baths. Such an arrangement of scattered billets could hardly be hoped to succeed, especially when it is remembered that in the earlier days the men were without uniform—a red, blue or white armlet alone denoting the exalted presence of a Sergeant, Corporal or Bombardier respectively. Yet gradually and steadily a change became visible ; slowly there appeared from out of the disorganised and shapeless mass of men a clear-cut, firm formation, a sense of discipline and orderliness, the beginnings of a unit of the British Army.

Inspections were numerous at this time ; during the months from March to July the Divisional Artillery was, in fact, inspected no fewer than seven times by Major-General Sir Francis Lloyd, Major-General Sir T. Perrott, and Colonel M. Peake. At the earlier inspections the men were still in civilian clothes, as was the 167th Brigade at the recruiting march on Peckham Rye which took place on May 1st, but shortly after that date a full supply of uniform was received, and the men were properly and thoroughly equipped in every way. Much could be related, incidentally, with regard to the recruiting march just mentioned ; it was the march of the men of a district through that district, and aimed at getting more recruits for the men's own unit. Suffice it to say that those recruits were obtained, and if the enthusiasm of the proceedings gave rise to some curious and amusing situations, if there rode upon the ammunition wagons (with which the batteries were now fully equipped) some whose right to ride there might well be questioned, who could object? The war was still young, enthusiasm was still high, men were still wanted.

It was probably in the first two weeks of August that Camberwell really grasped what the 33rd Divisional Artillery meant to it, for in those days it lost it. It is a curious irony of life that few things are really appreciated until they are gone, and then appreciation comes too late. Through all these earlier days of training the men had been living in or near their homes, but now there came a change, Adventure became Reality, for the batteries were moved for the rest of their training from London to Bulford. Night after night, from August 4th till August 10th, there crept out of Waterloo station trains bound for Bulford, packed with horses, men and wagons, setting out on the second stage of their work; night after night there were left in Camberwell homes very empty, hearts very dreary at the arrival of that time which all had known must come, but the coming of which was in no wise softened by this fore-knowledge.

Bulford wrought a tremendous change in the Divisional Artillery, which was now under the command of its own C.R.A. Brigadier-General Stuart. Here there was room to move; there was different country to work over each day; there were schemes on a far more elaborate scale than had been possible at Dulwich. The official syllabus of training was steadily worked through, and gradually this training became more interesting, more attractive as dull routine was left behind and sham warfare put into practice. The batteries were fully equipped with guns, even the 167th Brigade, which was a 4·5 in. howitzer brigade and had been greatly handicapped by a total inability to get howitzers from anywhere, being finally fitted out, and at last, in the early part of November, the batteries were given a chance of putting into effect on the practice ranges all that they had been learning by tedious and hard work during the period of training. One hundred rounds per battery were fired, and in most cases the results were very satisfactory when the shortness of training and the utter lack of previous experience were taken into account. The batteries were complimented by General Drake on the good service and drill at the guns, and returned to camp more anxious than ever to get to France, more keen than ever to fire a shot in anger now that they had fired one in cold blood. Rumour, already in high activity throughout the camp, became trebly busy since there appeared no further obstacle to keep the Division in England, and rumour was strengthened by the granting to the men of that last leave—overseas leave—which was given prior to departure for France.

It was in December that it came, December 6th to be quite accurate. Just a bald official order to proceed overseas, accompanied by a mass of typewritten time-tables, march tables and all the paraphernalia inevitable in a move of such dimensions. The great moment had arrived at last, the moment for which all had waited so long, so eagerly and with such excitement, and any pangs which might naturally have been felt at a parting such as this, any dark forebodings which a look into the future might have called up, were mercifully and naturally effaced by the bustle, the excitement, the " fever," if you like, of the whole affair.

On December 10th, at 4 P.M., the entraining of the batteries began at Amesbury and continued at intervals throughout the night. Fifty-one trains in all it took to move the batteries and their attendant ammunition columns, the last train leaving Amesbury at 4.5 P.M. on December 12th. Two days of bustle and excitement, two days of movement and stir around Amesbury, two days during which the station was crowded and packed with horses, guns and men sweating, heaving, swearing—and then silence. As though by a magic hand the 33rd Divisional Artillery was picked up and disappeared, and for a space it was hidden from the sight of man.

CHAPTER II.

FIRST EXPERIENCES OF WAR IN THE LA BASSÉE SECTOR.
(DECEMBER 1915—JULY 1916).

ON a foggy afternoon, typical of Flanders in December, there crept into Aire station a long and heavy train obvious even to the lay mind as a troop train, consisting as it did not only of ordinary passenger coaches, but also of innumerable horse boxes and a line of long open trucks crammed with guns and wagons. Every window was crowded with faces—the faces of British soldiers surveying with interest this, to most of them, new and strange land, listening with a thrill to the distant mutter of guns, looking with eagerness for signs of war and for a first view of the billets in which, for the next few days at any rate, they were to live. At Hazebrouck and at Lillers similar trains were pulling in, disgorging on to the track men, horses and guns in what might appear to be indescribable confusion, but which had in it all a method and a certain order. To the inhabitants there was nothing new in this sight; scores of times had they seen the arrival of fresh units from England in just this manner, but to the men themselves the affair was one of the utmost significance. As a unit they were making their first appearance within actual reach of the scene of war, and the unit was that one whose history the ensuing pages will endeavour to record; it was the 33rd Divisional Artillery once more, the batteries of which for days had been swallowed up, not exactly in the fog of actual war, but in the impenetrable maze of Lines of Communication. For days they had been just a memory, a rumour, an entry on the time-tables of various R.T.O.s, scattered about the railway line between Havre and Aire; for days they had indulged in wanderings which at times made them wonder exactly where the war was to be found, and at last in their estimation they had found it.

It must not be supposed that the journey of the Division from Amesbury to its billets in the " rest " area was one long, smooth, perfectly run affair. Far from it ! On arrival at Southampton it was found that two of the transports were in the wrong berths, while the engines of a third had broken down ; as a result, one brigade had to disembark and be broken up into small parties, each party going on to a different ship. On arrival at Havre mistakes had been made with regard to the accommodation of the men, and one wretched party which marched seven miles out to Harfleur had to return again over the same weary road before a shelter could be found. In fact, the journey in trucks marked " Hommes 40, chevaux 8 " (a phrase no less sinister in practice than in meaning) marked the termination of a period of discomfort and homelessness which few who shared therein will ever forget. When one remembers, however, the mighty forces which during these months were moved from England to France, the actual fresh units which came over railways overloaded with ammunition and supplies for troops already in the Line, one cannot help recognising the ability and organisation which enabled such work to be carried out, and which moved a division of artillery to scheduled time across a railway system already strained to breaking point.

It was on December 10th, it will be remembered, that the Divisional Artillery disappeared so mysteriously from England ; on December 16th, at 2.30 P.M., the concentration of the same Divisional Artillery was reported to be complete in the Aire-Thiennes area. The cloud of mystery was once more lifted : the batteries were known to be " somewhere in France." Actually, the area in which they were billeted was the rest area of the First Corps ; they were attached to the division in reserve, and were billeted in the villages of Mazinghem, Berguette, Guarbecque and Mt. Bernanchon.

The first few days in France proved rather a disappointment. Everybody (other than those who had been "out" before) had come full of ideas about the war, mostly taken from picture papers and so-called war stories ; most of the men had somehow expected to find themselves well within sight and hearing of the battle itself, with all the accompanying thrills of aeroplane fights, shelling in the distance, ambulances and what not, and what did they find? An ordinary village, rather dirty and very muddy ; a flat, uninteresting country and the usual routine of stables, watering, exercise and gun drill—just a continuation of the training which they had carried out at Bulford, with the difference that away on the horizon there was that continuous giant thudding, that heavy sullen muttering which betokened artillery at work, not now in mere practice but in grim earnest.

However, it was not of much good being in France unless use was made of the proximity of the war for instructional purposes, and so, two days after the completed concentration, parties were sent from each of the brigades to be attached to the 2nd Divisional Artillery, then holding the line on the La Bassée front from Givenchy on the north nearly to Fosse 8, the scene of such fierce fighting in the Loos offensive, on the south. These parties were conveyed by motor-bus to Cambrin, Annequin and Gorre, whence they were led on foot by guides to the positions of the batteries to which they were attached. Six parties in all went up from the brigades between December 18th and January 11th, the duration of stay in the line being usually four days, so that by the end of the second week in January all the officers, N.C.O.s, and gunners had had their first look at the war, had seen their first glimpse of the enemy lines, had had their first experience of shell fire.

About the middle of January the batteries were considered to have gained sufficient experience to merit their taking a more strenuous part in the war, and complete batteries were accordingly sent up in turn to take over the positions of the 12th Divisional Artillery (63rd and 64th Brigades R.F.A.) and of the 2nd Divisional Artillery (9th, 17th, 48th, 56th and 71st batteries), stretching from Givenchy down to Vermelles. As a rule three batteries were sent up at a time for six days, the wagon line work and ammunition supply being carried out by the batteries to which they were attached, while those not in the line continued training, with a few inspections and sudden wild rumours to help pass the time. Of inspections there were two :—on January 20th C/166 was reviewed by General Joffre, while on January 26th the 162nd, 166th and 167th Brigades were inspected by Lieut.-General Sir Hubert Gough, then commanding the 1st Corps. As, prior to this, the 156th Brigade had lined the route in December to bid farewell to Field-Marshal Lord French, the whole Division in its early days had an opportunity of seeing three great men whose names were to be connected so closely with the history of the war.

The demon Rumour held widespread popularity at this time ; rumours of sudden moves to a different part of the line ; rumours of a sudden advance to support our infantry—anything, in fact, which billet gossip could evolve on a quiet evening. Nor was this gossip entirely to blame if it gave rise to so many rumours, for official orders and counter-orders themselves gave plenty of scope for wonder to the average brain. As an example of the continual uncertainty which prevailed regarding future movements, the case of the Divisional Ammunition Column might well be taken. On January 26th it was ordered to stand by, ready for a sudden move ; this order was cancelled at 1.30 A.M. on January 27th, was revived

ORDER OF BATTLE.

DECEMBER 1915—MAY 1916.

H.Q.R.A.

C.R.A.	Brigade Major.	Staff Captain.
Brig.-Gen. C. F. Blane, C.M.G.	Major Sheppard.	Capt. T. Usher.

156th Brigade.

Lieut.-Colonel F. Hall, M.P. (*till February*).   Lieut.-Colonel Rochfort-Boyd, D.S.O.
Adjutant : Lieut. W. Holden (*till February*).   Lieut. W. G. Pringle.

"A" Battery.	"B" Battery.	"C" Battery.	"D" Battery.
Major Alcard (*till January*). Capt. L. R. Hill (*after January*).	Capt. R. D. Russell.	Capt. G. Lomer.	Capt. S. Talbot.

162nd Brigade.

Lieut.-Colonel J. F. Duncan.
Lieut.-Colonel O. M. Harris, D.S.O.
Adjutant : Lieut. T. D. Shepherd.

"A" Battery.	"B" Battery.	"C" Battery.	"D" Battery.
Capt. F. C. Packham.	Major R. G. M. Johnston.	Capt. A. van Straubenzee.	Major D. Stewart.

166th Brigade.

Colonel A. H. S. Goff.
Adjutant : Lieut. E. G. Lutyens.

"A" Battery.	"B" Battery.	"C" Battery.	"D" Battery.
Capt. D. M. Coffin.	Major T. E. Durie.	Capt. H. Freeman.	Capt. G. Fetherston.

167th Brigade.

Lieut.-Colonel Du Plat Taylor.
Lieut.-Colonel Harpur.
Lieut.-Colonel L. T. Goff.
Adjutant : Lieut. W. D. Watson (*till January*).   Lieut. H. C. Cory.

"A" Battery.	"B" Battery.	"C" Battery.	"D" Battery.
Capt. M. A. Studd.	Major Barkworth.	Major W. P. Bennett.	Capt. W. A. T. Barstow.

again at 5.30 the same evening with the additional information that it must be ready to move at two hours' notice, and was finally cancelled at 11.35 P.M. that night. Nothing immediate came of these rumours, and all through February the same training, now grown very tedious after the interest of a first visit to the Line, was carried on. A somewhat ambitious plan of two-day manœuvres was carried out in the First Army area around Estrée-Blanche and Therouane on the last days of January by those batteries which were not at the time undergoing training in the Line, but February 1st saw a resumption of the old billet life again.

Three units, however, escaped the general air of boredom which was now gradually pervading the Divisional Artillery—one at an early stage and the others later. C/167 (Major Bennett), as far back as December 30th, marched up to the Line and came permanently into action in a disused battery position about 150 yards south of the La Bassée Canal, midway between Vauxhall Bridge and Pont Fixe. It was attached to the 1st Corps Heavy Artillery for counter-battery work, and, covering as it did the wide front from Violaines on the north to Auchy on the south, with observation stations in Givenchy (" N "), Cambrin, "King's Clere " and " Mountain House," it had an excellent opportunity of learning accurately the whole of the front which the Divisional Artillery was at a later date to cover. The wagon lines were bad, but the battery position, despite the fact that it had to be built while the guns were actually there, was not too uncomfortable. An occasional shelling with whizz-bangs at that early stage did nothing more than arouse interest and teach a few healthy lessons, while the daily shelling of Pont Fixe, about 300 yards away, by a 5·9 in. howitzer was regarded as a free entertainment of great attraction.

A/162 (Captain Packham) and A/166 (Captain Coffin), the other two batteries to go into action independently, were rather later than C/167; they did not move into action until February 13th, when they were attached to the 1st Corps Heavy Artillery for counter-battery work and, having marched up through Béthune, Beuvry and Annequin, took up positions covering, with C/167, the same wide front.

At last orders came, on February 15th, for the whole of the 33rd Divisional Artillery to take over the line from the 12th Divisional Artillery. The relief began on February 23rd, when the first sections of the batteries relieved their opposite numbers in action; three batteries (C/156, C/162, A/166) which were already in the line for training stayed there, and on February 25th the remaining sections of the batteries came into action. C/167 vacated its position at

Cuinchy, marched to the wagon line on the night of the 23rd/24th and was split up, the right section going to D/167 (Captain Barstow) and the left to A/167 (Captain Studd) to form six-gun batteries. B/167 (Major Barkworth) had on February 14th been posted to the 1/4th London Brigade R.F.A. (T.F.), and was permanently struck off the strength of the Division.

At noon on Saturday, February 26th, the relief was reported complete, the 33rd Divisional Artillery under its C.R.A., Brig.-General C. F. Blane, assumed responsibility for the artillery support of the front covered by the 33rd infantry, and for the first time held the line entirely on its own. The front extended from Boyau 1 to Boyau 53, that is from Mad Point to just south of Givenchy. The four brigades, commanded by Lieut.-Colonel Rochfort-Boyd, Lieut.-Colonel Duncan, Colonel A. H. S. Goff and Lieut.-Colonel Harpur, were divided into two groups, " Z," the Northern Group, being commanded by Colonel Goff, " A," the Auchy Group, by Colonel Harpur ; the batteries of both groups were dispersed all along the front from the La Bassée Canal to as far south as Vermelles.

Here a slight digression may well be permitted. It will be noticed that Lieut.-Colonel F. Hall is not mentioned above as one of the Brigade Commanders. To the regret of all ranks he returned to England on February 15th, handing over the command of the 156th Brigade to Lieut.-Colonel Rochfort-Boyd. It would be impossible to over-estimate the work which Lieut.-Colonel Hall did in organising the recruitment of the 33rd Divisional Artillery in Camberwell ; without his work, and the work of Lieut.-Colonel Duncan who was also lost to the Division in March when he handed over the command of the 162nd Brigade to Lieut.-Colonel O. M. Harris, the brigades could never have been formed so rapidly as they were. In these pages, which perpetuate the history of the 33rd Divisional Artillery, it is essential that there should also be recorded the great effort made by Lieut.-Colonel Hall in raising the four brigades, an effort which was appreciated by His Majesty the King at a later date, when he bestowed upon him a Knighthood of the Order of the British Empire.

To return, however, to the war. The trench system here, as everywhere on the Flanders front, was situated in very flat ground, and O.P.'s in the front line were of little use except for shooting on the enemy fire trench. Providentially, along the rising ground a few hundred yards behind the front line there were a number of ruined houses dotted about at odd intervals, sometimes singly, sometimes in groups; all of these were practically destroyed by shell fire, but had just enough left standing to offer a precarious perch to anyone wishing to observe therefrom, and to provide a screen for such sand-bagging, strengthening and revetting as an ingenious mind, coupled with no small influence with the Sappers and a desire for greater comfort, might devise. " N " and Artillery House in Givenchy were but little used as they were rather too far to the north, but King's Clere and Mountain House (in Cambrin), Braddell Castle, The Ruin and the Four Hundred on either side of the La Bassée road, with Dead Man's House, Wilson's House, Ridge View and Maison Rouge stretching along the line just south of the road, made excellent spots from which, perched usually in the wreckage of the roof, one could direct fire on to every spot in the zone. The Ruin and, before it was rebuilt, the Four Hundred were trying in the extreme to the nerves, for they hung together in a manner which might have appeared impossible even to the ingenious mind of a Heath Robinson ; moreover, they were almost daily attended to by an ever-persistent German gunner with an unlimited supply of 5·9 in. ammunition and a nice taste in house removing, but King's Clere, a little further to the north, provided an excellent view of all the front and back areas, and had been thoroughly and effectively secured by means of cement and iron girders. This part of the front was, indeed, a most fascinating one for shooting over, provided a good O.P. was available. North of the canal had little of interest, save the ruins of Violaines and Canteleux, but to the south, and just on the bank, was the Railway Triangle with its mysterious tower and mound. Auchy offered several moderately undamaged houses whence, in the early morning, smoke could be seen issuing, while loopholes appeared and disappeared, or were camouflaged, with extraordinary frequency. Les Briques, with its dead trees and ruined house, struck a grim and forbidding note, but, just south of it, the green fields around Lone Farm were always full of possibilities. Many and varied were the ideas as to the use which was made of Lone Farm ; as a farm it had totally disappeared and suggested nothing more than a few dead trees and a mound of bricks, but underneath those bricks there must have been some splendid cellars. Every morning, just as day broke, parties of twenty or thirty Germans could be seen there, and every morning some battery or other, with an unexpected burst of shrapnel, used to lengthen the German casualty list in no small manner. It took the Germans an extraordinary time to learn the lesson of Lone Farm, and for quite a considerable period it was there that the newly-arrived battery officer from England saw the first grey-clad figures of the enemy ; there, as like as not, that he first saw his shells actually bring death. South of Lone Farm again came the Corons de Maron and the " Dump," or, to give it its correct title, Fosse 8 de

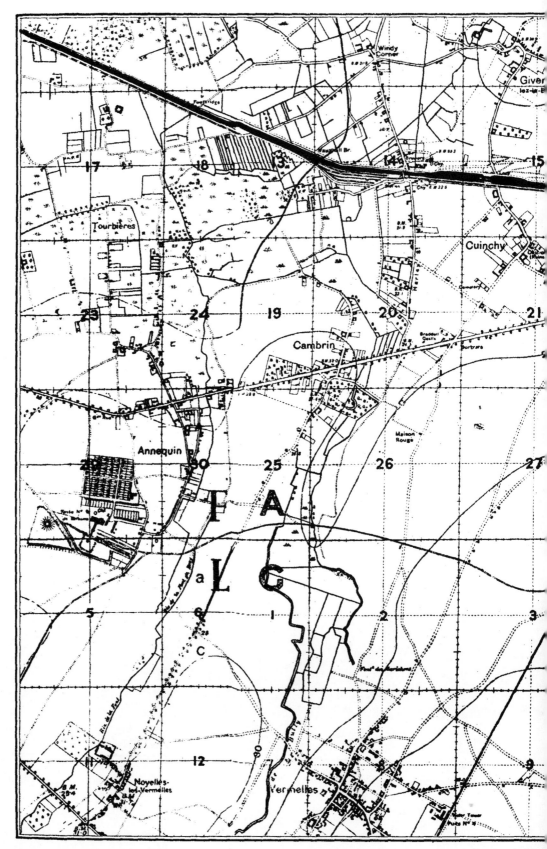

Scale 1:20,0

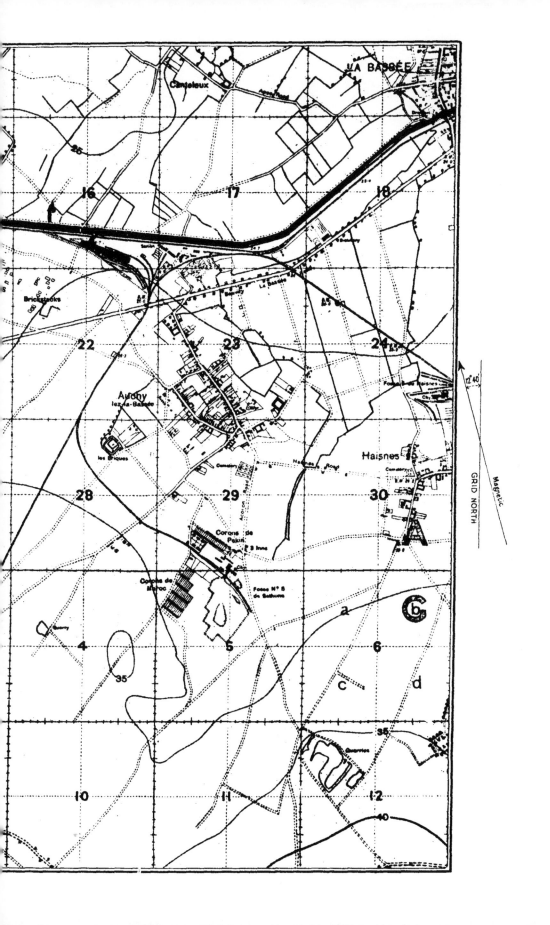

Béthune, but both of these were out of the zone of the batteries and had, therefore, to be left undisturbed.

Behind Auchy and Lone Farm could be seen Indian Well House, Haisnes, Douvrin and the road running up to La Bassée. For normal purposes this area was out of range, but was none the less interesting in that it afforded all manner of unexpected sights. A train, a lorry going along the road, a couple of horsemen trotting down a bridle path are commonplace sights in England, but when you are separated from that train or lorry by a network of ditches containing death in a hundred forms, when that train or lorry is carrying men who will probably to-morrow be trying their best to kill you, and whom you may, with considerable fortune, kill first, then the matter appears in a different light, and you feel an intense interest in the objects visible.

Up to the present this chapter has been devoted to a description of the front on which the Division was operating. It may be that too much space has been given to what is, after all, merely of personal interest, but it should be remembered that this was the first front upon which the Divisional Artillery served as a unit, and therefore the memory of it has been impressed upon the minds of both officers and men probably to a far greater extent than has any other portion of the British Front in France. Now, however, regard must be had for the tactical situation as it presented itself in the winter of 1915-16.

It will be remembered that, since the battle of Loos in September and October 1915, no attack on any large scale had been carried out by the British troops. Heavy fighting continued throughout the winter along the newly-formed salient at Loos, and this in itself proved such a drain upon the forces of both sides that the remainder of the 1st Army front was comparatively quiet. On December 19th the Germans launched a heavy gas attack in the Ypres salient, and on February 13th, in the same area, occurred the famous attack on the Bluff. The end of February saw the beginning of the great battle of Verdun, and it was therefore a natural result that the La Bassée front, situated as it was outside the zone of these different operations, remained in a state of comparative quiet, and was disturbed solely by the raids, mine explosions and artillery activity which were the invariable régime of trench warfare.

This period of the campaign saw the arrival in France of a great number of New Army divisions, and as far as possible these divisions, with one or two noteworthy exceptions, were placed in a part of the line which was not likely to be subjected to any large scale operations but which, by the opportunities it offered of raiding, patrolling and the like, formed an excellent training ground for troops not yet experienced in modern warfare. No better part of the firing line could, in fact, have been chosen than the La Bassée sector. The famous Brickstack area was a centre of great mining activities; raids were the order rather than the exception, and big trench minenwerfer were daily in action. The back areas of the German zone were in full view of the artillery observation stations whence practice could be obtained, day in day out, on every possible type of target. Salient features presented themselves for registration and calibration of the guns, and during these shoots the accuracy and drill of the gun detachments could be fully and carefully noted. Numerous houses, in a more or less advanced state of dilapidation, gave all ranks a good idea of the effect of modern artillery fire on fortifications, while working parties and moving targets of all descriptions taught observing officers and gun detachments the essential lesson of quick shooting without loss of accuracy, and the absolute necessity of a familiarity with every inch of the ground covered.

It has already been stated that the mining activities of both sides were very marked. Although this would appear to concern the infantry rather than the artillery, the effect on the latter was of great importance. The explosion of a mine was in many cases followed by an infantry raid, and for this reason gun detachments and officers on duty with the infantry were kept up to a high pitch of speed and smartness in putting down an immediate barrage. Moreover, this barrage shooting was most effective in instilling confidence in the accuracy and good shooting of gun detachments. It was a very strong but utterly fatal temptation to a battery commander to add twenty-five or even fifty yards to the range of his guns, to ensure that no shell fell short and inflicted casualties on our own infantry. To withstand this temptation needed the most complete confidence in the guns of the battery, but, on the other hand, to add the margin of safety almost invariably meant that the barrage dropped beyond its mark and inflicted no damage whatever upon the raiding party or trench for which it was intended. Gradually did the infantry learn completely to trust their gunners in barrage firing, and once and for all did the battery officers realise that there was only one range which would hit their target, and that any addition to that range, although satisfying their own peace of mind, would effectually wipe out any good which their efforts might have done, and would leave the infantry to the mercies of a hand to hand encounter with the enemy.

On March 8th an important alteration was made in the disposition of troops along the Divisional front. From this date two infantry brigades were kept in the line, each brigade maintaining two battalions in the front line. Each artillery section was divided into two sub-sections composed of two 18-pdr. batteries apiece, and it therefore worked out that each battalion of infantry in the front line had two 18-pdr. batteries to provide it with direct artillery support. This system appeared on paper excellent, and indeed from the point of view of establishing close co-operation between the Divisional Artillery and its own Infantry no fault in the plan could be found, but there was one tremendous handicap which every day made itself felt more vitally amongst gunners and infantry alike. Throughout this period the supply of ammunition for daily firing was most closely limited, and on March 18th the allowance was restricted to sixteen rounds per battery per day. It is not intended here to enter into the great ammunition controversy. Such a matter would be out of place in what is meant to be an historical record of an artillery unit throughout the war, but it is mentioned in view of certain remarks which will later be made concerning the mutual relations of the infantry with the artillery, and is one of the chief difficulties with which the artillery had to contend at this time.

March 18th saw the first attack of any dimensions which had so far taken place in the neighbourhood of the 33rd Divisional zone. After a short but very heavy artillery bombardment and the explosion of three mines, the Germans made an attack upon the 12th Division which was at that time on the right of the 33rd Division and was confronting the Hohenzollern redoubt. Apart from a heavy bombardment of Annequin with gas shells and the general searching with long range fire of all the roads leading up to the front, no material effect was felt by the 33rd Divisional Artillery. It gave the batteries, however, some idea of what would be expected of them in the event of a hostile attack on their own front, and, although conducted at a distance, enabled them by sight and hearing to realise the weight of shell fire to which they would be subjected if they were themselves attacked.

April 27th saw a much larger attack by the Germans, once again upon the right of the 33rd Division, and this time on the 16th Division in the Hulluch sector. Early in the morning of that day a very heavy bombardment began on the Division's right, and shortly afterwards a call for mutual support was received. A heavy mist lay upon the ground, but through it could be heard the throb and roar of a battle in progress, mingling with the nearer and more persistent thunder of our own guns and of the German retaliation. Gradually the mist thickened instead of clearing, and gradually did the firing become more intense; suddenly in the distance was heard the wail of a siren which was taken up by one closer at hand.   The Division had never before been subjected to a gas attack, and at first the true meaning of these sirens was only suspected and not fully realised, but a certain pungency soon made itself felt in the morning air.   The men began coughing and sneezing, the atmosphere became thick and unbreathable, and in a very few minutes all batteries were working under the protection of their gas helmets. The battle was over by the middle of the morning, and the batteries were able to return to the ordinary routine of the day, but a lesson and a valuable lesson at that had been learnt, and it was brought home even more clearly than before that the detachments must be prepared to work under more difficult conditions than they had as yet experienced.   Whilst on the subject of this gas attack it is important to note that, on the occasion in question, so dense were the gas clouds that they were even felt at the wagon lines as far back as Beuvry.

After this attack followed renewed trench activity and mutual retaliation.   On April 28th the wagon lines of the 166th Brigade at Beuvry were heavily shelled by a long range gun, and numerous casualties were suffered by horses and men.   The shelling of wagon lines is at all times most unsettling and likely to do great damage, but this particular case, being the first of its kind of which the batteries of the Division had had experience, created a great impression.

About this time a somewhat curious incident occurred between the German Air Service and our Artillery.   On April 28th a German aeroplane flew over the battery position of A/167 (Captain Studd) and dropped a long streamer to which was attached a message. This message stated that German headquarters were aware that No. 1 Harley Street (a big building used as a dressing station and situated in a road which derived its name from the number of aid posts which lay along it) was a dressing station, but that, owing to the great damage which was being done by the battery of howitzers in action behind this particular house, they were reluctantly compelled to destroy it by shell fire.   Apart from anything else, this was a considerable compliment to the work of A/167, the battery referred to, but it did not say much for the observation powers of the German aircraft.   A/167 was then in action on the eastern end of Tourbiers loop, and was at least 600 yds. from the dressing station in question.   Next day the bombardment of No. 1 Harley Street by aeroplane observation began ; a great number of direct hits were obtained, and, although the Red Cross was clearly visible, the building was entirely destroyed.   It is pleasant to note, however, that this incident did not pass unavenged. Early one morning a short time afterwards, the battery commander of A/166 (Captain Coffin) saw a large convoy of German ambulances proceeding along the road near Haisnes. A burst of high explosive blocked the front and rear of the convoy, a steady and destructive fire of high explosive and shrapnel swept the length and breadth of the road, and in a short time the debt owing to the Germans by the destruction of the dressing station in Harley Street was more than wiped out. The shelling of dressing stations and ambulances was not, at this time, a practice usually indulged in by our guns, but of late the enemy had been consistently shelling all our aid posts, our dressing stations and our field ambulances, and it was hoped that a short sharp lesson such as that detailed above might tend to lessen in the future the sufferings of our own wounded.

Quite soon after this incident another opportunity very fortunately presented itself of impressing upon the Germans our intention of brisk and immediate retaliation for any attacks on their part. Three big minenwerfers had, of late, been harassing our infantry to an undue extent every night from the vicinity of the Railway Triangle, Spotted Dog and Ryan's Keep, and it was decided to organise a really efficient shell storm to try and discourage the enemy from this particular form of attack. Accordingly it was arranged that, at 3.25 on a certain morning, a sudden and concentrated bombardment by 9·2 in., 6 in., 4·5 in. howitzers and 18-pdrs. should take place on the area from which the " Minnie " worked. By a great stroke of fortune, ten minutes before the bombardment was due to begin, the minenwerfer in question started its nightly bombardment. Hardly had it begun than from all sides there poured down shells of every description, trench mortar bombs and rifle grenades, and for upwards of twenty minutes the German trench system was one vast mass of smoke, flame and dust. Not for many days afterwards did that minenwerfer worry our troops, and the Germans must indeed have been impressed by the organisation which in the space of a few minutes brought down upon them such a concentrated and well-timed barrage.

On May 19th an important reorganisation of the Divisional Artillery took place. When the 33rd Division embarked for France its artillery consisted of four brigades :—the 156th, 162nd, 166th and 167th. Of these, the first three brigades were made up of 18-pdr. batteries, while the 167th was a 4·5 in. howitzer brigade. By an order which now was issued, the brigades were reconstituted to consist each of three 18-pdr. batteries and one 4·5 in. howitzer battery. The effect of such an organisation was that each Brigade

C

Commander had a small but complete tactical force under his direct command, and, in the event of open warfare and a moving battle, was so disposed that he had a percentage of both types of artillery under his control. Everything, in fact, was now clearly indicating the early resumption of active operations, and June 18th might be considered to mark the first step in this direction in the La Bassée sector.

On June 18th the 39th Division, then holding the line on the left of the 33rd, was withdrawn, and the 33rd extended its front northward as far as Grenadier Road in Givenchy. For one division this was an extraordinarily wide front, and necessitated the alteration and widening of gun pits, the establishing of new observation stations in Givenchy, with the consequent laying of telephone lines—a very heavy strain on the batteries who were responsible for the support and protection of such a widely spread body of infantry. The group system of batteries was reorganised into two new groups— Givenchy and Cuinchy—and the late Auchy group became a sub-section of Cuinchy group. As an example of the width of front to be guarded by the batteries, it may be stated that the howitzers had to cover a front of 120°. In addition to the extension of the front, preparations for operations on a large scale were ordered to be taken. Every battery had to make accommodation for keeping around the guns four times the amount of ammunition to what had previously been the rule; all ranks were made acquainted with the forward zone and the best lines of advance in case of a German withdrawal, advance positions were selected and the whole front began to seethe with an undercurrent of preparation and anticipation. To the inexperienced minds of the troops this appeared to indicate an offensive on the La Bassée front. Never before had the batteries been in a big battle; they did not know that, had an attack been contemplated on their front, the activity would have been multiplied tenfold. They did not know that, far away in the south, preparations on a vast and unprecedented scale were being made; that there were in the Somme area concentrations of artillery, infantry, ammunition and material which exceeded anything yet seen in war. They only saw their own preparations and formed their opinions accordingly.

On June 24th these suspicions, already fostered by the Higher Command in order to cover operations elsewhere, were more than doubled. On that day the whole of the British line burst into flame. From Ypres to the Somme a steady bombardment of the German trench system began, wire was cut and kept open, repairs to damaged trenches were prevented by persistent bursts of fire,

ORDER OF BATTLE.

May 1916—June 1916.

H.Q.R.A.

C.R.A.	Brigade Major.	Staff Captain.
Brig.-Gen. C. F. Blane, C.M.G.	Major H. K. Sadler, M.C.	Capt. T. Usher.

156th Brigade.
Lieut.-Colonel Rochfort-Boyd, D.S.O.
Adjutant : Lieut. W. G. Pringle.

"A" Battery."	"B" Battery.	"C" Battery.	"D" Battery.
Capt. L. R. Hill. Capt. Lutyens.	Capt. R. D. Russell.	Capt. G. Lomer.	Capt. M. A. Studd.

162nd Brigade.
Lieut.-Colonel O. M. Harris, D.S.O.
Adjutant : Lieut. T. D. Shepherd.

"A" Battery.	"B" Battery.	"C" Battery.	"D" Battery.
Capt. F. C. Packham.	Major R. G. M. Johnston.	Capt. A. van Straubenzee.	Major W. P. Bennett.

166th Brigade.
Colonel A. H. S. Goff, C.M.G.
Adjutant : Lieut. E. G. Lutyens.

"A" Battery.	"B" Battery.	"C" Battery.	"D" Battery.
Capt. D. M. Coffin.	Major T. E. Durie.	Capt. H. Freeman.	Capt. W. A. T. Barstow, M.C.

167th Brigade.
Lieut.-Colonel L. T. Goff.
Adjutant : Lieut. H. C. Cory.

"A" Battery.	"B" Battery.	"C" Battery.
Capt. S. Talbot.	Major D. Stewart.	Capt. G. Fetherston.

and in every sector did it appear that an attack was imminent; unless the German Headquarters could discover where the main concentration was taking place it was impossible for them to gauge the most probable place of assault. That they did discover it was realised, and realised bitterly, on July 1st and the succeeding days, but there is no doubt that the artillery activity along the whole front kept them in a considerable state of apprehension, nor did they dare to dispatch troops to the Somme in such a whole-hearted way as would otherwise have been possible.

Naturally, with both sides in such a state of activity, it was inevitable that a great deal of raiding should go on—raids by the Germans to try and discover in what strength we were holding the line, raids by our troops to determine the German order of battle and to follow, by identification, the arrival or departure of troops to and from the zone. On June 22nd, at 2 A.M., a tremendous mine was exploded by the Germans near the Duck's Bill in Givenchy. So great was the mine, which had been dug right underneath Company Headquarters of the 2nd Battalion Royal Welsh Fusiliers, that a complete company was almost annihilated. Following the explosion, the Germans raided the trenches under cover of a heavy barrage, and for several hours hand to hand fighting of the fiercest nature was carried on. Every gun which could be brought to bear upon that area gave such support to our harassed troops as was possible, and eventually the position was more or less restored. It is doubtful whether this raid had any connection with the forthcoming Somme offensive. It was conducted on such a large scale, and the mine shaft itself extended for such a distance, that preparations must have been begun some long time previously.

On June 27th it was our turn to harass the enemy by one of the swiftest and best planned raids which had yet been carried out. Two parties of the 9th Battalion Highland Light Infantry went across No Man's Land at Mad Point and, under cover of a barrage, entered the German front line at two spots some 250 yards apart. The barrage in this case was a most difficult one for the batteries to carry out, as not only had the two parties to be covered on their front and flanks, but the reserve trenches behind the gap which lay between the two parties had also to be blocked. This, however, was only the beginning of the affair. Gradually the Highlanders, having destroyed all the dug-outs, mine shafts and hostile troops within their reach, began to bomb their way along the trench inwards towards each other. Gradually such Germans as were not bombed retreated before the hostile raiders and congregated in a herd in the middle, with the raiding parties closing in on both sides and the barrage roaring over their heads to cut off all retreat. And then, when the Germans were crowded and wedged into one section of the front line, unable to move either way and awaiting a bombing attack from both flanks, the raiding parties suddenly ceased pressing on, a mine was exploded right underneath the spot where the Germans were assembled, and the raiding parties returned to our own trenches, all further work on their part being unnecessary. It was a triumph of organisation and accuracy, and fully merited the results it achieved.

On July 2nd the 2nd Battalion of the Worcestershire Regiment raided the enemy lines for one hour and a half, and inflicted numerous casualties on the enemy, and on July 5th the 2nd Battalion Royal Welsh Fusiliers raided the enemy opposite the Duck's Bill and remained in their trench system for over two hours. By now the German infantry were in an advanced state of nerves. Although the news of the offensive on the Somme had reached them and they realised that the main attack was to the south, the continued bombardment on their own front and the nightly raids gave them not one moment's peace of mind, nor dared they materially weaken this part of the line. The raid by the Royal Welsh Fusiliers on July 5th deserves rather more than a passing word. It will be remembered that, on June 22nd, they had suffered heavily at the hands of a German raid. On July 5th they were given a chance of retaliation, and never has a raiding party gone over the top with such a thirst for blood and revenge. Not only did the infantry attack, but with them went a party of the Tunnelling Company who were sore at the thought that the German miners had evaded their counter-mining and had managed to carry a shaft so far beneath the British trenches. It was not their fault—in that marshy ground the most up-to-date and scientific apparatus was necessary to carry a shaft to any depth beneath the ground. That apparatus the Germans possessed and we did not, and as a result they carried their shaft far deeper than we could reach, and blew up a company of British infantry with one touch of an electric contact. July 5th, however, proved an adequate revenge. For upwards of two hours the infantry bombed and bayoneted, the sappers blew up all the mine shafts, whilst the Cuinchy group of artillery alone fired 6,000 rounds, relays of detachments keeping the guns firing at " gun fire " practically all the time.

That operation proved to be the last carried out by the 33rd Divisional Artillery on the La Bassée sector. No hint had been received by the batteries of a move, no word of warning was given of an early departure, but suddenly, at about five o'clock on the afternoon of Thursday, July 6th, there came a bolt from the blue. Orders were received that the 33rd Divisional Artillery was to move down to the Somme, that it would be relieved forthwith by the 39th, and that the first half-batteries would march to the wagon lines at 2 A.M. on the 7th, *i.e.*, in eleven hours' time. Now the batteries had been in action in the same positions for nearly five months, and a few hours was but scanty notice to give in which to move out from long-inhabited trench positions, ready and equipped for fighting of any sort. Yet the order was complied with, and, when dawn broke the following day, all traces of the departure had disappeared, and away in the wagon lines were to be found the guns and men who, the previous evening, had been in action within, in some cases, 1,700 yards of the enemy.

Before the further activities of the batteries are followed, a word must be spoken in summary of the doings of the Divisional Artillery on this front during the five months in which they were in action. It may be complained that the foregoing chapter deals too fully with the action of the Division as a whole, and that not enough detailed information has been given concerning the daily life of the batteries. The answer is, that what concerned the Division vitally concerned the batteries, and that it has been considered more desirable to give a general *résumé* of the work carried out by the Division, for in that work the Artillery played a most active part. It would have been easy, and to a few people interesting, to have recorded the shelling to which the batteries were subjected, the difficulties and trials they had to undergo, and individual cases in which particularly brilliant or destructive shoots were carried out, but in so doing the general picture would have been lost and the value of this record greatly reduced. The period spent on the La Bassée front was a period of stationary warfare during which the batteries were hardened and experienced, and, as such, lacked the interest which the ensuing part of the campaign supplies. The description which has been given of the type of fighting carried out during this time will enable an idea to be gained of the work of the batteries, but two points in particular are worthy of record.

When the batteries arrived in France they were raw and untrained as far as actual fighting was concerned. The resulting strain upon all battery commanders was tremendous, for no man knows, until he has been under shell fire, the actual sensations of that experience, and no battery commander knew exactly how his men would bear the very great trial to which they were going to be put. In those five months every battery had to suffer such shelling and bombardment, had to carry out such accurate and wearying shooting, and to work under conditions of such difficulty as to satisfy commanding officers that the 33rd Divisional Artillery was indeed one of which to be proud, and that the men could be relied upon to undergo any trial, to meet danger and death in any form without deviating one inch from the work put before them. When the batteries moved south to the Somme there was but one feeling which pervaded officers and men alike, a feeling of complete confidence, of complete determination and of keenness to take part in real active operations which they fully realised, from the previous five months' experience, they were well qualified to take.

And the other lesson learnt—what was that? It was the most valuable one of co-operation and even of personal intimacy with the infantry. During the whole of the La Bassée period, with one short exception, the 33rd Divisional Infantry were holding the line. Day in day out, officers from every battery were attached to battalion and company headquarters, and the friendship of the infantry for the gunners and *vice versa* became very real. Even the N.C.O.'s got to know each other by name, and the resulting feeling of confidence and friendship was of the greatest value. It was difficult to maintain this practice in later days when casualties in the infantry and gunners increased by leaps and bounds, when old friends were lost and new faces were ever appearing, and when the batteries were continually being attached to strange divisions and were covering infantry other than their own; but the lesson had been learnt, and throughout the war the Divisional Artillery made it an aim and object to get to know the infantry it was covering, to live and fight with them, and to perfect that liaison which was so important, not only by the teachings of the cold official text books, but by the invariable lesson of human nature.

. . . . .

From the wagon lines to which they had marched on the night of July 6th-7th, the batteries moved to Mt. Bernanchon and Guarbecque, and there the Divisional Artillery concentrated. One day it spent in overhauling, refitting and inspecting, and on the 9th it entrained at Fouquereuil, Chocques and Lillers, and moved to the Somme, a unit no longer raw, inexperienced and untried, but a unit trained and hardened by five months' trench fighting, now setting off to take part for the first time in large scale operations, in pitched battle, open fighting and all the trials and sufferings attendant thereto.

CHAPTER III.

THE BATTLE OF THE SOMME.

(JULY 14TH—SEPTEMBER 6TH 1916).

EARLY on the morning of July 10th the long troop trains carrying the batteries of the 33rd Divisional Artillery drew into the stations of Longueau and Sallieux, in the neighbourhood of Amiens, and began to unload with every due speed. All ranks fully expected to march into action forthwith, and therefore with something akin to dismay it was learnt that the destination of the batteries was the area around Soues, Arouves and Le Mesge, villages some miles *west* of Amiens, and far away from the battle lines. The 156th Brigade and half of the 162nd Brigade marched first to Cardonette, but their stay there was only temporary, and on the evening of the 10th, after a long and exceedingly dusty march in great heat through Amiens, Ailly and Picquigny, the Divisional Artillery was reported concentrated in the area allotted to it. There it stayed during the whole of the 11th, resting, overhauling after the long journey and generally making preparations for the great battle which all realised was very near indeed at hand.

This was different country to the late surroundings of the batteries. Hills and valleys, pleasant little villages with orchards and pastures proved an agreeable change to the flat monotony of Flanders, and, keen as the men were to prove their mettle in the great struggle being waged over the far horizon, a day of rest in this quiet country proved very welcome. On the 12th, however, all was hustle and stir once again, and the four brigades marched together as a Divisional Artillery to the Vecquemont-Daours area. The heat was tremendous, and several inches of fine dust lay on the roads ; the result of a column, many miles in length, of horses and guns on the march under these conditions may well be imagined, and on their arrival—the 156th Brigade at Corbie, the 162nd Brigade at Daours, with the 166th and 167th Brigades at Vecquemont—all were covered and half choked with a mixture of dust and perspiration which nothing short of a dip in the neighbouring stream could remove. Here the batteries bivouacked for the night, while battery commanders were detached from the column to ride on at daybreak to reconnoitre the front and generally to learn the tactical position into which they must shortly lead their batteries; and from here at 8.0 A.M. on the 13th the column, after the previous night's halt, continued the march to Treux and the neighbouring Marette Wood, where the brigades waited and gained such rest as was possible in view of the fact that they were ordered to be prepared to move at thirty minutes' notice.

Not until 1.30 A.M. on the 14th were the expected orders to move received, and even then for one and a half hours the batteries stood tense and expectant, gunners by their guns, drivers at the horses' heads, while in the distance the throb and roar of the great attack on the second German line of defence came down to them. At last, at 3.0 A.M. in the half-light the 162nd, 166th and 167th Brigades moved off to Becordel-Becourt, the 162nd Brigade proceeding in the first place to Méaulte for a few hours, while the 156th Brigade moved off in the afternoon of the same day to Méaulte, bivouacking on the spot which the 162nd Brigade had just vacated on completing the march to Becordel. Now was the battle very close at hand indeed; the roads were choked with infantry, guns and transport moving up, always moving up, with their faces set towards the east where lay a mighty, seething cauldron, the melting pot of two great armies in mortal conflict. Against this never-ending stream came down, in a slowly moving column, the fruits—fruits indeed, though often very bitter—of victory. Ambulances, walking wounded, shattered guns, depleted and exhausted infantry battalions coming out to rest, and, a sight more cheering to the up-going troops, long lines of German prisoners. The appearance of this highway, one of the main arteries to the actual front line, brought home to the batteries, who were drawn up off the side of the road awaiting orders, a very grim realisation of the ordeal they were about to undergo, but detracted not one whit of eagerness from the minds of the men to plunge into that struggle just as soon as circumstances should permit.

At 4.30 P.M. on the 14th the brigade commanders of the three brigades at Becordel rode on to reconnoitre positions; it was generally understood that no move into action would take place until shortly before dawn of the following morning, and preparations were accordingly made for a night bivouac. It was a disturbed night; the road hummed and buzzed with traffic unceasingly, the battery horse lines were twice shelled by a 4-in. high velocity gun— once so heavily that the horses had temporarily to be withdrawn—

and at 1.0 A.M. on the morning of Saturday, the 15th, two brigades, the 162nd and the 166th, received orders to march into action at dawn.

Independently at 3.0 A.M. the batteries of these two brigades moved off in full fighting order, and, passing over the old front line system near Fricourt, headed for the positions which had been reconnoitred on the previous day on the slopes of the valleys running from Caterpillar Wood to Montauban and Bazentin. Gas hung thickly in the valley east of Fricourt and necessitated the wearing of P.H. helmets, while a thick fog rendered progress of the utmost difficulty, but gradually the batteries pushed their way up past the ruins of Mametz and, topping the ridge, moved down the slopes into the ill-famed and deadly Caterpillar Valley which, in the next few days, was destined to be subjected to the most ruthless of shell-storms. Here certain of the batteries in their innocence halted and prepared for action, and Providence for once smiled upon them. A few stray shells pitched over Mametz Wood, a few fell on the road ahead, but Caterpillar Valley at that particular hour remained untouched, and the batteries, after a short halt, continued unharmed. Signs of battle were now to be found everywhere ; the dead, friend and foe alike, lay all around, broken and twisted guns and transport, discarded equipment, rifles, bombs, all the disorder of battle were strewn about, while the shell-pocked ground offered that dead and forbidding appearance which is a characteristic only to be found in ground recently fought over.

Through the now clearing mist the batteries advanced and, as in open fighting, manœuvred in the manner so often taught in the plains around Bulford. A, B and C/162 took up positions on the northern slopes of the Caterpillar Wood–Montauban valley several hundred yards north of Montauban, as previously reconnoitred, but D/162, by an unfortunate misunderstanding, dropped into action just short of the crest of the slope four hundred yards north of Caterpillar Wood and about a mile to the left of the 18-pdrs., instead of falling in practically alongside them. This alteration was very regrettable, for, although for tactical purposes the range was the same in either position, D Battery and its teams almost immediately came under heavy fire directed at the cavalry in the valley between it and Caterpillar Wood, and lost its battery commander, Major W. P. Bennett, who was killed by a shell within the first few minutes. The 166th Brigade at the same time came into action two hundred yards east of Mametz Wood, and by 8.30 A.M. both brigades were heavily bombarding that portion of Switch Trench which ran west from High Wood. Of the remaining brigades the 156th

ORDER OF BATTLE.

JULY—AUGUST 1916.

H.Q.R.A.

C.R.A.	Brigade Major.	Staff Captain.
Brig.-Gen. C. F. Blane, C.M.G.	Major H. K. Sadler, M.C.	Capt. T. C. Usher.

156th Brigade.

Lieut.-Colonel Rochfort-Boyd, D.S.O.
Adjutant : Lieut. E. H. Prior.

"A" Battery.	"B" Battery.	"C" Battery.	"D" Battery.
Capt. Lutyens.	Capt. R. D. Russell (wounded). Lieut. W. G. Pringle (temporarily). Capt. Mansell.	Capt. G. Lomer.	Capt. M. A. Studd.

162nd Brigade.

Lieut.-Colonel O. M. Harris, D.S.O.
Adjutant : Lieut. Hill.
Lieut. B. R. Heape.

"A" Battery.	"B" Battery.	"C" Battery.	"D" Battery.
Capt. F. C. Packham. Capt. Hill.	Major R. G. M. Johnston (killed). Capt. V. Benett-Stanford.	Capt. A. van Straubenzee.	Major W. P. Bennett (killed). Capt. T. St. P. Bunbury.

166th Brigade.

Colonel A. H. S. Goff, C.M.G.
Lieut.-Colonel Murray.
Adjutant : Lieut. S. M. Wood.

"A" Battery.	"B" Battery.	"C" Battery.	"D" Battery.
Capt. H. A. Littlejohn.	Major T. E. Durie.	Capt. H. Freeman.	Capt. W. A. T. Barstow, M.C. (wounded). Capt. Maxwell.

167th Brigade.

Lieut.-Colonel L. T. Goff.
Lieut.-Colonel C. G. Stewart, C.M.G., D.S.O.
Adjutant : Lieut. H. C. Cory.
Lieut. J. S. Campbell.

"A" Battery.	"B" Battery.	"C" Battery.
Capt. S. Talbot.	Major D. Stewart.	Capt. G. Fetherston.

marched through Fricourt during the morning in rear of the 19th Infantry Brigade (33rd Division), halted in reserve and reconnoitred the whole position, while the 167th Brigade moved to a position of assembly midway between Caterpillar and Bazentin-le-Grand Woods, experiencing great difficulty *en route* in getting past our heavy batteries which, in many cases, were in action off the side of the road and firing directly across it.   These two brigades came into action on the night of the 15th/16th, with the exception of A/167 which was not in action till 7.0 P.M on the 16th, and took up positions at 1.0 A.M., the 156th Brigade just north of Bazentin-le-Grand village, the 167th Brigade close together in line half a mile north of Caterpillar Wood.   The wagon lines of all batteries lay immediately west of Becordel.   Thus, by dawn on the 15th, two brigades were in action, while at dawn on the 16th the whole of the 33rd Divisional Artillery was in the very midst of the Battle of the Somme, and was bombarding the enemy to the utmost of its ability.

It is now necessary, in order to understand what follows, to turn our attention from the affairs of the batteries, and to endeavour to grasp the tactical situation as it presented itself at 4.0 A.M. on July 15th 1916.   At dawn on July 14th the great attack had been launched on the German Second Line from Contalmaison on the left to Longueval on the right.   This line covered the important villages of Bazentin-le-Petit, Bazentin-le-Grand and Longueval, while to the rear of it lay the sinister woods of Bazentin, High Wood and Delville Wood.   The actual assault was carried out by the 23rd, 7th, 3rd and 9th Divisions, the 23rd being on the left opposite the northern end of Bazentin-le-Petit, while the 9th Division on the right faced the village of Longueval.   At 3.25 A.M. the great attack began, and the German Second Line on a front of three miles was broken ; the flanks remained firm, however, and before the advance could be carried further it was considered essential that the gap should be widened by an attack towards Pozières on the left, and against Ginchy and Guillemont on the right.   In addition to this, certain local operations had to be carried out upon the front from Bazentin-le-Petit to Longueval, which embraced the zone covered by the 33rd Divisional Artillery, and it is with these operations that we must necessarily concern ourselves.

By nightfall on the 14th the whole of Bazentin-le-Petit Wood, village and windmill, Bazentin-le-Grand and the southern portion of Longueval were in our hands, our line running just to the north of these places ; but High Wood, although reached and captured by a gallant charge of cavalry supported by infantry, proved too tough a nut to crack, and remained in German hands together

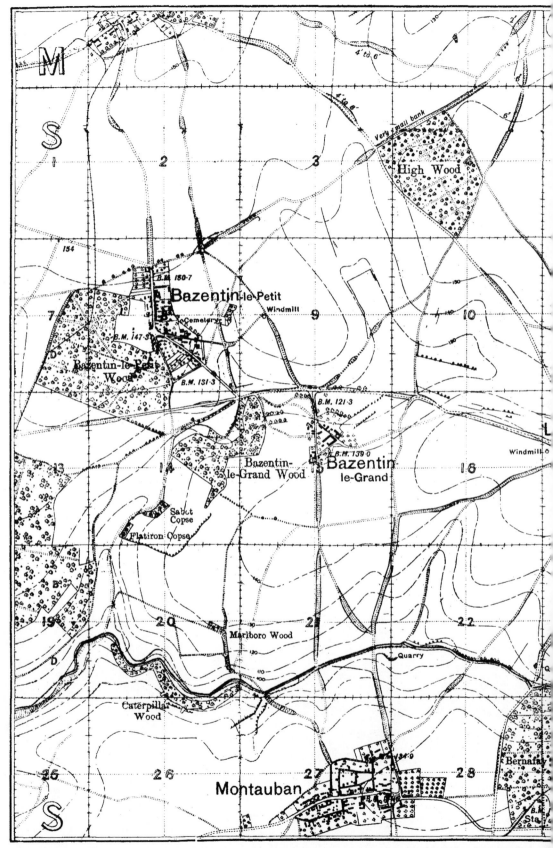

Scale 1:20,000.

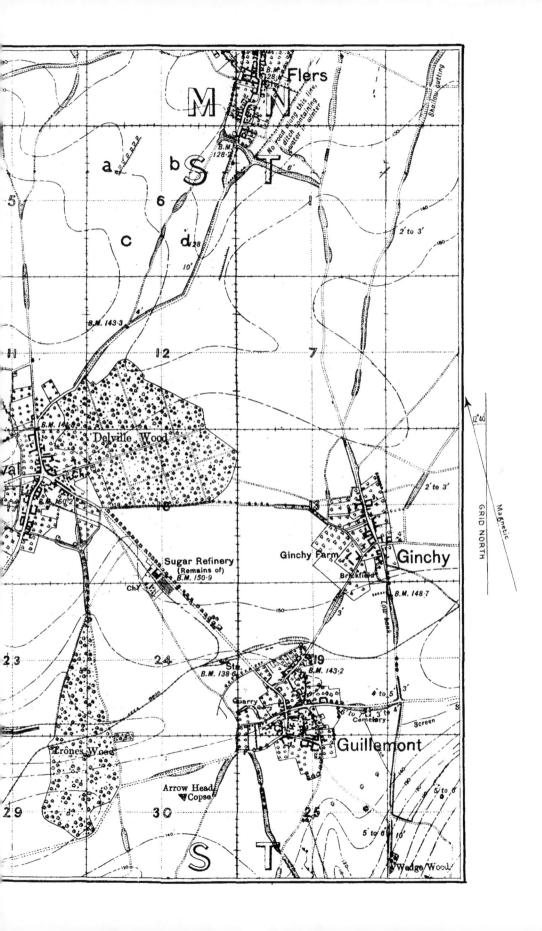

with the still uncaptured Delville Wood and the northern end of Longueval Village which was under the fire of enemy machine guns in High Wood. To clear these two woods and the remainder of Longueval was essential, and therefore, on the morning of July 15th, an advance was ordered by the 98th and 100th infantry brigades of the 33rd Division upon that portion of Switch Trench which ran westwards from High Wood, while a South African brigade was ordered up from Montauban to capture Delville Wood and the northern part of Longueval which still lay in German hands. With the latter attack, which indeed culminated into a battle of assaults and counter-assaults spread over several days, we cannot concern ourselves now. This history aims at perpetuating the deeds solely of one unit, and, to preserve the sequence of events, it is manifest that the operations upon that unit's immediate front must receive the closest attention; for this purpose we shall turn to the attack on Switch Trench launched on the morning of the 15th by the 98th and 100th infantry brigades covered by the guns of, amongst others, the 162nd and 166th Brigades of the 33rd Divisional Artillery, the first big attack in which these brigades took part.

From 8.30 A.M. for one hour the guns of both brigades bombarded Switch Trench where it ran west from High Wood, and at the end of the hour lifted on to Martinpuich, while the infantry assaulted the objectives which had just undergone this short but intense shelling. On the left the 98th infantry brigade reached its objective, but the 100th brigade was held up by machine-gun fire on the flanks and, after suffering some casualties, returned to its original line; the 98th brigade, with its right flank left thus in the air, had to follow suit, and by ten o'clock in the morning the battle had died down, leaving the guns free, apart from the usual day firing and registration, to get slightly more settled in their new surroundings. It should be remembered that the batteries had been marching, travelling by train and marching, day in day out, since the early morning of the 9th, and now, plunged into a great battle, it might have been hoped that at least a few hours' rest could have been obtained. This was not to be, however; no sooner had the batteries ceased co-operating in the infantry operation above referred to than they set to digging rough shelter trenches for the men in case of bombardment, digging pits for ammunition, camouflaging the guns as far as possible, getting up from the wagon lines heavy dumps of ammunition, and generally trying to get the battery positions into such a condition as would enable the guns to inflict the maximum of damage upon the enemy with the minimum of casualties to themselves. Open warfare was still the order of the day, and at any moment orders might be received for a further advance by the batteries, but on the other hand those orders might never come, and all ranks had already seen sufficient of the fierceness of the enemy's barrage to give them will to urge their already tired limbs to further efforts at self-protection.

As events turned out, no further assaults were made by the infantry on the zone covered by the 33rd Division batteries till the 20th; for five days the batteries were able to register accurately every outstanding feature and point of importance on their zones, while communications were elaborated and perfected from the somewhat rough and ready open warfare methods which had been set up when first the brigades came into action. O.P.'s were established in the old German second line between Longueval and Bazentin, from which points very clear observation upon High Wood and the ground lying to right and left thereof could be obtained, although the ground, consisting as it did of open undulating downs, offered but few salient objects upon which to register; there were, however, one or two points—the corner of High Wood, the orchards north of Longueval and the mysterious iron gate standing on the sky line between High Wood and Delville Wood—which enabled every battery commander to divide his zone up into areas each containing at least one fairly clear reference point, while to the left of High Wood an odd bush or tree and an occasional view of Switch Trench served the same purpose.

It must not be supposed, however, that because there was no infantry assault the guns had little to do. From the 15th until the night of the 19th/20th every battery kept Switch Trench under continual fire, cutting wire, bombarding the trench itself and generally rendering that line of defence as difficult and as uninhabitable as possible to the enemy. By night Switch Trench and Martinpuich were kept under intermittent bursts of fire, and it is safe to say that at no moment between the dates given above were all four batteries of any one brigade silent. This was no trench fighting position; the enemy had been got on the move, he must be kept on the move, and to do this every battery was firing more ammunition in twenty-four hours than had been normally fired by a whole brigade in a week on its late front opposite to La Bassée. On the 17th C/156 (Captain Lomer) was forced to withdraw to Flatiron Copse, 800 yards south of Bazentin-le-Petit Wood, as part of High Wood was still in German hands, and the battery, being under direct observation, was not only subject to a galling fire but was in serious danger of being rushed by a counter-attack on the part of the enemy. B (Captain Russell) and D (Captain Studd) batteries of the same brigade stuck it out until the early morning of the 21st, and then, the operations of the 20th which we shall shortly describe being over, withdrew to south of Bazentin-le-Petit Wood and Flatiron Copse respectively. As A/156 (Captain Lutyens) had in the first place dropped into action at the northern end of the valley running from Caterpillar Wood to Bazentin, the result of this movement was that the whole of the 156th Brigade was now behind, that is south of, Bazentin-le-Grand Wood, and no longer in the exposed position north of the village which it had hitherto occupied.

It has already been stated that, from the O.P.'s in the old German second line, a very fair view of the ground to the right and left of High Wood could be obtained ; this was indeed a fact, but with such skill had the Germans sited their main front line—the ill-omened Switch Trench—that it was exceedingly difficult to observe the actual effect upon it of the shelling to which it had been subjected, nor was the condition of the wire visible even through powerful field-glasses. Accordingly it was ordered that one officer per artillery brigade should advance from the outpost line of our infantry and make such examination of the German wire by daylight as was possible at close range. The opposing infantry were still in a condition of open fighting—sentry groups and outposts being the order of the day, with the main front line some distance behind them ; shortly before dawn on July 19th, therefore, the officers in question crawled out from our sentry groups and, passing in some cases right through the line of German outposts, made an examination, as careful and thorough as the proximity of the enemy in broad daylight would permit, of the condition of the Switch Trench wire. The examination was not reassuring ; in many cases the wire stood firm and untouched, and it was realised that further and strenuous efforts by the batteries would be essential that day if the coming attack was to have any chance of success. It is a regrettable duty to relate that one of the officers (Lieut. Elliott) who made this reconnaissance never returned ; having passed beyond a German sentry group he was severely wounded, and, although his orderly dragged him into a shell-hole and left him in such shelter as it offered while he went for help to bring him back into our lines, his body was never again found. The whole of the day was, indeed, a bad one for the 33rd Divisional Artillery. Colonel A. H. S. Goff (166th Brigade) was wounded and evacuated ; all the batteries were heavily shelled, in particular the batteries of 162nd Brigade which wilted beneath a storm of shrapnel during the entire day, while the head-quarters of the same brigade received a three-hour bombardment of lachrymose gas shell, making the carrying on of the administration extremely difficult. None of this, however, was allowed to cause any interruption of the day's work, and by nightfall all batteries of the Division had received orders for the following day's assault upon High Wood, and had made the necessary preparations.

At 3.25 A.M. on Thursday, July 20th, the first infantry operation took place in this zone since the attack on the morning of the 15th. Following on a half-hour bombardment by the 33rd and 21st Divisional Artilleries (XV. Corps) which began at 2.55 A.M., the 19th infantry brigade advanced to the assault of High Wood. Two thousand rounds of 18-pdr. and 500 rounds of 4·5 in. howitzer ammunition per brigade were fired in support of the infantry, the target of the batteries being High Wood until " zero " hour (3.25 A.M.), when the batteries lifted to the northern or enemy edge of the wood, bombarding it for half an hour until 3.55 A.M. and then making the final lift to the far side of the wood. The assault was successful, the wood was carried, but during the whole day the infantry were subjected to the most intense and galling artillery fire by the enemy guns, light and heavy. All day long our batteries searched the roads and approaches from Flers, and the hollows north of the wood — anywhere whence an enemy counter-attack might develop — and, with the exception of one which was launched at 12.30 P.M. and beaten back by artillery and infantry combined, this fire was successful in keeping the enemy at bay.

The hostile artillery fire, however, was terrible; not one inch of the wood but was torn and swept by high explosive shell, rent by shrapnel and rendered completely uninhabitable to any human being. At 6 P.M. the effect of this shell-storm came to a head, and for half an hour our batteries put down a heavy barrage along the northern edge of the wood, under cover of which the infantry retired to the southern half; it was no hostile counter-attack which thus drove them back — it was the sheer weight and force of the thousands of shells which, from all around, the enemy poured into the wood, and which smashed and shattered the unfortunate troops who were trying to hold what they had so gallantly won. At first the report came through that the whole of the wood had been evacuated and that the infantry were back in their original line in front of Bazentin, but this was proved to be erroneous, and the southern half of High Wood at any rate was retained in our grasp. At 9.30 P.M. the enemy opened a vicious gas shell barrage on the ridge in front of D/162 and on the batteries of the 167th Brigade, and at 11 P.M. followed this up by a counter-attack on the scene of the morning's fight. After three hours' firing the situation became quieter, and in the morning the position on the whole had not changed since dusk the previous evening.

For the next two days there ensued another period of comparative inactivity as far as infantry assaults were concerned. Both sides paused, as it were, to draw breath, but not for one moment did this cause a lull in artillery activity. The enemy, as well as our own Higher Command, was beginning to realise more and more the immense importance of counter-battery work, and these intervals between the attacks were, from the gunners' point of view, almost more to be feared than the attacks themselves. Morning, noon and night first one battery and then another would be subjected to a sudden burst of intense fire, while at other times a ponderous and deliberate bombardment of a fixed area in which a number of batteries were in position would be carried out—a system which had the most harassing effect upon the men, and to the success of which an ever-lengthening casualty list of guns and gunners bore eloquent testimony. July 21st was a typical day of this sort; starting at 10 A.M., a prolonged and widespread enemy bombardment was carried out during the whole day with 4·2 in. and 5·9 in. upon the valley running from Longueval to Montauban, and its adjacent slopes. The 18-pdr. batteries of the 162nd Brigade, together with the headquarters of the brigade itself, came heavily under fire, and a long casualty list was only averted by the use of the shelter trenches which by this time had been dug in all the battery positions. While this was in progress the 167th Brigade, farther to the left, was also undergoing a severe bombardment by 5·9 in. howitzers. Direct hits were obtained upon B/167 (Major Stewart), and in all the batteries, including D/162 which lay just behind the 167th Brigade, a number of casualties were sustained. Murderous fire was, at the same time, opened upon Caterpillar Valley, from the fork between Mametz and Caterpillar Woods down the entire length of the valley nearly to Mametz village itself, and at times during the day it was almost impossible to see a single battery position from which the smoke, flame and dust of bursting shells were not flying. Nothing could be done; it was a case of " wait and see "—the hardest test to which troops can be put—and to the eternal credit of the men it may be said that they waited on this, as on all other similar occasions, with quiet philosophy and with a stoicism which it would be hard to equal.

Meanwhile, what of our friends the infantry ? On the morning of the 21st the hard-pressed 33rd Division was withdrawn from the line and was succeeded by the infantry of the 51st Division (153rd, 154th, and 155th infantry brigades). At the same time the zones of the 33rd Divisional batteries side-slipped to the right and, coming under the 51st Divisional Artillery for tactical purposes, covered the line to the right (*i.e.* east) of High Wood. Day firing was carried out upon Switch Trench, the new zones were registered and night firing, consisting of 500 18-pdr. and 75 4·5 in. howitzer rounds per brigade, was directed upon the hollows in rear of and approaches to the divisional zone. At 10.15 P.M. Caterpillar Wood and the neighbouring localities were heavily bombarded by gas shell and high explosive, and all communications of the 167th Brigade were cut; lamp signalling was immediately taken up, however, and proved itself entirely reliable as a means of communication, despite the gun flashes all around and in the sky.

The morning of July 22nd was devoted to further registration and short bombardments. From 3.0 A.M. until 3.30 a general bombardment of Switch Trench was ordered at the rate of 2 rounds per minute from the 18-pdrs. and one round per minute from the howitzers, totalling upwards of three thousand rounds fired by the fifteen batteries. At the end of the bombardment the 162nd Brigade stood by to carry out a registration by aeroplane, but no machine ever appeared and soon afterwards normal firing for the day was continued, D/162 shortly after one o'clock carrying out a destructive shoot on some machine guns and dug-outs to the west of High Wood which were, by their enfilade fire, holding up the whole situation and preventing an advance in the neighbourhood. Their destruction was essential, for an advance had been ordered for the following day, and at 7 P.M. in the evening the whole of the front burst into flame in preliminary bombardment for the assault. At the rate of 80 rounds per battery per hour the guns of the XIII., XV. and III. Corps bombarded the positions which troops of the 5th (on the right), 51st and 19th (on the left) divisions were to attack next day, the objective of the 51st division, which was covered by the guns of the 33rd Divisional Artillery, being the N.E. and N.W. edges of High Wood, together with a portion of Switch Trench running E. and W. therefrom.

"Zero" was 1.30 A.M. on July 23rd, and seven minutes previous to that hour the fire of the batteries was increased to intense rate. At half-past one to the second the infantry went over the top, and the batteries searched back by short lifts to a line 200 yards beyond the objective. For half an hour was this searching fire continued, and at two o'clock the batteries slowed down and set up a protective barrage 200 yards beyond the late German trench, under cover of which it was hoped the infantry would be able to consolidate their position. Such, however, was not the case. Although in places the attacking troops had gained their objectives, at many points our men had been held up by machine gun fire and, by their failure to advance, had compelled their more successful comrades to retire to their starting place. All along the line the assault failed, and when at 5 A.M. the enemy counter-attacked fiercely the guns shortened their range and bombarded Switch Trench once more. By 8.30 A.M. all was quiet again, the attack was over—and our infantry were back holding the same line from which they had advanced earlier in the morning.

From July 23rd–27th there ensued another of those lulls which have already been described; for the moment our advance was checked and held up while the Higher Command appeared to be seeking a solution to the very determined and successful opposition which the enemy showed to our troops in this sector, and during the interval which elapsed the usual harassing was carried out night and day by the now rapidly wearying batteries. Two thousand rounds by day and 700 by night were poured on to the German defences by each brigade, and in return the German batteries gave no peace to our guns, daily subjecting the area in which the batteries were located to a vicious and effective bombardment. Mametz and Caterpillar Woods, the valleys running from Caterpillar Wood to Bazentin on the one hand and Montauban on the other were daily ploughed from end to end by shells varying in calibre from 77 mm. to 12 in., while the valley running from Longueval to Montauban, together with the ridge to the west thereof, became a veritable death trap. It was of no use seeking to move the battery positions; one place was as bad as another, and there was nothing to do but to sit tight and trust that, before our batteries were completely wiped out, a further advance might check the ever-increasing storm of German shells.

There was another, and a very serious, difficulty to be faced at this time also; owing to the enormous strain placed upon the guns by the incessant day and night firing, the running-out springs began to give way and to fail, and great difficulty was found in obtaining new ones. Previous to the war almost all these springs had come from Germany, and, with this source of supply cut off, British manu-facturers at home had found it impossible as yet so to organise their output as to meet the ever-increasing and insistent demands from the various theatres of war. As an instance of the seriousness of this trouble it may be mentioned that on July 26th only five guns of the 162nd Brigade were in action, the remainder having no service-able springs left, whilst of these five two had to be pushed up by hand after the firing of each round. Such a state of affairs, which cut down the volume of fire of the brigade by over one half, was bound to reflect seriously upon the preliminary bombardments and barrages in any attack, nor was the trouble confined to the 162nd Brigade alone.

On July 24th the 33rd Divisional Artillery ceased to work in contact with the infantry, and was put under direct orders of the XV. Corps to carry out counter-battery work on the whole Corps front, searching hostile battery positions, hollows and approaches, and in addition answering any S.O.S. call when required upon all portions of the Corps front. Such duties naturally incurred still more firing and work ; two batteries (A and B) of the 162nd Brigade were unable to get sufficient right switch to cover the now wider front, and were forced to move further up the slope, new O.P.'s in front of Longueval had to be reconnoitred and linked up with the batteries by telephone, while the new zone which stretched from the south of Martinpuich to Delville Wood had to be registered before dusk. Hardly had this been done than, at 8.30 P.M., a report was received that the enemy were leaving their trenches between High Wood and Delville Wood, and the batteries immediately opened a rapid rate of fire to break up the expected counter-attack which, surely enough, was launched at 8.45 P.M. under a very heavy barrage. Both sides bombarded with the utmost fury, and ultimately the counter-attack melted under our fire, but not till midnight were the tired batteries able to report "all quiet," and even then night firing was carried on in the usual way. The 51st Divisional Artillery was at this time responsible for the direct support of the infantry, and it was by way of co-operation that this bombardment of the hostile trenches was carried out.

It has been previously stated that from the 23rd to the 27th a lull occurred in the infantry operations. This, broadly speaking, is a fact, but it must not be supposed that during that time our front line troops were entirely inactive. Bit by bit each day they had been bombing their way through Longueval, sometimes without artillery support, sometimes assisted by the guns, as on the 26th when for one hour from dawn the guns poured shells into the northern end of the village. It was slow work, this gradual penetration, but by the evening of the 26th a very appreciable advance had been made, and, when orders were received at 4 P.M. that a general assault on Delville Wood and the orchards north of Longueval would take place next day (27th), our troops were in a far more favourable position for "taking off" than they had been a week earlier.

The assault was delivered at 7.10 A.M. on the morning of Thursday, the 27th, and was preceded by an artillery bombardment beginning at 5.30 A.M. For this bombardment 1,500 18-pdr. and 400 4·5 in. howitzer rounds were fired by each brigade, and were directed mainly upon the trenches to be assaulted and the back areas thereof. To the 5th Division was entrusted the capture of the objectives on the front directly under the guns of the 33rd Divisional Artillery, and the line of this ran from the north-west edge of Delville Wood through the enclosures 150 yards north of Longueval village, along the sunken road running west from these enclosures to the High Wood–Longueval road. The chief interest of the attack, however, lay in the fact that the creeping barrage, as already practised in the opening days of the Somme battle, was now being more and more carefully elaborated. It had not yet reached that high stage of perfection which, in the offensives of Arras and Passchendaele in 1917, enabled the gunners to provide what was almost an ever-moving curtain of fire advancing yard by yard in front of the infantry, but it did even now remain upon one point until the very last moment and then lift off, but scarcely creep, to the next point to be attacked while the infantry stormed the first.

All day long fierce fighting continued but, although on the right of the line the 2nd Division gained their objectives, on the left the men of the 5th Division were held up at points. The climax of the day was reached at six o'clock in the evening, when a heavy counter-attack was launched all along the line by the enemy, but this counter-attack, in common with a similar one launched at 10.30 P.M. on the following night (28th), broke up under the fire of our guns. During this attack green flares were lighted all along the front by our foremost infantry at specified times, and although it was difficult to persuade them to do this, inasmuch as they considered that the flares would be equally useful to the enemy as well as to our guns in showing up their position, the information thus obtained of the progress of the assault was of very great value.

During the 28th and 29th the batteries busied themselves in preparing for future operations. Casualties in men and guns had been severe throughout the fighting, vast quantities of ammunition had been expended, and all this had now to be replaced. On the morning of the 27th a 5·9 in. shell had exploded directly in the pit where the men of B/162 (Major Johnston) were getting their breakfasts, killing and wounding every man in the pit, while on the afternoon of the 29th D/162 (Captain Bunbury) was heavily shelled and lost one and a half detachments who were practically blown to pieces. A 5·9 in. shell burst right upon a pile of ammunition beside one of its guns and exploded a number of rounds; in addition to the wiping out of the detachments, the gun itself was completely destroyed by the explosion, and only the piece and a portion of the spade were ever found afterwards. It is curious to note that the force of the explosion, which made a huge crater in the ground, threw a complete wagon of ammunition so high into the air that it came down some 150 yards from the battery, yet not a single round in the wagon exploded. As, in addition to this, all the guns of C/167 (Captain Fetherston) were out of action and the other batteries had suffered the usual daily casualties which now had become inevitable, it will be seen that the Divisional Artillery was in a fairly serious plight. However, the work had to be carried on, and on the afternoon of the 29th the batteries set themselves to the now familiar task of bombarding Switch Trench with 45 rounds per gun, in preparation for another attack which was due to take place on the morrow.

The bombardment proper for this attack began at 4.45 P.M. on the 30th, but previous to this there had been the short burst already referred to and another similar effort in the early morning from 3.15 to 5.15. At the same time our heavy artillery carried out a series of destructive—or, at least, would-be destructive—shoots on the enemy batteries; this was a most essential procedure, for the work of the batteries had been greatly impeded all the morning by an intense hostile gas shelling of the positions while, during the whole of the afternoon, the batteries on the ridge north of Caterpillar Wood were raked from end to end by high explosive. At last, however, the final bombardment opened, and from 4.45 P.M. till 6.10 P.M. the German defences between High Wood and Delville Wood were subjected to 800 rounds per 18-pdr. battery and 400 rounds per 4·5 in. howitzer battery all along the front. Seven minutes before zero, which was at 6.10 P.M., fire was quickened to intense rate, and at zero hour troops of the XIII. and XV. Corps advanced to the attack, having for their objectives the sunken road running from the N.W. face of Delville Wood to the east corner of High Wood. The XIII. Corps, who were on the right, reached their objectives successfully, but the XV. Corps, advancing on the left of the XIII., were not so fortunate; enfilade machine gun fire from strong points near the orchards north of Longueval held them up, while their left, although successful in reaching the sunken road near the corner of High Wood, was subjected to such a perfect hell of high explosive that it was shelled out and forced to retire. Thus at 8 P.M., when firing was reduced to normal, the situation was but little different to what it had been before the attack.

The attack of the 30th was very typical of the tactics in practice at this time in the Somme battle. The same thing had been seen in the previous assaults of the 20th and 23rd, and the same thing was to be seen in subsequent operations; small attacks on limited areas—perhaps only on a two division front—were launched and, nine times out of ten, were doomed to failure by their narrow scope. There is no doubt that individual strong points were holding up the general advance and had to be overwhelmed before any more ambitious plans were undertaken, but there is also no doubt that, when these unfortunate battalions went over the parapet upon some purely local undertaking, they were immediately subjected to machine gun fire in enfilade from the flanks, where no attack was taking place, and to overwhelming shell fire from batteries on neighbouring zones, which, owing to the undisturbed state of their own zone, were able to add to the already heavy volume of fire on the front attacked. It may be that the Higher Command was right in its handling of the situation, but for the men on the spot it was heart-breaking to see battalions of the finest material launched to certain death on an attack which, by the narrowness of its front, was doomed to failure before it ever began.

July 30th and 31st contained nothing more of importance than three S.O.S. calls from Delville Wood, and on Tuesday, August 1st, at 5.30 A.M. orders were received with dramatic suddenness for the 162nd and 166th Brigades to be relieved by the 78th and 79th Brigades of the 17th Divisional Artillery. In a fever-heat of expectation the batteries of the two brigades waited all day long for the orders to take effect; at last, between four and seven o'clock in the afternoon, the incoming units arrived, and with heartfelt thanks the batteries, taking their guns with them, marched back to the wagon lines. It was unfortunate that D/78 should have chosen the moment to relieve D/162 when four low-flying German aeroplanes were right overhead, but choose it they did, and the price had to be paid. The incoming battery was a little ahead of its time, and, as a result, when the teams and limbers of D/162 appeared on the scene the shell storm for which the aeroplanes had called was just beginning. Whizz bangs, 4·2 in. and 5·9 in. shell poured down upon the battery position and horses for over half an hour, and how the battery escaped with such light casualties as it did, was a marvel. One gun and one ammunition dump were destroyed, several drivers and horses were hit, but in no way was the relief disorganised, and D/162, after manœuvring under a hail of shells, ultimately withdrew towards the Montauban flank. For the rest of the evening Caterpillar Valley all around and south-west of Mametz Wood was deluged with shells, and the batteries who chose that route for their outgoing march had an extremely unpleasant time. All got away in the end, however, and after a short halt at the wagon lines continued the march. Dernancourt, which was the destination of the batteries, was reached at 2.30 A.M., and here they remained till the 11th resting, refitting and generally cleaning up after the ordeal of the past eighteen days.

Only two brigades were now left in the line—the 156th and the 167th—and, as Headquarters staff of the 33rd Divisional Artillery had gone into rest at Dernancourt, these two were put under the command of the 51st Division. The zone covered by the 156th Brigade extended along the High Wood–Bazentin-le-Petit road southwards from the north-west corner of the wood, while the 167th Brigade looked after the road running south-east from the eastern edge of High Wood; D/156 (Captain Studd) carried out counter-battery duties. From August 1st to August 11th little of importance in the way of operations occurred. Hostile attacks on Bazentin-le-Petit on the 2nd and against High Wood on the 10th were repulsed by our fire, while on the 4th and the 7th minor infantry engagements were carried out by our troops on the orchards and houses along the north-west edge of Delville Wood and on High Wood respectively.

Very heavy firing took place throughout this period, and during the week ending August 17th the 156th Brigade fired no less than twelve thousand rounds, while the German artillery must have flung something like the same amount into our positions. B/167 (Major Stewart) was shelled out and had to move on the 3rd to a position six hundred yards east of Caterpillar Wood, where it was joined next day by Captain Fetherston's battery (C/167) which had also undergone a severe gruelling at the hands of the enemy. A/167 (Captain Talbot) proved no less unfortunate than the other two batteries, and on the 5th, after a very heavy shelling which lasted all day, it was compelled to move to a position alongside "B" and "C," where it went to form two six-gun batteries instead of three consisting of four guns each. At the same time the brigade was temporarily handed over to the command of Major Stewart, for Lieut.-Colonel L. T. Goff had on the previous day been evacuated sick to England. Thus the two brigades remained shelling and being shelled, day in day out, until August 11th, when the other two brigades (162nd and 166th) came up into the line from the Dernancourt rest area and relieved them. The 156th and 167th had been in action continuously since July 16th under the most trying and harassing of conditions. They had been subjected to shelling more severe than any yet experienced in the war, and, when they marched out to rest on the evening of the 11th, they were utterly exhausted, utterly worn out, a party of very tired and weary men.

On returning to the line on the 11th the batteries of the 162nd Brigade did not reoccupy their old positions but, after reconnaissance by Lieut.-Colonel Harris, formed two six-gun 18-pdr. batteries under the command of Major Johnston and Captain van Straubenzee, and took up positions on the southern slopes bordering Caterpillar Valley, at a point about three hundred yards N.N.W. of Montauban. At the same time D/162, which from the 8th onwards had been sending parties up from Dernancourt to dig gun-pits and prepare the place for occupation, came into action under the northern bank of Caterpillar Valley about five hundred yards to the right front of the other two batteries, which was the position it had originally been intended to occupy on July 15th. The 166th Brigade took up positions 500 yards north of Caterpillar Wood.

While these two brigades had been out at rest a change had taken place amongst the infantry, and the guns now covered the 33rd Division (forming part of the XV. Corps), with the 14th Division on the right and the 1st Division on the left, the tactical command of the batteries being in the hands of the 14th Divisional Artillery. From the 11th until the 18th the lull in infantry fighting, which had been noticeable in this sector since the beginning of the month, continued, but the work of the guns was as usual very heavy. In addition to counter-battery work and minor bombardments, four hundred and fifteen 18-pdr. rounds by day and five hundred by night had to be expended by each brigade on searching and sweeping roads and hollows behind the brigade zone, while the 4·5 in. howitzers carried out the same work to the extent of two hundred and thirty-three rounds by day and one hundred and sixty-six by night. The zone in question was the extreme right of the 33rd Divisional front, along the enemy front line known as Wood Lane. Fortunately for the batteries, hostile shelling upon the gun positions was far less violent than had been the case before the two brigades went into rest, and it was now possible to get through a very fair amount of registration without interference from enemy shell fire ; this was important, for the guns had to be ranged upon a number of new points owing to the change in position, while a wireless set which had been installed at Brigade Headquarters enabled numerous " N.F." calls to be picked up from our aeroplanes, all of which were acted upon by the howitzer batteries of the respective brigades.

On the 16th orders were received for an attack to be delivered on Friday, the 18th, and in preparation for this the ammunition allotted for night firing was doubled on the nights of the 16th and 17th, while by day the guns bombarded Wood Lane, cutting the wire and shelling not only the trench but also No Man's Land in front thereof, lest the German machine-gunners should creep out forward and thereby escape our barrage. At 2.45 P.M. on the 18th the attack was launched by the 33rd Division, with the 14th Division on its right. In addition to the preceding two-days shelling, the whole of the morning of the attack, with two short forty-minute intervals, was devoted to barrage firing on the enemy trenches, the barrage of 18-pdrs. lifting at three given times to suggest an impending assault, whereupon the 4·5 in. howitzers, a few minutes after the "lift," dropped back on to Wood Lane (the enemy front line) to catch such of the enemy as had manned the parapet to withstand an attack. Immediately prior to zero hour there was no bombardment; it was hoped to start the attack simultaneously along the whole front, and the best means of achieving this was considered to be an opening of the barrage at zero itself, without any bombardment during the preceding five minutes.

The order of battle in this attack showed the XIII. Corps on the right, the III. Corps on the left and the XV. Corps in the centre. The two flank Corps successfully gained their objectives, as did also the right of the XV. Corps, but the 33rd Division was held up partly by flank machine-gun fire and partly by hostile machine guns which had, after all, succeeded in pushing forward into shell holes in No Man's Land, and had thus avoided our barrage. The objective of the 33rd had been Wood Lane Trench, from about 150 yards north-west of its junction with Orchard Trench to the cross-roads just outside the western corner of High Wood; at 3.15 P.M., when the failure of the infantry to gain the objectives was realised, the batteries of the 162nd and 166th brigades dropped their range from the protective barrage they had established four hundred yards beyond Wood Lane Trench, and put down a heavy barrage along a line two hundred yards north-east of the trench. This was maintained throughout the afternoon until, the position on the right being somewhat obscure, the batteries were requested by the 14th Division to lengthen their range by one hundred yards. A situation report was received shortly afterwards, however, which entirely justified the original shortening of the range, and this was resumed till half-past seven in the evening when normal night firing was begun. Once again the attack had been beaten off by the deadly and ubiquitous machine guns, and once again our infantry looked at the grim and forbidding Wood Lane Trench across a No Man's Land thick with dead and wounded.

On the 19th the zones of the batteries side-slipped two hundred yards to the right, and for two days registration, in addition to the usual harassing fire, was carried out on the new zones. Teams were at work day and night to replenish ammunition which the past few days had seen so lavishly expended, and, thus reinforced, a further effort was made on the 21st to advance our line in the neighbourhood of Wood Lane and Tea Trench (running N.E. from Wood Lane), while the 14th Division advanced to the capture of the last line of enemy defences in Delville Wood.

Once again we were defeated; after a short preliminary bombardment Wood Lane was assaulted at 3.30 P.M., while at 1.30 A.M. on the following morning (22nd) the attack on Tea Trench was carried out, but in neither case were we able to advance. The enemy front line was stiff with men and machine guns, and our troops were swept away by a blast of fire before they were even able to get to grips with the enemy. Thus ended a tragic series of short attacks on portions of the enemy trenches, attacks which failed in their objects, which wore out our troops—infantry and gunners alike—and which cost us many thousands of lives that we could ill spare.

On the afternoon of August 22nd signs and portents were not lacking of a new and great effort all along the line to continue the advance which latterly had been so severely held up. The previous day Lieut.-Colonel Harris (162nd Brigade) had been ordered to reconnoitre a position for a forward gun which should be able, at a range of not more than 2,000 yards, to enfilade the new German trench running north-east from Wood Lane, and such a position had, after taking bearings from various O.P.'s, been chosen. Now, at 4 P.M. on the 22nd, the gun was ordered into action, and was accordingly brought into position in a shell-hole on the southern edge of the road which ran east and west due north of Bazentin-le-Grand. Three hundred rounds were dumped alongside it, the whole was placed under command of Lieutenant V. Benett-Stanford (C/162), and a most satisfactory registration was obtained with seventy rounds burst immediately over and into the enemy trench in true enfilade at a range of 1,600 yards. Following on this, on the morning of the 23rd, the 156th Brigade came out of rest and went into action about half a mile south-west of Montauban, as a group under Lieut.-Colonel Rochfort-Boyd; to this group was added A/167 which took up a position in the same area, and later B/167 which, on the 25th, joined the 156th Brigade group in a position near A/167. The 167th Brigade, now under the command of Lieut.-Colonel C. G. Stewart, did not come into action as a unit, but kept its remaining battery out at rest to replace casualties as they might occur.

On the 23rd the orders for the attack were received. This time it was to be the biggest operation since July 14th, the order of battle showing the French to attack on the right from the Somme itself to Maurepas, the XIV. Corps from south of Guillemont to the western edge of Ginchy Village, the XV. Corps from a point in the Longueval–Flers road north of Delville Wood to the western edge of High Wood, and the III. Corps from that point westwards to the extreme left of the attack.

On the immediate front of the batteries (of which the 156th group was attached to the 7th Division, the 162nd and 166th to the 14th Division), the right infantry brigade (100th) of the 33rd Division was to establish itself in Wood Lane, while the 14th Division was to advance the right of its line so as to connect up with the left of the XIV. Corps, to clear the remainder of Delville Wood, to establish a line outside the wood from the position already held by the Division in Beer Trench to the Longueval–Flers road, and there to connect up with the right of the 33rd Division. The bombardment began at 3.45 P.M. on Thursday, the 24th, and, so far as the batteries of the 33rd Divisional Artillery were concerned, consisted in shelling New Trench (behind Wood Lane) and the ground in rear thereof, Tea Trench, Tea Lane and Tea Support (west of the Longueval–Flers road), but chiefly Tea Trench, while the advanced enfilade gun of the 162nd Brigade was ordered to sweep New Trench in enfilade from 5.45 P.M. until the moment of attack. The average rate of fire was one round per gun per minute, but towards the close of the bombardment the rate gradually quickened up until, at zero, the rate of fire became intense.

Zero hour was at 6.45 P.M. on the 24th, and, two minutes after the infantry had gone over the top, a general lift was started by the guns. The howitzers lengthened their range straight away and bombarded the Flers–Longueval road, while the 18-pdr. barrage gradually crept forward by 25 yards at a time, until it finally came to rest along a line about 200 yards north-east of the infantry objective. At a quarter-past six the rate of fire dropped to the original one round per gun per minute, while at half-past ten the close barrage was terminated and intermittent searching and sweeping of the enemy zone was adopted in its stead.

Meanwhile, how had the day gone with the infantry ? On the extreme right the French had won a great victory and had swept all before them ; the XV. Corps had gained all its objectives save the extreme eastern corner of Delville Wood and a small portion of Beer Trench, while on our own immediate zone the infantry had at last swept over the objectives they had for so long striven to capture ; the enfilade gun in particular did tremendous damage, the infantry reporting numbers of the enemy found dead in New Trench and thereby testifying to the great effects which may be expected of field guns firing in true enfilade.   All night long till 7.30 A.M. on the 25th the batteries stood by to answer S.O.S. calls, and kept a slow rate of fire on their zones whilst the infantry consolidated the position, but no counter-attack materialised, and in the morning we still held firmly the ground we had captured the previous day.   Great praise accrued to infantry and gunners for the success of these operations ;   in particular the G.O.C. R.A. 14th Division sent personal congratulations to Lieut.-Colonel Harris (162nd Brigade) who, from his observation station near Longueval whence all the battle could clearly be viewed, sent back situation reports which reached the General Officer commanding the 33rd Division before reports came in from any other source, thereby enabling him to deal quickly with every new point as it arose.   There was only one disappointing feature in the whole of the attack, and that was the enormous number of " dud " shells fired by our heavy artillery.   Not more than 40 per cent. of their shells burst properly, whilst the German heavies obtained at least 95 per cent. detonations which caused the most appalling destruction wherever they occurred.   It was a sidelight—but an important one —of the battle, nor, for many months, did this serious state of affairs right itself.

Hitherto the enemy had not shown many signs of retaliation for the operations of the past few days, but at 8 o'clock on the morning of Friday, the 25th, the storm broke.   Every battery position was heavily bombarded throughout the day with shells of every calibre up to 8 in., and this at a time when it was essential that ammunition wagons should be able to reach the guns to refill their depleted stocks.   All day long the storm raged so severely that in certain cases the detachments had to be withdrawn from the guns.   Major Johnston of B/162 was killed whilst sending his men into cover— a loss which the brigade ill could suffer—and many of the detachments were killed and wounded ; so violent, indeed, was the shell fire that the 18-pdr. battery positions of the 162nd Brigade, churned up from end to end, were rendered quite uninhabitable, and during that night and the following day new positions were taken up about 500 yards further to the north-east.

While this was going on, the batteries of the 156th Brigade group were also changing positions, but this time for tactical purposes. In order to be able to bombard Ginchy, new positions 1,500 yards south-east of Longueval and along the sunken road running from that village to Bernafay Wood had been reconnoitred, and were now taken up, while the zones of the other brigades at the same time side-slipped 800 yards to the right and covered the ground immediately north-east of Delville Wood. Fearful weather, moreover, broke over the whole battlefield. Rain and wind in endless storms turned the countryside into a vast sea of mud, and, catching the batteries of the 156th and 162nd Brigades in their new and only partially prepared positions, caused them not merely extreme discomfort but real difficulty in being able to fight their guns at all. No roads led to the batteries, but merely dry weather tracks across roughly beaten-down shell holes and trenches, and for a time it seemed as though they must be cut off from all sources of ammunition supply. Nevertheless, during the 27th and 28th the wagons of the batteries, aided by our own D.A.C. and the Column of the 7th Division, struggled through the mud with load after load, gunners and passing infantry helping the teams to reach the positions, and by the evening of the 27th not only had all the batteries refilled their normal gun-line dumps, but the 156th Brigade had gone even further and had brought up 6,000 rounds per battery in conformation with an order they had only received 24 hours previously ! It had been intended on the 29th to resume the offensive with the French and Fourth Armies, and indeed the 156th Brigade group did actually carry out a seven-hour bombardment of Ginchy before the order to stop reached them ; the weather was too bad, no infantry could have attacked with any hope of success, and accordingly the operations were postponed until finer weather should supervene.

This lull was very welcome, for it gave the batteries an opportunity of digging in and of draining their positions so as to render them slightly more habitable. The infantry of the 14th Division had, on the 26th and 27th, bombed their way with only minor artillery support right through the remaining corner of Delville Wood, and now held the entire wood together with a portion of Beer Trench which hitherto had successfully resisted capture. The position therefore seemed entirely favourable for a renewal of the attack if only the weather would clear, but this it showed no signs of doing.

As a matter of fact, the first renewal of hostilities came from the German side. On the 30th the 33rd Division infantry had been relieved by the 24th Division, and hardly had the latter settled into their trenches when, at 1 P.M. on the 31st, the Germans launched a big attack along the whole line from High Wood to east and south-east of Delville Wood. A heavy barrage was immediately opened upon them, while Captain van Straubenzee and Lieut. Body, who were at the O.P. at the time, got all the guns of the 162nd Brigade to bear with tremendous effect upon a large force of the enemy in Cocoa Lane, and the infantry on the front of the 33rd Divisional batteries held their ground. For a long time the situation was obscure and, indeed, extremely anxious; the final report, however, showed that the part of Tea Trench lying west of the Flers Road and a portion of Wood Lane had been evacuated by our infantry, but that elsewhere no serious encroachment had occurred on our front, although serious reports were heard of the state of affairs to the east of Delville Wood.

So ended the month of August, and with September there came an improvement in the weather, and a consequent promise of further operations. On the afternoon of the 1st the expected orders were received; once again the French and the Fourth Army were to attack, once again was an attempt to be made to beat down the stubborn German resistance. The bombardment was due to begin on the 2nd, but before this could be done a slight rearrangement of the batteries had to be carried out. On the night of August 31st, from 11 P.M. till 4 P.M. on the morning of the 1st, thousands of lethal and lachrymose shells had been poured down upon the batteries of the 156th Brigade group, and especially upon A and B/167. Casualties from gas poisoning were fortunately slight owing to the immunity offered by P.H. helmets, but B/167 proved an exception and suffered so many casualties, including its battery commander, that it had to be withdrawn immediately from the line, its place being taken by C/167 which, it will be remembered, was still out at rest. At the same time Lieut.-Colonel C. G. Stewart took over the command of the 166th Brigade in place of Lieut.-Colonel Murray, who was evacuated also suffering from gas poisoning.

The bombardment for this new attack began at 8 A.M. on the 2nd, operation orders showing that it was to be on a great scale, extending along the whole of the Fourth Army front from Thiepval on the left to Guillemont on the right, and from there being carried on by the French to as far south as the Somme. The Fourth Army attack was to be carried out by the XIV. Corps (on the right), the XV. (centre) and the III. Corps (on the left), the objectives of the XIV. Corps being Falfemont Farm and Guillemont, and from there to advance and establish a line along the Wedge Wood–Ginchy road to as far north as the right of the XV. Corps. The XV. Corps aimed at capturing Ginchy and its surrounding trenches, also Vat Alley, Pint Trench to its junction with Ale Alley, and Ale Alley itself. Further to the left the 24th Division were ordered to capture Beer Trench from its junction with Ale Alley, or such portions as had not been previously captured, to retake the portion of Wood Lane which they had lost during the previous two days and to link up with the 1st Division on their left, the objective of which was the north-east half of Wood Lane and the German intermediate line both to High Wood and to a point 200 yards west thereof. The 162nd and 166th

Brigades were supporting the 24th Division, while the 156th Brigade group bombarded Ginchy.

All the day and night of the 2nd and during the morning of the 3rd the guns bombarded their allotted targets—the enemy front and support line and the hollows in which his reserves might congregate. Very special injunctions had been issued by the Commander-in-Chief for every possible step to be taken which would lead to success, and all ranks were to be fully impressed with the necessity of knowing what was expected of them. In addition, every care was to be taken to nurse guns and howitzers during the bombardment, so that as many as possible might be in action when the infantry assault took place.

Zero hour was noon on Sunday, September 3rd, and it is most satisfactory to note that, as the infantry went over the top, every gun and howitzer in the brigades was in action, firing at intense rate and none the worse, owing to careful attention, for the heavy work of the previous days. Lieut.-Colonel Harris observed and reported upon the battle during the entire day from his observation station in an old German trench west of Delville Wood, and from his position informed Divisional Headquarters of the somewhat sensational events of the day, sensational in victory upon most parts, in unexpected reverses around High Wood.

At first the attack swept forward unchecked; at 12.15 P.M. Cameron Highlanders of the 1st Division were seen to advance into Wood Lane almost without opposition; parties proceeded round the east corner and along the north-east face of the trench* and reached, towards the east, a point fifty yards beyond the enemy trench. At the same time parties crossed Wood Lane and were seen to jump into the trench running eastwards along the crest. At 12.30 P.M. a second infantry battalion left Black Watch Trench, about three hundred yards south-west of Wood Lane, and advanced towards the latter under heavy machine-gun fire from the right flank; the Camerons were still seen to be advancing over the sky-line east of High Wood, and seemed to be working towards New Trench which ran at right angles to Wood Lane. At 1.25 P.M. these troops appeared to be held up by parties of the enemy, but the Camerons surrounded the latter to the north and bombing encounters took place; the whole of the remainder of the Camerons then disappeared over the sky-line towards Switch Trench, where they were stopped and suffered heavy casualties. During all this time there was very little hostile artillery activity except for a medium barrage of 5·9 in.'s

---

* *The front-line here ran north-west and south-east.*

upon Delville Wood, and the infantry attack continued successfully and uninterrupted, the depth of assault being small.

At two o'clock in the afternoon, however, came the first hint of the turn of the tide. A report was received that large numbers of the enemy were collecting in Switch Trench along two hundred yards of its length east of the Flers–Longueval road, and the howitzers opened a fifteen minutes' intense bombardment for their dispersal. At twenty-five minutes past three the enemy were seen to advance on Wood Lane, our infantry retiring about two hundred yards in front of them. The Germans came from a north-easterly direction, entered the east corner of High Wood, the north-west portion of Wood Lane and the trench running east along the crest; we still held the southern portion of Wood Lane. As soon as this was seen, nine guns of the 162nd Brigade were pulled out and switched round on to the enemy counter-attack which, however, did not advance over the crest but halted on reaching the trench running along the crest. At the same time small parties of the enemy were seen advancing westwards from the gate which stood out on the sky-line midway between High Wood and Delville Wood. By 3.35 P.M. the enemy were occupying the whole of the sky-line from High Wood for three hundred yards eastwards, and appeared to be unmolested by any artillery fire except that of the nine guns already referred to. No other battery or brigade appeared to get on to them or even to observe them, and this extraordinary and quite inexplicable state of affairs lasted for a considerable time. Not till very late was any sort of barrage put down upon them, and even then it was a long way over the crest and very meagre in quality. In the meantime the enemy dug themselves in again, and at ten minutes to six about one hundred of our men were seen actually retiring from the direction of Switch Trench.

Thus, on this front, the whole attack was rendered utterly fruitless by the assaulting troops being apparently ignorant of the nature and locality of their objective; consequently, finding little resistance, they overran the points to be taken, and were cut up on retiring. The attack itself in its initial stages was as fine as there ever has been, and had the promise of a great victory, but the final result of the whole day's operation was that our line at seven o'clock in the evening between High Wood and Delville Wood was the same as before the attack, while the sacrifice and loss of life had been appalling. It was all the more difficult to bear this disappointment, moreover, when news of the battle on the rest of the front was received. All along the line great successes had been achieved both by our troops and by the French; the roll of prisoners and captured guns was

E

appreciably swelled, and a considerable and important advance had been made. Only on the High Wood–Delville Wood sector did the front remain unchanged; there the two woods, black, forbidding and grim, shattered by shells and burnt by both sides to clear the appalling stench of the dead, stood like two sentinels barring all further progress, obstacles of the most deadly type.

It was not granted to the batteries of the 33rd Divisional Artillery to see these two woods completely and permanently in our hands. On the morning of the 5th the battery commanders of the 1st and 2nd New Zealand Field Artillery Brigades came up with one section apiece, and began to take over from the 33rd battery commanders. Next day, Wednesday the 6th, the relief was complete; New Zealanders took over our positions together with the support of the front, and the batteries wound their way wearily back to the wagon lines, whence, after a short halt, they continued the march to Bonnay (156th and 162nd Brigades) and to Neuville (166th and 167th Brigades).

Thus closed a chapter in the life of the 33rd Divisional Artillery. For eight continuous weeks—with one rest of ten days in the middle—they had been in action in the Battle of the Somme, the greatest offensive undertaken up to that date. For eight weeks they had continuously bombarded the enemy and had, as continuously, been raked by hostile shell fire in return. It would be impossible to estimate the number of shells—which ran into tens of thousands—which the batteries had fired in that period; suffice it to say that in spite of nervous and physical exhaustion, in spite of the fact that seldom could more than two hours' sleep in twenty-four be obtained, that food was oft-times short, that daily the men saw their comrades maimed, shattered, blown to pieces before their eyes, and daily waited for their own turn to come; despite all these trials and horrors not one single order was ever issued to the batteries, not one single request was ever made by the infantry which was not immediately acted upon by the guns. Eight different divisions were covered by the batteries during the period July 15th to September 6th; fourteen separate attacks were carried out during that time and, whether acting under the orders of their own C.R.A. or of the C.R.A. of a strange division, the part allotted to the batteries was invariably carried out to the letter.

From August 1st onwards the headquarters of the 33rd Divisional Artillery had remained out at rest, and the tactical handling of the brigades had, during all the remainder of the time and in all the succeeding battles, been under the control of other and strange divisions. In view of this, it would be impossible to praise too highly the Brigade commanders who throughout the operations were responsible for the handling of the batteries; to the battery commanders there was always—even in the worst of times—the supreme comfort of knowing that behind them was their own brigade headquarters, and that whatever happened they were amongst friends; but to the brigade commanders there was the great responsibility, the great burden of knowing, during the final five weeks, that above them, watching them, relying upon them, was a strange division with whom they had never co-operated before, whose officers were, in many cases, unknown to them.

Yet the real and full measure of praise was due and was agreed by all to be due entirely to—the men. No words can aptly describe their splendid courage and endurance maintained right up to the end of these eight weeks of continual battle; those men who, some of them twelve months before, had been ordinary civilians, who in the early days of July had marched from Cuinchy and Cambrin, full of enthusiasm and eagerness, up to this their first battle, *they* were the real victors. As they marched back now to the wagon lines, a body of tired and weary men with the strain of the past weeks writ deeply in their faces and in their eyes; as they turned their backs upon the battery positions, where the torn and shell-strewn ground held many a rough cross and many a mound to bear silent but eloquent testimony to the sacrifices which had been made, they presented a spectacle to silence for ever the pessimists and pacifists at home who, by their whining and selfishness, were undermining the morale of the nation. If the men of England, half-trained, inexperienced, civilians of twelve months ago can perform such deeds as these, then must England indeed live!

CHAPTER IV.

DAINVILLE, HEBUTERNE AND THE BATTLE OF THE ANCRE.

(SEPTEMBER TO DECEMBER 1916.)

IN the foregoing chapter the doings of the Divisional Artillery in the Battle of the Somme have been chronicled, and, in view of the very heavy strain undergone by all ranks, it might be expected that at least a short rest would have been granted before the batteries went into action again. This, however, was not to be, for the wastage of men was tremendous at the moment, and so great was the necessary concentration of guns for any attack that every available battery was kept in the line. The nearest approach to a rest that could be hoped for was the taking over of some part of the line which was quiet — changing places, in fact, with batteries on some other portion of the front, and this is practically what was done by the artillery whose doings we are following.

On September 6th, as already noted, the brigades moved out of action and spent the night around Bonnay and La Neuville (just north of Corbie). On the 7th the whole Divisional Artillery, under orders to go into action on the Arras front, marched northwards and, passing through La Houssoye, Behincourt, Molliens-au-Bois and Villiers Bocage, spent the night at Havernas (156th Brigade), Wargnies (162nd Brigade) and Flesselles (166th and 167th Brigades). Next morning the march was resumed, and the night of the 8th was passed at Le Meillard (156th and 162nd Brigades), Outrebois (166th Brigade) and Occoches-le-Petit (167th Brigade). On and on they went, stopping on the 9th at Grouches, Lucheux, Bout-des-Pres and Le Marais Sec, and on the 10th at Hauteville, Wanquetin and Montenescourt, the day's march as a rule beginning about 9.30 A.M. and finishing shortly after two o'clock in the afternoon. A short halt was called in the Wanquetin-Montenescourt area on the 10th, nor was any further move made till the 13th, the time being occupied in a reorganisation of the Divisional Artillery.

It will be remembered that just before the Battle of the Somme a change had been made in the formation of the brigades, and that

ORDER OF BATTLE.

SEPTEMBER—OCTOBER 1916.

H.Q.R.A.

C.R.A.	Brigade Major.	Staff Captain.
Brig.-Gen. C. F. Blane, C.M.G.	Major H. K. Sadler, D.S.O.	Capt. T. C. Usher.

156th Brigade.

Lieut.-Colonel Rochfort-Boyd.
Adjutant : Lieut. E. H. Prior.

"A" Battery.	"B" Battery.	"C" Battery.	"D" Battery.
Major S. Talbot.	Major M. A. Studd, M.C.	Major G. Lomer, D.S.O.	Capt. W. G. Pringle (4-gun).

162nd Brigade.

Lieut.-Colonel O. M. Harris, D.S.O.
Adjutant : Lieut. T. D. Shepherd.

"A" Battery.	"B" Battery.	"C" Battery.	"D" Battery.
Major Hill [struck through, handwritten annotation]	Major V. Benett-Stanford, M.C.	Major A. van Straubenzee, M.C.	Capt. T. St. P. Bunbury.

166th Brigade.

Lieut.-Colonel C. G. Stewart, C.M.G., D.S.O.
Adjutant : Lieut. S. M. Wood.

"A" Battery.	"B" Battery.	"C" Battery.	"D" Battery.
Capt. H. A. Littlejohn.	Capt. Hon. T. P. P. Butler. Capt. Dust.	Capt. Freeman.	Capt. B. McCallum, M.C.

167th Brigade.
Broken up.

the 167th Brigade (until then a 4·5 in. Howitzer Brigade) was so split up that the four brigades each had three 18-pdr. batteries and one 4·5 in. howitzer battery, each battery consisting of four guns. Very early in 1916, however, B/167 had been posted away to another division, and therefore, after the reorganisation of the brigades before the Battle of the Somme, the 167th Brigade consisted only of the three 18-pdr. batteries which it had received from each of the brigades in return for the 4·5 in. howitzer battery it had sent to them. It was now ordered that all 18-pdr. batteries should consist of six guns, and therefore from September 11th the 167th Brigade ceased to exist. Sections of each of its batteries were sent to the 156th and 162nd Brigades, Lieut.-Colonel C. G. Stewart assumed command of the 166th Brigade, and on September 13th, with six-gun batteries of 18-pdrs. (except for the 166th Brigade), but with the 4·5 in. howitzer batteries still consisting of only four pieces each, the Divisional Artillery resumed its march and moved into action once more on the Arras front near Dainville. One section per battery went up on the first night and began taking over from the 37th Divisional Artillery, and on the night of the 14th/15th the remaining sections of the batteries moved in, assuming, from 6 A.M. on the morning of Friday the 15th, responsibility for the artillery support of the infantry on their front ; the 156th Brigade covered the 35th Division, the 162nd and 166th Brigades the 12th Division, each brigade for fighting being under the control of the C.R.A. of the Division behind whose infantry it lay. In addition, the artillery on the front was divided up into groups, and Lieut.-Colonel Harris, from his headquarters in the white house on the Arras–Doullens road, controlled not only his own batteries but also C/63 and D/64 which, together with the 162nd Brigade, went to form " G " group. " H " group was administered by Lieut.-Colonel Stewart.

At the beginning of this chapter it was stated that, owing to the huge concentration of artillery on the " live " sectors of the front, no batteries could be spared to go into the rest area, and that therefore the best which could be hoped for was a comparatively quiet time on a peaceful part of the line. This was what the batteries at Dainville were hoping for, and this was what they badly needed after the strenuous days of the Somme fighting ; it is therefore interesting to note what happened to them in the following few days, for it will give a good idea of the worry and hardship which thoroughly bad staff work can give, and which it did give, to men already tired by fighting.

By their northward march the batteries had left the XV. Corps of the Fourth Army and were now under the orders of the XVII.

Corps, Third Army. On the night of September 14th/15th, after six weeks' heavy fighting and four days' marching to follow, the batteries moved into action ; at seven o'clock on the evening of the 15th, just eleven hours after the batteries had assumed responsibility for the defence of the front, orders were received to move out of action and to march south to the VII. Corps area to cover the infantry of the 33rd Division, the 12th Divisional Artillery taking over the Dainville sector. This in itself was not so very bad ; it is true that, as a result of the orders, leave which had just reopened both for England and for the Boulogne rest camp was stopped, and it was generally felt that the batteries might equally as well have marched to the VII. Corps area in the first case. There was the consolation of knowing, however, that once again the batteries were to cover their own infantry, and occasional mistakes of this kind were not altogether unusual.

This, unfortunately, was not all. On the night of the 15th/16th one section per battery withdrew from action and moved to the Coullemont–Warlincourt–Couturelle area, the remainder of the batteries, except those of the 156th Brigade, following on twenty-four hours later. The next night the leading sections marched into action as ordered on the Gommecourt front, relieving the batteries of the 17th Divisional Artillery, and twenty-four hours later, on the night of the 17th/18th, they were joined by the remaining sections who had left the Dainville positions vacant ; at the same time the 156th Brigade marched to Gaudiempré and came into action, on the morning of the 19th, north-east of Sailly-au-Bois. Thus on September 19th all the batteries were in action on the Gommecourt front, and wagon-lines had been established around Gaudiempré and Pas.

So far, so good, but now chaos set in. On the 20th, after the batteries had been in action just twenty-four hours, orders were received for the 162nd Brigade to sideslip and relieve the batteries of the 78th Brigade, forming the northern group. This was done by one section per battery and was to have been completed on the 21st, but was cancelled late on that evening; instead of sideslipping, the batteries were ordered to return to their old positions on the Arras front which they had quitted five days previously, were relieved by the 46th Divisional Artillery and retired to their wagon-lines at Pas, while at the same time half-batteries of the 156th Brigade moved out of the line to wagon-lines around Wanquetin and Montenes-court. At noon on the 22nd the remaining sections of the 46th Divisional Artillery relieved what had been left in the line of the 33rd, and the batteries of the latter returned to their old wagon-lines around

Wanquetin and Sombrin. Two sections per battery (156th and 162nd Brigades) moved into action the same night (22nd/23rd) in the Dainville sector and were joined by the remaining sections next day, while on the 24th the 166th Brigade came into action between Dainville and Arras, forming once again " H " Group of Artillery in the Dainville sector. Thus after a general shuffle, numerous orders and counter orders, general disturbance and three days' marching, the batteries were in exactly the same positions which they had occupied ten days before. They had marched all the way to Gomme-court for nothing—merely to inhabit positions for twelve hours and then to return to Arras and Dainville again. Yet these were tired men who ached for rest and a little comfort.

It may be thought that at this stage the Higher Authority would have been able to sort matters out and to run their administration on slightly more efficient lines, but nothing of the sort was experienced. On October 1st, six days later, the good game of battle-dore and shuttlecock between XVII. and VII. Corps was continued, and orders were again received to march to the VII. Corps area, the scene of the previous excursion. On the 3rd the leading sections of the batteries set out over the now well-known road and, after establishing themselves once more in wagon-lines around Gaudiempré on the 4th, came into action on the Gommecourt front on the 5th, where they were joined 48 hours later by the remaining sections which had stayed behind at Arras to cover the move. Thus, in order to carry out the apparently simple work of transferring a Divisional Artillery from the Arras to the Gommecourt front, somebody amongst the Higher Command had forced the unfortunate batteries to march down from one front to the other, sideslip, return along the road to their original Arras front, and then march all the way down again to the zone they had been in after the very first march !

Strange to say, the batteries really did remain now on the Gommecourt front, and, as they took part from there in operations connected with the Battle of the Ancre, it will be well to examine their positions carefully.

The 156th Brigade established itself around Sailly, the 162nd just south of Fonquevillers, and the 166th Brigade north of the same village, the advantage of these positions being that the hostile trenches west of Gommecourt could be barraged in enfilade —the deadly effect of which had already been proved in the Battle of the Somme—while the batteries could also cut wire on various parts of the front east of Hebuterne to as far as Rossignol Wood. This wire-cutting was, indeed, the main occupation of the batteries,

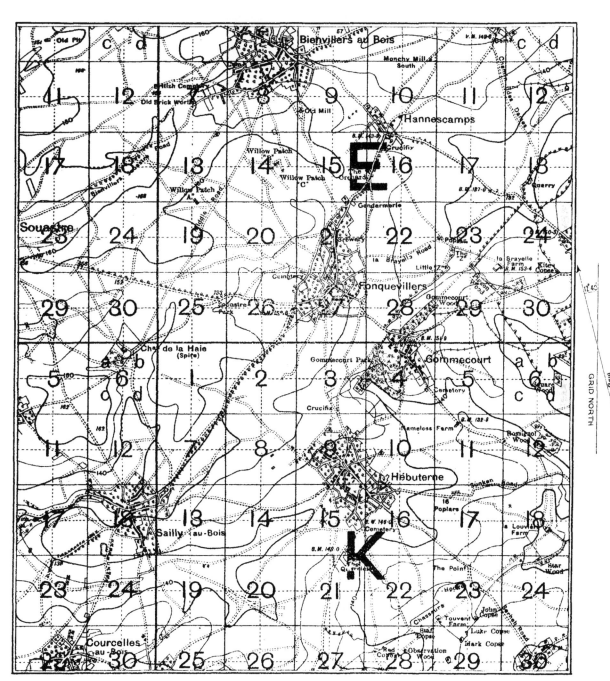

Scale 1:40,000

and every moment of good visibility was utilised to carry out the tedious and extremely difficult work.

The 49th Division was holding the line at the time, and the batteries working under 33rd Divisional Artillery Headquarters (who in its turn was controlled by the 49th Division) covered the front from " The Z " to the south-west corner of Gommecourt Park, wire-cutting being carried out mainly just below and south of the Gomme-court–Fonquevillers road. From the 7th till the 11th, when the wire-cutting was finished, the work went on daily without interruption ; on the 8th D/162 (Major Belgrave) had exchanged positions with a battery of the 48th Division and had moved into Hebuterne itself, while on the 9th the batteries were placed under control of VII. Corps direct, and were relieved of the responsibility of covering the 49th Divisional front as far as infantry support was concerned, but apart from these small interruptions no distraction of any importance was suffered. Hostile artillery was sufficiently active to be rather troublesome—the tactics employed being occasional short bursts of shelling and sniping rounds into the battery positions, a procedure which kept all ranks unpleasantly on the *qui vive*, and it was with a feeling of satisfaction that the report was made on the 11th that wire-cutting was complete.

Here the batteries had a slight rest from the continual firing of the previous days, but not so the brigade commanders. On the 12th orders were received that the brigade commanders of the 33rd Divisional Artillery should supervise the wire-cutting of the 79th Brigade, and no sooner was this done than positions had to be recon-noitred for the batteries on the neighbouring Serre front. The recon-naissance was carried out on September 18th, and the following day the batteries moved into positions from which they were destined to take part in the Battle of the Ancre. The move in this case was of no magnitude whatever ; the batteries of the 156th Brigade lay east of Sailly-au-Bois, the 162nd Brigade took up positions south of Hebuterne, with the exception of " D " battery which was in Hebuterne itself, while the 166th Brigade shifted to the north of the same village. Once again wire-cutting was the order of the day. The front covered by the batteries, held at this time by infantry of the 31st Division, extended from west of Puisieux to as far south as Serre, and wire-cutting was concentrated on the zone stretching from the cross roads south-east of The Point to 300 yards north-east of John Copse, the batteries being under direct control of the XIII. Corps.

From October 20th until November 13th the batteries were kept in a state of high activity. Every day wire-cutting was continued, and bursts of fire were directed day and night upon the gaps cut in the wire to prevent the repair thereof. At the same time all the hostile approaches, communication trenches and trench junctions were constantly bombarded, and here again every endeavour was made to prevent the enemy from putting right such damage as had been done. These tactics naturally used up a large amount of ammunition, and as naturally evoked swift retaliation from the enemy. Every night, as the ammunition wagons toiled up from the wagon-lines around Couin and St. Leger with supplies for the guns, they met the blast of the German shells searching the approaches around Sailly, Colincamps and Hebuterne. Nightly did the Germans take their toll of men and horses engaged upon the work of ammunition supply, while an ever-lengthening casualty list in the battery positions showed that the enemy, provoked to wrath and apprehension by the obviously deliberate and premeditated cutting of his wire, was not replying in vain. He knew, from the destruction of his wire, that an attack was imminent, and realising this he turned the full blast of his attention upon the batteries; they were the chief danger at the moment, whereas the infantry could be attended to later when the day of assault grew nearer at hand.

The tactics of the enemy were as before; not usually long bombardments, but sudden short bursts of fire upon the battery positions, catching men unawares and making them dread even the narrow open spaces between the guns. Every day these bursts— sometimes only a few sniping rounds—cut down the effectives at the gun positions, until Hebuterne became a word of ill omen to all. Still the work continued; the back areas of the enemy system began to receive attention, Puisieux was bombarded on the 22nd in conjunction with the heavy artillery, and on the 26th the first infantry raiding party went over to obtain identification of the troops opposite and to examine the effect of the previous six days' wire-cutting. After two half-hour bombardments, with an interval of two hours between, a party of the 93rd Infantry Brigade set out to enter the hostile lines, but an enemy better known almost than the Germans and in its way equally deadly, the enemy Mud, prevented them from even reaching the German parapet. So heavy was the going in No Man's Land that it became a physical impossibility to get across, and after many efforts the infantry returned to our own trenches.

Once again wire-cutting and trench bombardment were resumed, and now the enemy became more violent still in his reply. Nightly did he pour thousands of gas shells into the battery positions, forcing the men to wear their box-respirators during what little rest they could achieve and depriving them of their badly-needed sleep. Practically every day the villages of Sailly and Hebuterne were shelled by 15 cm. and 10 cm. howitzers, while a deliberate bombardment of batteries and brigade headquarters was carried out during the last three days of the month. On November 2nd another attempt was made by the 31st Division to raid the enemy trenches east of Hebuterne, and throughout the night of the 2nd/3rd a heavy flank and covering barrage was kept up by the batteries to support the infantry in their hazardous task. Once again, however, failure had to be confessed. The utter impassability of No Man's Land, owing to mud and water-filled shell-holes, combined with very brisk enemy opposition forced the raiding parties back to their trenches again, and once more were the batteries left in ignorance of the effect of their work.

It was essential, however, that the enemy lines should be penetrated, for the non-success of the previous two raids had led to a lack of knowledge of the hostile troops opposite, and had prevented an examination being made of the German wire. Accordingly, on November 6th, a third and this time in part successful attempt was made. After a 20-minute bombardment during which three raiding parties crept into No Man's Land, a hurricane barrage for six minutes was carried out, under cover of which the raiders set out for the enemy trenches between The Point and the Sunken Road. Heavy machine-gun fire was encountered and the two raiding parties on the left were held up, but on the right the party covered by the 162nd Brigade forced its way into the enemy line, bombed dug-outs, examined the wire and returned safely to its own trenches bringing with it, for purposes of identification, five prisoners, of whom one died on arrival.

Matters now began to move rapidly. From the 7th to the 10th the enemy bombarded Sailly and Hebuterne heavily, and on the night of the 9th fired 4,000 gas shells into our battery positions; on the 10th also began the final three-day bombardment by our batteries before the launching of the assault to be known in history as the Battle of the Ancre. The 10th, 11th and 12th, designated in the secret operation orders as W, X and Y days, marked a doubling and trebling intensity of bombardment on the enemy trenches; the German front and support lines were pounded and flung in all directions, wire was cut, gaps and breaches were kept under constant bursts of fire to prevent repair, and when November 13th dawned it seemed that no more could be done, and that, in view of the bad visibility and weather existing during these days, every possible preparation had been made.

Zero hour on Monday, the 13th, was a quarter to six in the morning; sharp to the second the guns roared forth the barrage, the infantry advanced to the assault and the Battle of the Ancre, which for so long had been fomenting, burst out in all its fury. The 33rd Divisional Artillery was covering the extreme left of the battle line, its zone extending from John Copse on the right through the Touvert Farm–La Louverie Farm road to the left of the line of assault, and was supporting the infantry of the 31st Division by whom the attack was to be made. On the front of the batteries the wire was found to be completely and successfully cut, the barrage proved entirely satisfactory and the infantry, assaulting and passing over the German front line, advanced to their next objective—the German second line—along the whole of the front from Puisieux to as far south as Serre.

On the whole the hostile barrage was not severe until noon, when No Man's Land and our front system were very heavily bombarded. Every morning from 5.45 till 6 A.M. for the previous three days a heavy barrage had been fired on the German trenches so that, after the first two occasions, the enemy grew used to these barrages and could not tell whether an attack was coming or not. During the assault itself, which was helped by a heavy fog, the chief casualties were suffered from rifle and machine-gun fire coming from the German second line, while heavy mud in No Man's Land made the advance extremely tedious. The German front line, as already noted, was successfully captured in spite of these difficulties, the enemy in most cases being caught by surprise and surrendering on close fighting, and it was not until the advance on the second line began that real trouble was met.

The 3rd Division, to whom had been allotted the capture of Serre, was unable, owing to the mud and heavy enemy opposition, to reach its objective, and the 31st Division found itself with its right flank in the air. All day long fighting continued, our casualties being terribly heavy, while the batteries barraged with all their might in the hope of protecting the 31st Division until such time as the 3rd Division, by advancing on the right, should secure the flank. It was all of no avail, however; after twelve hours of raging battle orders were received from Corps Headquarters to evacuate the captured ground, and this was done in the evening under a protective barrage from the guns of the 33rd Divisional Artillery. Thus on this particular front no advance was made, while the casualties were so heavy that strong patrols had to be sent out during the night to cover the bringing in of the wounded. It should be remembered, however, that the operations described formed only the extreme left of a great battle, and that, although the flank was held up, the centre advanced with such success that Beaumont-Hamel was captured together with 3,000 prisoners, while an advance was made on to the outskirts of Beaumont village itself. Therefore, in considering the results of the Battle of the Ancre, the foregoing narrative which concerns only the batteries on the extreme flank must not be taken alone, but in connection with the history of the rest of that day along the whole front of assault.

Next day, after firing a dummy barrage in the early morning in co-operation with an attack further to the south, the batteries of the 33rd Divisional Artillery gave up their part in the Battle of the Ancre and began to retire to their wagon-lines. Two batteries per brigade—" C " and D/156 with " B " and " D " of 162nd and 166th —moved out on the night of the 14th/15th to the area around Couin and St. Leger, and on the following night were joined by the rest of the brigades. Here they remained till the 22nd, cleaning, reorganising and resting, with occasional very unwelcome returns to their old battery positions to remove ammunition; here with the most profound regret they bade farewell to Lieut.-Colonel Rochfort-Boyd, whose gallantry and personality had won for him a firm affection and friendship in the hearts of all ranks, and who now, on handing the command of the 156th Brigade to Major Bridges, went to take over a Horse Artillery Brigade with the 1st Indian Cavalry Division (there to meet his death while directing the batteries in the Cambrai offensive of 1917); and from here they marched on November 22nd through Villers Bocage and Talmas to Airaines, to enjoy in this, the middle of November 1916, the first rest which they had been granted, with the exception of ten days during the Battle of the Somme, since they had gone into action nine months previously.

At Airaines they remained till December 5th, when they set out once more with their faces turned towards the east to relieve the French and to hold, throughout the winter, the ground wrested from the Germans in the Battle of the Somme. The story of that long and trying winter in bitter cold and deep mud, the tale of how the Germans were so continually harassed by artillery fire that they were forced to carry out the retreat of February 1917 to the famous Hindenburg line, belongs to another chapter in the life-story of the batteries, and as such must be relegated thereto.

CHAPTER V.

FROM November 23rd, the date of arrival at Airaines, until December 5th when the first units began the march back to the line again, a complete rest was enjoyed by the batteries, and badly was it needed. Clothing, harness and equipment had to be overhauled carefully, casualties amongst men and horses replaced, while many of the reinforcements lately arrived from England were not fit to take their place in the gun detachments or teams, and needed a thorough drilling to change them from the half-raw condition in which they had left England to something more nearly approaching the necessary smartness and accuracy required in the field. Moreover a certain staleness, the inevitable result of a long period of continuous fighting, had descended upon the batteries as a whole, and it needed a period of brisk training interspersed with half-holidays, concerts and games of every description to bring back the old spring and confidence.

On November 29th the first hint was received of the destination of the batteries when fighting should once more become the order of the day, for on that date Brig.-Gen. Blane set off for Maurepas —the extreme left of the French on the Somme—there to hold a conference with the French General commanding the artillery of the French XX. Corps. On December 1st the full facts were known, and a warning order was received that the 33rd Division was to take over the line from the French from Sailly-Saillisel to a point opposite Bouchavesnes, the batteries occupying the positions of the 127th French Regiment of Artillery. Further it was learnt that the artillery support of the line was to be carried out by the combined brigades of the 33rd and 40th Divisions, each Division keeping two artillery brigades in the line and one in rest.

On Tuesday, December 5th, the move began. A/162 and C/156 with No. 2 Section of the Divisional Ammunition Column set off early in the morning on what was to be a three-day march, and passing through Picquigny and Ailly-sur-Somme, halted for the first night at St. Sauveur. The second day saw them leave Vecquemont and Corbie behind them, and on the third day, after spending the previous night at Vaux-sur-Somme, they arrived at Camp 14 on the Corbie-

ORDER OF BATTLE.

OCTOBER 1916—FEBRUARY 1917.

H.Q.R.A.

C.R.A.	Brigade Major.	Staff Captain.
Brig.-Gen. C. F. Blane, C.M.G.	Major H. K. Sadler, D.S.O., M.C.	Capt. W. E. Bownass.

156th Brigade.

Lieut.-Colonel Bridges.
Adjutant : Lieut. E. H. Prior (*until January*).
Lieut. F. L. Lee.

"A" Battery.	"B" Battery.	"C" Battery.	"D" Battery.
Major S. Talbot.	Major M. A. Studd, M.C.	Major G. Lomer, D.S.O.	Capt. W. G. Pringle (*till January*). Major W. A. T. Barstow, M.C.

162nd Brigade.

Lieut.-Colonel O. M. Harris.
Adjutant : Lieut. R. H. Pavitt.

"A" Battery.	"B" Battery.	"C" Battery.	"D" Battery.
Major G. Fetherston, M.C.	Major V. Benett-Stanford, M.C.	Major A. van Straubenzee, M.C.	Major J. D. Belgrave, D.S.O.

166th Brigade.

Lieut.-Colonel C. G. Stewart, C.M.G., D.S.O.
Adjutant : Lieut. S. M. Wood.

"A" Battery.	"B" Battery.	"C" Battery.	"D" Battery.
Capt. H. A. Littlejohn, M.C.	Capt. Dust.	Capt. H. Freeman.	Capt. B. McCallum, M.C.

Bray road some few miles west of Bray itself.   So the move went on ;
on December 8th B/156 and C/162 shook the dust—or rather mud—
of Airaines from off their feet and followed the first two batteries
by the same stages ;   next day A/156 and B/162 followed suit, and
on December 10th the two remaining batteries—D/156 and D/162
—turned their backs upon the rest area, arriving at Camp 14 two
days later.

While this march was in progress matters had been moving up
in front, for on December 8th the 156th and 162nd Brigade commanders (166th Brigade had been left in rest at Airaines) went up
to take over from the French the headquarters and battery positions
of the 127th Regiment of Artillery.   Taking over from the army of
another nation was a somewhat more lengthy business than an
ordinary relief on the British front ;   the trouble of language was not
insuperable, but the difficulty of reconciling their methods of communication and control with our own, and of making the alterations
necessary to fall in with the usual practice of brigade and battery
administration was by no means light, nor were matters simplified
by the oft-recurring phrase " ça ne marche pas " when discussing
some important telephone line from brigade to battery or O.P.

However, by December 12th all was ready for the arrival of the
batteries, and on that day there marched into action two sections
each of C/156, A/162 and C/162 who had left Camp 14 on the previous
day and had established wagon-lines at Camp 21, one mile south of
Maricourt, on the Suzanne–Maricourt road.   They were followed
on December 13th by A/156, B/156 and B/162, while the 15th saw
the arrival of the " D " batteries, so that exactly ten days before
Christmas the whole of the Divisional Artillery was " back to work "
again.   Camp 14 had only been used as a very brief halting place in
the scheme ;   it acted, in fact, merely as a place for the partial concentration of the batteries, and it was well that this was the case, for a
worse spot and a more unsuitable artillery camp it would be difficult
to find.   Some distance from the road, approached only by the
roughest of tracks, it lay in a valley and quickly showed itself to be
a veritable mud-trap.   The horse-lines were bad, the men's quarters
were worse, and the effort of pulling into the camp off the road, and
of struggling back on to the road again when the march was resumed,
more than counteracted any benefit which might otherwise have
accrued from the two days spent there in rest.   It was with a feeling
of relief, therefore, that the batteries turned their backs upon this
much-hated spot and set out for Camp 21, their permanent wagon-
lines whilst in action.   Nothing could be worse than Camp 14 ;
perhaps Camp 21 might be better.   Perhaps !

As events turned out, Camp 21 between Suzanne and Maricourt was a slight improvement, but very slight. It was on ground which had been the scene of the summer and autumn offensive, and nothing could solidify the earth which had been so torn and shattered by high explosives. The least suspicion of rain—even of damp—turned everything into mud, while the neighbourhood of the water-troughs, unless built up from a timber foundation, became absolutely and completely impassable. Certain of the batteries, in fact, which were forced to establish their wagon-lines on the west of the road struck such fearful conditions that a number of horses were actually drowned in the mud. It was not the fault of the batteries or brigades—they were ordered to establish wagon-lines in a certain spot and perforce they had to do it, nor could the most strenuous of efforts put things right in a few days. To whomever the fault was due, it was heartbreaking to battery commanders to see the effects of a three weeks' rest being wiped out almost in as many days by the impossible conditions in which some of them found themselves.

To return, however, to the tactical situation. By December 16th all the batteries, less one section in some cases, were in action in the Maurepas–Bouchavesnes area. Only two brigades—the 156th and the 162nd—of the 33rd Divisional Artillery were in the line, for the 166th Brigade had been left behind at Airaines, but to General Blane's command were added two brigades of the 40th Divisional Artillery—the 178th and 181st—in action in Anderlu and Marrières Woods respectively, and with these four brigades it was considered that sufficient artillery support for the divisional front would be forthcoming. The batteries of the 162nd Brigade, with the exception of " D " Battery, lay just west of the Clery–Le Forest road and about half-way between the two villages ; D battery, for reasons to be discussed presently, took up a position two hundred yards east of Hospital Wood, while the battery positions of the 156th Brigade were congregated in the area around and east of Le Forest.

In taking over from the French a portion of the line, as was done in this case, very considerable difficulties had to be faced from the brigade and battery commanders' point of view. The French field batteries consisted almost always of four guns, and to relieve them with six-gun batteries involved either the digging of further gun-pits and shelters for the men or the splitting up of the batteries into two portions. In this case the 33rd Divisional Artillery was relieving three groups (the 3rd, 4th and 5th) of French artillery, each group consisting of three four-gun batteries, and accordingly it was resolved to take one section each from " B " and C/156 and to combine them into a third four-gun battery, while " A " and B/162 carried out the same procedure in the other brigade ; two guns of C/162 relieved on their own a French battery, and A/156 was fortunate enough to take up a position in which it was possible to keep all six guns in action together.   Thus it will be seen that the brigades were thrown into rather a disorganised condition, but this was not all.   The French Army did not maintain any batteries of field howitzers, and therefore the 4·5 in. howitzer batteries of the two brigades found themselves nobody's children, left out in the cold with nobody to relieve, no battery position to take over.   They were forced on this, as on another later occasion, to buckle to and dig their own position, and for this reason D/162, as already stated, came to the edge of Hospital Wood and dug itself in under a small bank.

By the 16th and 17th of December the main work of establishing the positions had been overcome, and, preliminary registration being completed, the batteries had a chance of looking around them.   The surroundings were not inspiring ; they had been wrested from the enemy during the Somme offensive and, in common with the rest of the battlefield, were torn and pitted with shell-holes in all directions. The autumn and winter rains had turned the whole countryside into a vast sea of mud, mud so deep, so thick and of such peculiar con-sistency that it was altogether impossible to remove it, drain or even dig through it.   Conditions were, indeed, pitiable ;   every yard walked was an effort involving absolute wading ;   thigh gum-boots were powerless to keep the men dry ;   ammunition, rations and mail had to be brought to the battery positions by pack-horse, for no wagon could approach, and on top of all this it rained, rained con-tinuously and steadfastly during the whole period.   It was indeed a wretched place, rendered more wretched by the knowledge that Christmas—a season usually associated with comfort and merry-making—was fast approaching.

For some time after the arrival of the batteries on this part of the front there was no war, for the simple reason that war was impossible.   The battery positions consisted merely of six semi-dry platforms for the guns, separated and surrounded by apparently bottomless mud ; the men lived in wet and muddy shelters and dug-outs, and were scarcely ever dry ; telephone lines forward ran through mud which made the repair of breaks a clumsy, maddening business, while up with the infantry there were no trenches, no dug-outs, nothing but mud and water.   Along the whole of the divisional front there were only about four places where anything approaching the semblance of a communication trench could be found, and these were so bad as to be rather deeper of mud than the surrounding ground. There was only one way to reach the front line—a ditch full of water with a little wire in front—and that was to walk straight over the open up to the fire trench itself, and there, if a new arrival, drop in; if an old hand, sit on the parados.

This state of affairs may sound fantastic and even an exaggeration, but it is only too true an account. The French, finding conditions were well-nigh impossible for fighting, decided philosophically not to fight, and arranged with the enemy accordingly. It was muddy for them, but just as muddy for the enemy; it was a beastly business wading up communication trenches which were practically non-existent to a front line which was scarcely habitable, but it was just as beastly for the Germans; therefore, forward observing officers going up to visit the infantry had the strange experience of walking up to our front line over the open, of sitting on the parapet in full view of the enemy one hundred yards away, and of seeing the enemy doing exactly the same thing themselves. So extraordinary were the conditions, in fact, that a battery commander of the 162nd Brigade walked over the open with one of his subalterns not only up to the front line but over it at a spot where it was deserted, and had got well into No Man's Land before a sentry in one of the adjoining bays called him back.

Whether the French method of thus maintaining an unofficial truce was a good one need not be debated in these pages. It certainly led them to give up making any effort to dig communication trenches at all, even in spots where with trouble it would have been possible, and it by no means helped to foster the "cultivation of the fighting spirit," the importance of which was being impressed so busily upon all ranks at the time. On the other hand it gave them a tiny measure of comfort which made life just endurable, and by resuming active operations and reducing the enemy to a state of misery they would have let themselves in for similar wretchedness.

When the 33rd Division took over the line, however, the question was left in doubt no longer. Where there was war there was to be real war and no unofficial truce; the French protested, they tried in vain to prevent the infantry sniping, but it was of no avail. One morning a whole platoon of Germans marched calmly down to the front line over the open, following the custom of bygone days; the temptation was too great, and a Lewis gunner, hastily putting together the gun he had been cleaning, raised it on to the parapet and browned the lot! From that moment onwards not a head dared show above the parapet, and everybody living in the front line or visiting it endured discomfort and hardship beyond imagination.

Gradually, as the 33rd Division settled in, hostilities increased and boiled up. Even so the majority of the firing was upon the back areas, for the forward trench system—engulfed in a sea of mud—offered no target whatever. Duckboard tracks, valleys hidden from infantry and artillery observers where the enemy might walk about in the open, suspected battery positions, cross-roads and other similar targets received as a rule the attention of our guns, while the enemy administered the same treatment to corresponding features behind our lines. The actual front covered by the batteries extended from the enemy trenches on the Bouchavesnes ridge northwards through Moislains Wood to the great wood of St. Pierre Vaast. From observation stations along the ridge east of Aiguille Ravine (in which was the artillery forward telephone exchange) a very good view of all the enemy system could be seen except in the extreme north of the zone, though the trenches behind the support line were hidden owing to the steep valley which ran down towards Moislains.

Thus the year drew slowly to a close. On Christmas Day the brigades took part in an artillery bombardment carried out along the whole Corps front to show that "Peace on Earth, Goodwill toward Men" was not considered to apply to Germans. In reply, the enemy increased in violence his sniping with whizz-bangs of any portion of duckboard track and road where he might catch ration parties or artillery teams toiling up with ammunition from Plateau Siding, and then, on December 31st, the 166th Brigade arrived from Airaines and relieved the batteries of the 156th. By the system already outlined one brigade of each Divisional Artillery was kept in rest, and beneath the envious eyes of the 162nd Brigade, whose turn was not yet, the 156th turned their backs to the mud and marched away to the rest and comparative comfort of G.H.Q. reserve.

The first fortnight of January proved uneventful. The same harassing fire was continued, the same mud prevailed everywhere and the greatest problem of all to be contended with at the time was not the enemy, but the weather. An alarming increase in the number of cases of trench-feet and frost-bite began to show itself, not only in the infantry but in the artillery. For the infantry special drying rooms were erected and dry socks were issued to every man on leaving the trenches, but the gunners were thought to be better off, and for them there were no such arrangements. Consequently there fell upon brigade and battery commanders a very great strain, a strain which had to be withstood at the time when more work began to show itself in the offing.

More work there certainly was. On January 2nd General Blane, on the relief of the 33rd Division by the 40th, had handed over control of the brigades to the C.R.A. 40th Division and had gone with headquarters into rest at Belloy-sur-Somme. On January 10th there came a warning order from his headquarters that a side-slip of the division to the right was about to take place, and that brigade commanders were to visit the French positions along the actual borders of the Somme next day. Close on the heels of this came directions for the batteries to withdraw from the line, the 166th getting away first on January 12th, followed by the 162nd Brigade four days later, and January 16th found both brigades in rest at their wagon-lines—Camp 21, west of Maricourt.

The following six days were spent at these wagon-lines, and during the period yet another reorganisation of the Divisional Artillery took place. Since September 1916 there had been three brigades, the full establishment of a brigade being three six-gun 18-pdr. batteries and one four-gun 4·5 in. howitzer battery. It was now decreed that a Divisional Artillery should consist of two brigades, each brigade to be of the same composition as before but with six-gun howitzer batteries, and not four as previously. To bring this about the 166th Brigade was broken up. One section of D/166 went to D/156, the other to D/162 ; A/166 (Captain Littlejohn) marched to Mirvaux and became part of the 26th Brigade, while B/166 (Captain Dust) joined the 93rd Brigade at Morlancourt and was merged in that unit. The Divisional Artillery did not lose all its old friends, however, by this breaking up. Major Barstow was transferred to the 156th Brigade, as was also Lieut.-Colonel Stewart who, with the whole of the staff of the 166th Brigade H.Q., came to 156th H.Q. ; the late headquarter staff of that brigade took over the nominal command of 166th Brigade—now a brigade in name only and not in substance—and awaited orders at Belloy as to future movements.

While this change-about had been going on, the batteries at Camp 21 had been busy in other respects as well. Cold, dry weather had set in, and, remembering the mud of Bouchavesnes and realising that similar conditions existed in the positions which were shortly to be occupied on the banks of the Somme itself, teams had been out every day making use of the good going occasioned by the hard weather, and filling up the ammunition pits at the battery positions which by now had been reconnoitred by battery commanders themselves. It was the only advantage which the 162nd Brigade, deprived by this move of the rest for which it was nearly due, managed to gain over the 156th Brigade who were now marching up from the rest area to the new wagon-lines around Vaux Wood and Eclusier.

On January 22nd the move into action began. From the wagon-lines west of Frise the batteries marched up to take over the defence of the line from the River Somme itself on the right to the junction with the 4th Division, some three-quarters of a mile south of Bouchavesnes, on the left.   The infantry had relieved the French 17th Division two days previously and had been supported temporarily by the French batteries, but now on the 24th the guns came up and, taking over from the groups of Commandants de St. Paule, Le Gros and Rouziers of the 30th, 29th and 49th Regiments of Artillery, assumed responsibility for the support of the line from eight o'clock on the morning of the 24th.   Under the control of General Blane at P.C. Jean the batteries were split up into two groups;   the left group, commanded by Lieut.-Colonel Stewart, consisted of the 156th and the 14th Brigades, while the 162nd and the 33rd Brigades, at first under the control of Lieut.-Colonel Nevinson but ultimately, from the 31st, commanded by Lieut.-Colonel Harris, went to form the right group, each group covering one brigade of infantry in the front line.

Battery positions on the south of the Somme had been very difficult to find, for on clear days Mt. St. Quentin, which was in German hands, commanded the whole of the countryside, and the concealment of flashes was a practical impossibility.   After a certain amount of debating Major Fetherston's battery (A/162) took up a position just south of Buscourt Cemetery, with D/162 (Major Belgrave) two hundred yards in front under the shelter of a bank; C/162 (Major van Straubenzee) lay between Buscourt Cemetery and the river, while Major Benett-Stanford established his battery (B/162) with four guns to the south-east of these positions, the remaining section being detached for enfilade work about seven hundred yards south of Feuillières.   With Brigade headquarters situated in an old German second-line trench one hundred yards behind " C " battery, the whole of the 162nd was thoroughly compact and well together and, from the point of view of administration, excellently placed.

The 162nd was the only brigade of the 33rd Division lying south of the Somme.   The batteries were, in fact, the first British guns to return there since the very early days of the war, and it fell to them now to occupy the extreme right of the British line in France, just as they also occupied the extreme left of that same line on the beach at Nieuport some six months later.   The batteries of the 156th Brigade all lay to the north of the river, " A " and C/156 (Major Talbot and Major Lomer) to the east of Howitzer Wood and 2,000 yards N.W. of Clery-sur-Somme, " B " and D/156 (Major Studd and Major Barstow) south of the same wood, and from here they continued the good work of harassing the enemy in the position to which he had been forced back by the offensive of the foregoing months.

On January 25th battery commanders studied and registered their new zones. The German line here ran from the river Somme to the west corner of Limberlost Wood, and on through Freckles Wood in a north-easterly direction. Observation stations north of the river were situated on the high ground west of Hersfeld Trench, while to the south of the river, from a high hill running sheer down to the water about 1,200 yards due west of Halle, a magnificent enfilade view right down on to the front covered could be obtained, and also an extensive back area view of the country round Péronne, Mont St. Quentin, Feuillaucourt, Allaines and along the Paris-Lille road in the direction of Nurlu. The line just here offered an extraordinary feature which was to be found in very few other places along the front; owing to a big " hair-pin bend " of the river and to the fact that the two arms of the bend enclosed a marsh, the trenches ran straight down to the river on the north side and there ceased altogether, reappearing on the southern bend again some 2,500 yards further down. It was impossible to dig trenches or to keep men in the marshes enclosed by the bend of the river, and similarly it was practically impossible for men to get across to raid our lines, but a danger—and a very serious one—now presented itself, for a spell of intensely cold weather set in; the river, the canal and the marshes were all frozen solid, and the situation suddenly arose that between the batteries and the German lines there lay nothing but two isolated machine-gun posts. Our old ally, the marsh, which had hitherto proved a safe defence against hostile raids on the guns, now offered a perfectly secure passage. So feasible in fact did a raid appear, that plans were actually being formulated for a descent upon the German batteries opposite this bend by our people—plans which in the end had to be abandoned, as two howitzer batteries, at the request of the infantry, shelled the frozen river and with sixteen rounds cut a channel thirty yards wide across the ice.

The weather had indeed turned intensely cold. Every night some thirty degrees of frost were registered, and the ground was deeply covered, in snow. It was, of course, exceedingly healthy, but involved a great deal of suffering, while the handling of guns and ammunition, the cold metal of which seemed to bite right into the flesh, was a matter to be taken by no means lightly. Fortunately there was but little activity at the time. Hostile minenwerfers and rifle-grenades worried our infantry to a large extent, but prompt retaliation, coupled with the arrival into action of X, V and Y/33 trench mortar batteries, reduced this source of trouble to a minimum.

Apart from this the batteries were more or less left to themselves to register such targets as they chose until February arrived, bringing with it a more definite sequence of events.

February heralded the commencement of more active operations, but before these started the period in the rest area, for which the 162nd Brigade was due, began to be granted to certain of the batteries. On February 1st A/162 stored its guns in the northern part of Marrières Wood, leaving them there under a guard and eventually handing them over to the 33rd Brigade. At the same time orders were received to build positions east of Marrières Wood for the guns stored there, while the 8th Division got positions ready south-west of Rancourt to be taken up at a later date by "A" and B/156. A/162, with its guns stored away, marched out to rest at Vaux-sur-Somme, to be followed on the 7th by D/162 which went into billets at Sailly-le-Sec; in the latter case, however, two guns were handed over *in situ* to the 55th Battery to be served by them from there, while the remaining four were left under a guard until such time as the battery should return to man them once more.

With two batteries out at rest, the remainder found themselves engaged in rapidly increasing work. On February 2nd a lengthy bombardment of the enemy trenches was carried out by field and heavy artillery, and the next day began the deliberate cutting of the enemy wire by the 18-pdrs., which was to extend over a very considerable period. To carry this out more effectively the enfilade section of B/162 (which had been in action south of Feuillières) moved to a point on the south side of the Somme east of Clery, where the canal lock adjoined the river; the old position south of Feuillières was taken over by a section of C/162 which moved thither from east of Chapter Wood. At first hostile retaliation was slight, and until about the 8th, with the exception of a severe lachrymose shelling endured by B/162, the work went on more or less unhindered. Gradually, however, the enemy grew apprehensive over the continued cutting of his wire, and his anger was brought to a culminating point on the 7th when the 9th H.L.I. raided the trenches and, after killing ten machine gunners and bombing two dug-outs full of men, returned to their own lines with two prisoners and a machine-gun as proof of their exploit. For their assistance in this raid the batteries received the thanks of General Baird (100th Infantry Brigade) who was especially pleased with the way in which the wire had been cut.

On February 10th, after a further interval of wire-cutting, another bombardment of the enemy trenches took place. From 1.0 P.M. on that day until 6.15 A.M. the following morning a long and deliberate artillery attack was carried out, finishing with a fifteen-minute

ORDER OF BATTLE.

FEBRUARY—MARCH 1917.

H.Q.R.A.

C.R.A.	**Brigade Major.**	**Staff Captain.**
Brig.-Gen. C. F. Blane, C.M.G.	Major H. K. Sadler, D.S.O., M.C.	Capt. W. E. Bownass.

156th Brigade.

Lieut.-Colonel C. G. Stewart, C.M.G., D.S.O.

Adjutant : Lieut. F. L. Lee.

" A " Battery.	**" B " Battery.**	**" C " Battery.**	**" D " Battery.**
Capt. S. Talbot.	Major M. A. Studd, M.C.	Major G. Lomer, D.S.O.	Major W. A. T. Barstow, M.C.

162nd Brigade.

Lieut.-Colonel O. M. Harris, D.S.O.

Adjutant : Lieut. R. H. Pavitt.

" A " Battery.	**" B " Battery.**	**" C " Battery.**	**" D " Battery.**
Major G. Fetherston, M.C.	Major V. Benett-Stanford, M.C.	Major A. van Straubenzee, M.C.	Major J. D. Belgrave, D.S.O. Capt. A. E. G. Champion.

166th Brigade.

Broken up.

intense bombardment which crept over the enemy front line as though to be followed by an assault, and then suddenly dropped back on to the fire trench again to catch such infantry as might have manned the parapet.   The enemy was now fully aroused ; all day he bombarded the right brigade zone and especially 162nd Brigade Headquarters, and from this day onwards he was always ready to retaliate heavily for any operations carried out against him.

A raid on the 14th by the 4th Suffolks round Pekly Bulge (south of the Clery–Feuillaucourt road) did not tend to calm the increasing activity which was now becoming general, and, although no prisoners were brought to our trenches (four, with their escort, were killed by a heavy German trench mortar while crossing No Man's Land), a great deal of damage and many casualties were inflicted upon the enemy in their dug-outs.   On the 19th, however, matters ought to have reached their climax, for on that day should have taken place the attack on Hersfeld Trench, in preparation for which all the previous bombardments and wire-cutting had been carried out.   It was postponed, however ; postponed until the 22nd because foggy weather had prevented any full examination of the condition of the wire after its bombardment, and because the mud in No Man's Land was so bad as to prevent the infantry from reaching the gaps.   In point of fact this attack was again postponed on the 22nd, and finally, after being fixed for March 2nd, was abandoned altogether.

The work now resolved itself into a slow but ever-persistent harassing of the enemy.   "A" and D/162 returned into action on February 20th and joined in the general artillery attack which was in progress all along this portion of the front—an attack the result of which ultimately showed itself in the great German retreat to the Hindenburg Line early in March.   The operation on Hersfeld Trench had been abandoned, but a new assault by the 8th Division further to the north had been in course of preparation for some time, and now definite steps were taken to carry it out.   It will be remembered that at the beginning of the month the 8th Division were preparing battery positions for " A " and B/156 south-west of Rancourt ; on the morning of the 21st the leading sections of the two batteries moved up to these positions, and at the same time the right group, temporarily under the command of Major J. D. Belgrave while Colonel Harris was on leave, pushed forward an advance gun of A/162 to a position two hundred yards east of Clery, whence wire-cutting on the group zone could more effectively be carried out.   Although no attack on the 33rd Divisional front was to be launched it was essential to employ tactics which would mislead the enemy, and by continual harassing to prevent him from concentrating all his attention upon the 8th Division.

There was, however, another reason for this continual bombardment. Rumours began to circulate that the German Higher Command, finding the present positions if not untenable at least strategically unsound, intended to withdraw to the great trench system known as the Hindenburg Line which for a long time past had been in preparation well to the rear, and which was supposed to be a model of siting and fortified field-work. At first rumours were vague and of doubtful origin ; but gradually it became evident, from the explosions which every day could be seen behind the enemy lines, that a great deal of destructive and demolition work was being carried out, all of which pointed to the fact that the area was shortly to be evacuated.

Under these circumstances it was necessary that information should be obtained as to the strength in which the enemy was holding the line, and for this purpose a series of raids was carried out. On the night of February 27th/28th the 2nd Worcesters raided the enemy trenches around Pekly Bulge in two parties, the first party going over at 8.40 P.M. and remaining in the trenches for half an hour, while the second raid started at 1.0 A.M. and lasted for sixty-five minutes. Rumour had it that many of the first party—who were nearly all old hands, and for whose benefit the first raid was said to have been organised—went over again with the second party to complete a few odd jobs which they had not had time to finish thoroughly earlier in the night ! Whatever the truth of this story may be, the raid was eminently successful. Twenty-two prisoners were taken, thirty-six of the enemy were killed in hand-to-hand fighting and six dug-outs full of men were bombed. Moreover, the prisoners proved to be men of the 2nd Guards Grenadier Regiment, and this identification, together with the discovery that the German line was still strongly held, was of the greatest value to Headquarters.

On March 1st the hostile trenches were again raided, this time by the 2nd Argyll and Sutherland Highlanders, and on March 3rd the attack by the 8th Division was carried out on the left with the object of securing a jutting-out portion of the enemy front and support lines. The attack was too far to the north to permit of the 33rd Divisional Artillery batteries taking any share therein, except for " A " and B/156 who had on the 1st completed their move to the left to reinforce the artillery supporting the assault. The 33rd Division did, however, carry out a feint bombardment synchronising with the barrage of the 8th Division, and this in itself was of considerable value since once again information was obtained concerning the strength of the enemy.   The infantry in and on the left of Limberlost Wood not only let off smoke during the feint attack, but also fired rockets of every conceivable colour and variety, and the effect of this upon the enemy was surprising.   Completely mystified, very nervous and on edge, he bombarded the trenches held by the 33rd Division with all his might and main, and disclosed the strength of artillery which he still held upon the front.   This strength was, indeed, quite normal and seemed to belie any ideas of an early retreat on his part, but one feature stood out prominently.   Artillery officers from each of the brigades, who were sent down to the infantry to report on the hostile artillery strength, pointed out that the entire retaliation was carried out by field-guns and 10 cm. howitzers ; of heavy guns and even 15 cm. howitzers there were none.   Perhaps, after all, this supposed retirement was near at hand.   Whether it was or was not, from the 4th until the 9th a steady bombardment was kept up upon the enemy communications.   Infantry patrols reported the line lightly held, and the sniping and movement going on was suspected of being carried out by a few picked men moving from place to place in the trenches and utilising fixed and automatically-fired rifles to the full.   Even a raid by the enemy in the early morning of the 8th did not wipe out this idea ; the opinion was formed that it was sheer bluff, and that only a very few machine-guns and individual gunners, making a lavish use of Very lights, were maintaining the appearance of strength on the enemy's part.

The 33rd Divisional Artillery never saw the climax of this affair. On the morning of Friday the 9th, half batteries of the 156th and 162nd Brigades were relieved by the 178th and 181st Brigades respectively of the 40th Division.   The remaining half batteries withdrew on the 11th, and the two brigades, turning their backs upon the battlefields of the Somme, marched into rest at Vaux-sur-Somme and Sailly-le-Sec.   Rumour had it that they were to go into training for some great battle shortly to take place, a battle in which the line was to be broken, open fighting was to be the order of the day, the German line was to be turned and British arms were to be victorious over the enemy once and for all.   Rumour, as on all such occasions, ran wild amongst the men, but where the attack was to be and when, whether it was in connection with the expected German retreat or elsewhere was kept from all except a favoured few.   Officially it was said that there was to be fighting, and open fighting at that, and that the batteries must train accordingly ; more than that they were not to know.

From the 11th until the 25th the batteries trained hard in every form of exercise ; gun drill, driving drill, flag and lamp signalling, battery staff work and movement into action over open ground were carried out day by day, while in the evening concerts and sing-songs were interspersed with lectures to build up the fighting spirit of the men, to raise their morale to the highest and to give them that quiet confidence and assuredness of being the better man which is so essential to troops who have a battle lying before them.

Moreover, the fighting spirit of the men was raised in other ways than by lectures. The batteries, drawn up in hollow square at church parade, saw the Corps Commander decorate officers and men for gallantry; heard the citation which accompanied the Order of the Crown of Italy awarded to Lieut.-Colonel O. M. Harris; heard the Corps Commander tell them how, shortly after they had been withdrawn from the line, infantry patrols had discovered the enemy trenches to be unoccupied; learnt how, with the enemy in general retreat, the whole of our line southwards from Arras was pressing forward on the heels of the enemy, and even as he spoke was occupying and advancing east from Péronne. It was no concern of the men's that the enemy was relinquishing very bad ground merely in order to take up a vastly superior and stronger position which he had, under the most favourable circumstances, been preparing for some time. They returned to their billets feeling that the enemy really was the under-dog, that his tail was down and consequently that theirs was decidedly up.

Only one incident of this period marred the pleasure of the rest which was being enjoyed. Before the batteries moved northward they lost their C.R.A., Brigadier-General C. F. Blane who, on undertaking new duties, left the Divisional Artillery with whom he was so closely connected. General Blane brought out the (then) four artillery brigades to France in their early raw state in 1915. He helped to mould and to shape them, and, after leading them through all the hazardous times of the Battle of the Somme and through the dreary and trying conditions of the winter, he now handed them over, a splendid fighting unit, to his successor. General Blane did a tremendous amount towards building up the 33rd Divisional Artillery, and in its future history the name of the man who did so much for it in its earlier stages must always be remembered.

The orders to move were ultimately received in the fourth week of March. On the 24th the C.R.A., Brigadier-General Stewart, who had succeeded General Blane in the command of the 33rd Divisional Artillery, set out in a motor bus with his brigade and battery commanders to make a preliminary reconnaissance of the new front on which the batteries were to operate. Next day the latter in full fighting order moved off towards the north on the four-day march which was to terminate at Arras, and was to bring them to the positions from which they would assist in the great offensive of April 9th—the battle of Arras and Vimy Ridge.

CHAPTER VI.

THE BATTLE OF ARRAS AND VIMY RIDGE.

(APRIL—JUNE 1917.)

THE march of the batteries from the Somme to Arras proved very exacting; not only were the weather conditions rather more than bad—intense cold and wet being experienced the whole time— but also the batteries, already deprived of their commanders, were further depleted on the second day of the march, when an order was received for one officer and twenty men from every battery to go forward by motor lorry to work upon the positions which had been allotted for occupation. A measure of praise is due to those, in many cases, junior officers who under difficult conditions, short of personnel and in foul weather led the batteries over the long road through Talmas and Bealcourt towards Arras, now at last disclosed as the goal of the 33rd Divisional Artillery.

All along the line of that march the direction of the coming battle was clearly indicated. Vast columns filled the road, columns of infantry, guns and transport, columns of motor-lorries and ambulances, all with their faces set towards the north, all forming part of a great moving stream inexorable in its progress. Even to the inexperienced the sight of these masses moving up, with scarcely a single vehicle passing in the opposite direction, indicated a great concentration in progress, a mighty gathering of the storm clouds, and only two questions remained unanswered; exactly where, and how soon ?

While the batteries were marching steadily along, pondering over these questions, the brigade and battery commanders, who had covered the whole distance on the 24th, were busily engaged in examining the positions they were to occupy and the zones to be covered. The 15th Divisional Artillery, who were in the line at the time, had already in part prepared the positions to be occupied by the 33rd, and the work and trouble they had expended thereon won for them a very deep feeling of gratitude amongst the officers and men who were to benefit by their labours. Until the arrival

ORDER OF BATTLE.

APRIL—MAY 1917.

H.Q.R.A.

C.R.A.	Brigade Major.	Staff Captain.
Brig.-Gen. C. G. Stewart, C.M.G., D.S.O.	Major T. E. Durie, M.C.	Capt. W. E. Bownass.

156th Brigade.

Lieut.-Colonel B. A. B. Butler.
Adjutant : Capt. B. L. Oxley.

"A" Battery.	"B" Battery.	"C" Battery.	"D" Battery.
Major Lutyens. Major H. McA. Richards, M.C.	Major M. A. Studd, M.C.	Major G. Lomer, D.S.O. Major Barker.	Major W. A. T. Barstow, M.C.

162nd Brigade.

Lieut.-Colonel O. M. Harris.
Adjutant : Capt. R. H. Pavitt.

"A" Battery.	"B" Battery.	"C" Battery.	"D" Battery.
Major G. Fetherston, M.C	Major V. Benett-Stanford, M.C. (*wounded*). Major H. C. Cory, M.C.	Major A. van Straubenzee, M.C. (*wounded*). Capt. W. G. Pringle. Major L. Hill.	Major W. P. Colfox.

of the working parties who had been detached from the batteries on the line of march, however, no material work could be done, and accordingly the time was spent in studying the zone to be covered and in reconnoitring the best O.P.'s from which to shoot.

The strategical cat was now well out of the bag. A great attack, it was learnt, was to be launched upon the whole German system from and including Vimy Ridge on the left to a point well south of Arras on the right. The 33rd Divisional Artillery was to be responsible for the zone immediately south of the river Scarpe, and, after taking part in the preliminary bombardment, was to advance in support of the assaulting infantry so as to keep in touch with the foremost troops throughout the battle. With this knowledge the importance of a thorough acquaintance with the enemy lines was realised, and many hours were spent in front line and observation station studying the hostile wire, trenches and all the back areas. For wire-cutting and bombardment of the German front line our own fire-trench was the best place, and from it a very clear view of the objectives could, in certain parts, be obtained. In order to see the opposing support lines and back areas, however, a higher view point was necessary, and for this purpose certain ruined houses were utilised in the Faubourg St. Sauveur—an outskirt of Arras on the Cambrai road—together with the ruins of Blangy and some tall factory chimneys on the eastern edge of Arras.

The latter offered the most hair-raising experiences at times. On normal occasions the top of a tall chimney sways in a most noticeable manner with every gust of wind ; when, as was often the case here, a deliberate shoot was carried out upon it by the enemy, and 5·9 in. shells were bursting around its base, it really seemed to the wretched observer, perched on an iron cross-bar at the top, that the chimney must sooner or later sway right over and break in two, even if a well-aimed shell did not by a direct hit effect the same result. Moreover the inhabitants of these chimneys, being quite near to the enemy trenches, had often the pleasure of hearing a shell, aimed at some object behind them, whisk past their ears in the course of its flight so close that it seemed inevitable that ultimately the chimney must be hit.

With the arrival of the working parties on March 27th real activity set in. Not only did the pits, platforms and dug-outs begun by the 15th Division require to be completed, but also accommodation for twelve thousand rounds of ammunition in every battery position had to be made ready, while the ammunition which was already there needed sorting. Moreover, the word was passed round to hurry—time was short, and the day of attack was not far off. Hurry, indeed, was the watchword, and for four days the men toiled unceasingly; on the 30th work was redoubled, for on that day the remainder of the gunners of each battery, which had arrived at Duisans the previous night, came up into billets at Arras and continued the work of preparation. In addition to making ready the battery positions in Arras, advanced positions were ordered to be dug and ammunition dumped just behind our own front line, whither the batteries would advance as soon as the first objective in the attack had been secured. This work was of necessity slow, for detection was easy and by day hostile aeroplanes caused a maddening series of interruptions.

On the 30th/31st the first guns of the Divisional Artillery came into action. "A" and B/156 (Major Lutyens and Major Studd) placed advanced wire-cutting guns five hundred yards behind Arras Cemetery, while Major Fetherston (A/162) put a forward section in the garden of a house on the eastern outskirts of Arras, with the task of cutting wire just south of the river Scarpe on the enemy second and third lines. Wire-cutting was immediately begun, and from this date the 33rd Divisional Artillery started to take its active share in the forthcoming battle.

By April 1st the remaining guns of the brigades which had been left at the wagon lines were brought into action. From their headquarters in 6, Rue Jeanne d'Arc and 34, Rue des Capucins, Lieut.-Colonel Butler, who had just been posted to the 156th Brigade, and Lieut.-Colonel Harris directed the work of the batteries, which was now exceedingly heavy. Work on the positions was still in progress, wire-cutting—always a slow business—was continued day in day out, ammunition needed constant replenishing, registrations had to be checked and renewed, and gunners and drivers were being instructed in the route by which the advance to the forward positions would be made. The brigades lay between the Baudimont Gate and St. Nicholas, and the advance from there must inevitably take the batteries over a canal bridge and through narrow winding streets before they could reach Blangy. Whether that bridge would be intact when the time came and whether the streets would not be blocked by shell-torn houses remained to be seen; the route was laid down for the batteries, and that route had to be known by all ranks.

On Wednesday, April 4th, began the bombardment proper, the five-day bombardment which was to precede the launching of the Spring offensive. In secret orders it was known as "V" day, the succeeding days being designated "W," "X," "Y" and "Z"— "Z" representing zero. From this it will be seen that originally

G

April 8th was fixed for the attack ; on the 6th, however, orders were received that between " X " and " Y " days there should be a " Q " day, for the attack was postponed for twenty-four hours and it was necessary that the code system should be continued. Each day had its own special programme with targets, rates of fire and hours of bombardment fixed.   One day was devoted to the destruction of all woods, another to trench-junctions, a third to villages and cross-roads, and so on ; the enemy front and support line and his wire were at the same time kept under continual bombardment by day and night, and every night prolonged gas-shelling of known and suspected battery positions was carried out.

The " village " day was a wonderful sight ; all around behind the enemy lines great clouds of smoke and brick-dust hung heavily, in which every now and then further explosions took place.   From Tilloy on the right —handed over to the mercies of a 15 in. howitzer — from Athies, Feuchy, Fampoux and numberless others these mighty columns of destruction could be seen rising, and the casualties amongst the enemy in the villages, which until now had been left more or less untouched, must have been tremendous.   The enemy retaliation was not heavy ; in fact, its weakness gave rise to the rumour that he, knowing what was coming, had filled his trenches with wire and had retired to a rear position.   Patrols, however, proved the falsity of this, as did also the harassing fire which was intermittently directed upon the 33rd Divisional batteries, and which, although not heavy, was sufficient to cause casualties and give rise to great worry lest some of the vast piles of ammunition in the positions should be exploded.

Gradually the day of attack —now definitely fixed for the 9th— drew near.   On the 5th the last armoured telephone cable was laid to the batteries through the wonderful sewers of Arras, those sewers which, converted into underground passages and lit with electric light, acted as routes to the front line and afforded under-ground shelter for all the reserve troops when the attack was launched. On the 8th the wagon-lines were advanced from Duisans to a position just west of Arras ; on the 8th also took place the final reconnaissance of the routes forward which were carefully marked out with flags— one colour for infantry, another for guns and a third for cavalry. On the evening of the 8th tanks, lumbering across country, passed the batteries en route for their position of assembly, and early on the morning of Easter Monday, April 9th, the tired detachments, after shelling the enemy battery positions with gas all night long, set dial sight and range drum for the opening rounds of the barrage. Huddled under shelter of the gun shields from the cold drizzle which was falling, they peered out through the gradually thinning darkness, listening for the blast of the whistle which would herald the opening burst. All around hung a strange silence ; in every battery position sights were being set and checked, ammunition prepared, the last necessary arrangements made. In every gun pit along the whole of that long front Nos. 1 stood waiting for the signal which would turn the countryside into a roaring volcano.

Sharp to the second at 5.30 A.M. the thin blast of countless whistles cut the air, long sheets of orange flame stabbed the darkness, and with a roar and a crash the hundreds of guns burst out, lighting up the countryside, drowning all other sound and putting down a furious barrage to protect the infantry who, at the same moment, advanced in long lines to the assault. Standing in the eastern outskirts of St. Nicholas, the scene was wonderful. Dark night was of a sudden converted into day by the flashes of countless guns ; with a vast eruption the mine prepared under the enemy trenches opposite Blangy flung skywards what once had been solid ground, while to the flashes and tumult were now added countless rockets and Very lights, fired despairingly by the enemy when he realised that the expected attack had indeed been launched. At the same time the ominous rattle and clatter of machine-guns broke out with increasing intensity as the enemy strove to avoid the hand-to-hand fighting which, above all others, he dreaded the most.

The front covered by the 33rd Divisional Artillery ran southwards from the river Scarpe and was assaulted by the 44th and 45th Infantry Brigades of the 15th Division. To the right of this Division the 12th and 3rd were advancing to the assault, while the left of the 15th Division kept in touch with the attacking troops of the 9th to the north of the Scarpe. The 15th Division formed part of the VI. Corps, with the VII. Corps on the right and the XVII. on the left. The attacking troops of the 15th Division were faced by the 10th Grenadier Regiment of the 11th German Division, and it was estimated that six German battalions were in the actual front line between the river Scarpe and the village of Tilloy.

The first objective to be taken was the German forward system, and this was quickly overrun, our troops capturing many prisoners and establishing themselves along the so-called "Black Line" as arranged, which ran from the Scarpe, through Fred's Wood and southwards to Tilloy. Here they halted for a space while our protective barrage roared over their heads, and then at 7.30 A.M., the scheduled time, they advanced once more with their ranks reorganised to assault the German Second Line, known as the "Blue Line," which ran down between the Railway Triangle and Watery

Wood, and was continued along Observatory Ridge to the Cambrai Road. This line was known to be more strongly held than the first objective, and here it was feared that our troops would be held up, for there were many formidable obstacles, such as the Railway Triangle, to be overcome before the objectives could be secured.

As events turned out, these expectations were in part realised. When the infantry went over the top at the beginning of the day a subaltern from each of the artillery brigades accompanied the foremost assaulting line, while a Captain from the same brigades was attached to each battalion headquarters. In addition to this, from every battery of the 33rd Divisional Artillery one subaltern was sent with the attacking troops, to advance with them and to act as a duplicate source of information with the other F.O.O.'s; as all these officers were accompanied by telephonists, signallers and linesmen it was expected that at least some of them would be able to keep their telephone lines uncut, and would thereby be able to supply first-hand information of the immediate tactical situation. It was from this source that information now arrived.

The Railway Triangle just south of the river had proved, as was expected, the first serious obstacle to the 15th Division. Here stiff opposition was met, for the enemy machine gunners in their dug-outs in the embankment escaped unscathed from the barrage, and succeeded in bringing heavy fire to bear upon the attacking troops before the latter were able to get to grips with them. What followed was one of the inevitable results of a creeping barrage, but also gave occasion for a very fine feat of arms on the part of the batteries. The barrage automatically crept on towards the German second line, leaving the infantry, held up by machine-gun fire, farther and farther behind it. The forward observing officers, however, seeing the crisis which had arisen, got news back to the batteries; urgent orders were sent to all the guns concerned, and the barrage, moving away towards Feuchy, suddenly halted and returned to the Railway Triangle. Back it came to drop mightily, inexorably upon the embankment itself, pounding and blasting away at the hostile machine gunners who had been the cause of all the trouble, until at a given moment, hastily arranged with the infantry, it lifted and crept forward again, and the programme from there onwards was continued once more. As a result of the operation the capture of this very important strategical position was effected at the second assault with the loss by our infantry of only three men wounded; every living soul on the embankment had been wiped out by the second visit of the barrage, and the advance was resumed unchecked! It was a very fine example of the tactical handling of guns, and fully

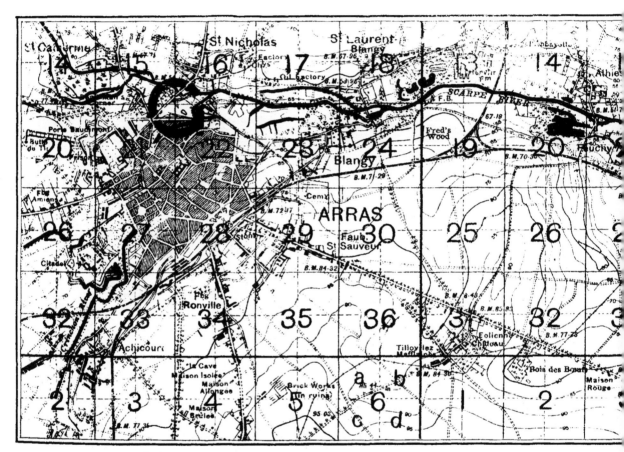

Scale 1: 40.000.

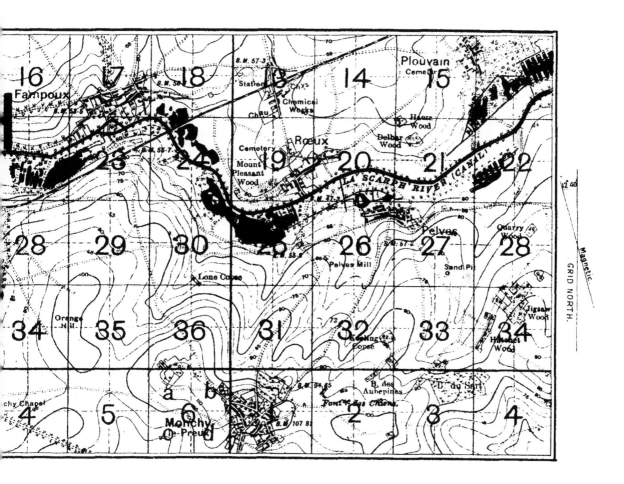

deserved the long accounts given of it in the newspapers two days later.

With the fall of the Railway Triangle the German second line was quickly captured, and here, on the immediate front covered by the 33rd Divisional Artillery, the weary men of the 44th and 45th Infantry Brigades halted. The assault upon the third German line, the "Brown Line," had been entrusted to the 46th Infantry Brigade who, during the attack on the first two systems of defence, had issued forth from the cellars and sewers of Arras into a position of assembly in the German front line, and this brigade now advanced to the attack.

As soon as the German second system had fallen, the batteries began to advance so as to keep touch with the infantry. The delay occasioned by the holding up of the latter at the Railway Triangle had until now rendered any move of the guns impossible, for it was essential that every piece should be brought to bear upon the obstacle which was stopping the progress of the infantry. Now, however, the move forward began ; one section at a time, the guns advanced to the positions already prepared for them in Blangy just behind our original front line, battery commanders going forward to register the guns immediately the trails were dropped. As soon as the first sections were registered and in action, the second sections began to advance ; directly they were in action and firing, the third sections joined them, and thus every battery maintained four guns in action throughout the move forward, and was able to keep a barrage in front of the infantry who now, in the afternoon, were advancing to the assault on the German third line.

Strange to relate, the advance of the batteries, which of necessity was carried out through the outskirts of Arras, was not greatly hampered by shell fire. It was generally anticipated that the enemy would bombard the eastern exits of the town as soon as ever the attack was launched, for he must have known that troops would be issuing forth from there, and, as the route of the batteries lay over a bridge and through some very narrow streets, it was fully expected that casualties would be suffered in this operation. It was therefore with a feeling of relief that battery commanders saw the whole of their batteries in action in the new positions around the eastern edge of Blangy, bombarding throughout the afternoon the defences between Orange Hill and the river Scarpe.

Throughout that afternoon it did indeed seem as though British arms were winning the day. All around troops appeared to be pressing forward ; up the road from Arras there suddenly came squadron after squadron of cavalry which wheeled into a big field in Blangy, dismounted, halted for a space while reconnoitring parties pushed on ahead, then mounted and pressed away on over the captured ground for some advanced objective.   Long columns of infantry, transport, ammunition columns and all the necessary material of war poured steadily out of Arras and moved on ever towards the east, until it seemed as though the whole of the front were pushing forward. The batteries in Blangy, firing though they were upon the enemy as hard as they could, felt somehow that they were being left behind, and longed to receive the order to limber up and join more closely in the pursuit which was now going on.

Orders were not long in coming for the 162nd Brigade at any rate.   Leaving the other brigade still in action around the eastern outskirts of Arras, it threw forward reconnoitring detachments in the middle afternoon, and by evening had begun to advance to new positions—the third occupied that day—around the Railway Triangle which, a few hours before, had been the scene of such close infantry fighting.   All day it had been raining on and off ; now it started to snow, and for the batteries of the 162nd Brigade there began a night of real heartbreaking work.

Ground which has been barraged, captured and counter-barraged a few hours previously, rained upon all day, trampled by cavalry and countless advancing reserves ; ground which consists of shell-torn earth hastily shovelled down by a pioneer battalion to make a rough track, and carried over trenches by arched wooden bridges or not at all ; ground of this nature churned up into deep sticky mud is, for tired horses and men, a difficult obstacle over which to drag guns and ammunition on a rapidly darkening night.   Yet it had to be done ; the infantry were thought to be still advancing, and unless they were covered by the guns they must, sooner or later, meet with disaster.   All that evening the four batteries of the brigade struggled and fought their way through the rapidly increasing throng on the track ; pushed their way past the inevitable broken-down wagons they met ; manhandled each gun in turn through and over trenches which were not bridged, and ultimately, soaked with mud and perspiration, utterly worn out but victoriously aware of the fact that they were still the most advanced batteries and that there were none ahead of them, they arrived at the Railway Triangle and dropped into action, A/162 on the eastern side of the embankment, " B," " C " and " D " on the western.   Here they remained throughout the night of the 9th/10th waiting for daylight to come for the advance to be resumed.

Thus ended the first day of the great Spring offensive.   The infantry, pushing on all the evening towards the German third line, had established posts on the northern slopes of Orange Hill (N.W. of Monchy); the guns were still keeping touch with them despite the rapidity of the advance and the appalling weather conditions; many prisoners and guns had been taken, a considerable number of the enemy lay dead on the captured ground, and nothing, so far, seemed to be holding up the advance of our troops.

On the morning of Tuesday, the 10th, the infantry occupied the remainder of Orange Hill. They had, in the first day of battle, engaged in very heavy fighting; they had made a rapid advance and now, tired out, were unwilling to continue until all the batteries were not only in a position to give them close support, but were in better communication with them. For this purpose the 156th Brigade advanced up to the Railway Triangle, while the 162nd pushed forward once again, this time bound for positions on the western slopes of Orange Hill.

Fortunately there was very little fighting during the 10th; the infantry were busy consolidating, reorganising themselves and carrying out reliefs, and therefore it was possible to spend the day in getting all the guns well forward, replenishing ammunition and making arrangements for thorough support of the infantry in their next advance.

It was well that the whole of the day was available for this, or rather it was inevitable that it should be. So fearful was the mud east of the Railway Triangle, where the Scarpe had helped the rain and snow to form a bog, that the batteries had to make their way across country to the outskirts of Arras once again, and, crossing the railway, worked up towards Monchy along the Cambrai road. The congestion was terrible everywhere, and movement along the road, which was double-banked by traffic in both directions, proved maddeningly slow. Not till the early morning of the 11th did the batteries arrive in their new positions after a night of bogging and digging-out guns, of marching along chaotic roads, of urging tired men and tired horses to further work; but now, grouped on both sides of the road which ran from Feuchy to Feuchy Chapel cross-roads on the Arras–Cambrai road, they were right up close behind the advancing infantry on the western slopes of Orange Hill itself, and were in the best of positions for observation and close artillery support.

On Wednesday, the 11th, the battle broke out again. The 37th Division, who had been in reserve hitherto, took up the attack and assaulted Monchy-le-Preux from the north; at the same time the cavalry advanced on the village from Orange Hill, and after severe fighting Monchy was captured. This cavalry action was much criticized at a later date; it was an attempt to get through a supposed gap in the enemy line, and consisted of a mounted advance across some seven hundred yards of perfectly smooth and open ground dipping slightly and then rising again.   In this advance fairly heavy casualties were suffered both from machine gun and shell fire—the latter being mainly time high-explosive burst the height of a man's head in the saddle—and the operation ended in a dismounted action around Monchy ; it certainly proved a valuable distraction from the 37th Division attacking on foot, and, had not the cavalry put their horses in the village itself when they adopted dismounted action, it is probable that their losses would not have been so severe.   While this operation, which advanced our line four hundred yards east of Monchy and up to the river Scarpe, was in progress, the flanks also tried to advance, but were held up and were forced to return to the trenches they had left.

During the 11th the 156th Brigade came on from the Railway Triangle and dropped into action slightly to the north of the 162nd Brigade, and between it and Feuchy.   At the same time the wagon-lines of the brigades were brought forward and were kept right up close (in the case of the 162nd Brigade, 500 yards) behind the battery positions, for it was expected that the advance would soon be resumed. Although the Army on the right, which had captured Bullecourt and Riencourt, had been driven out again to its original positions, the Army on the left had taken and held the Vimy Ridge, and it seemed that, with the fall of this important feature, further progress must very soon be made.

Now, however, the advance, which for three days had been so brilliant, began to be checked.   On April 12th the 29th Division on the right and the 9th on the left tried to advance their line, but were beaten back.   Hostile artillery, so comparatively silent since the 9th, began to show increasing activity in barraging our troops and in carrying out counter-battery work.   It was manifest that the enemy, after two days of disaster, was pulling himself together, and after losing the majority of his artillery on April 9th and 10th, had now rushed up fresh guns to stiffen the support of the front.

This opinion was strengthened on the 13th, when every battery and wagon-line was heavily shelled, the enemy fire being directed not upon any particular unit, but in a great shell storm over different areas in which the guns and horses were congregated.   It was clear that a determined resistance was going to be offered to any further attack, and accordingly the order was circulated that on this part of the front the line should be held until the flanks had made further progress.   Since this course removed the possibility of any sudden need of teams for a quick advance, the wagon-lines were ordered to return immediately to the eastern outskirts of Arras, only a small number of animals for pack-work being maintained by each battery in forward wagon-lines at the Railway Triangle. With a sigh of relief battery commanders saw their teams wind their way down Battery Valley to Arras again ; the neighbourhood of Orange Hill was no place for horses.

The wisdom of thus removing the horses was very soon put beyond all manner of doubt. All through the early morning and day of the 14th the batteries were heavily bombarded with gas shell and high explosive, especially heavy punishment descending upon the area where the horses had been. Serious casualties would inevitably have been suffered if they had remained there, but as matters stood the only casualties sustained were those in the gun positions themselves, and even these did not prevent the batteries from opening a smashing fire upon the enemy when in the evening he delivered a violent counter-attack upon Monchy, a counter-attack which was broken up under our fire, melted away and failed completely.

The batteries now settled down to what was to be temporarily a " holding " job, and from the 12th until the 23rd nothing more than the usual harassing fire and registration was carried out. The brigades were placed under the administration of the 17th Divisional Artillery and were ordered to dig themselves in, for heavy casualties had of late been suffered amongst the detachments, and it was vital that no more wastage should occur. Digging in was, in the present surroundings, extremely difficult ; two feet below the surface thick solid chalk was met with, and every shovelful thrown up offered an unmistakable mark to the keen eyes of the enemy aeroplanes which were now actively patrolling the front. Not to dig in meant casualties from the usual shell-fire to which the batteries were inevitably subjected ; digging in meant increased safety for the men but also, despite the fullest use of camouflage, the attracting of further bombardment by the enemy. Surely a choice between the devil and the deep sea !

In front of the batteries, on the forward slopes of Orange Hill and in Monchy, excellent O.P.'s were obtainable and were made full use of. The weather—hitherto bitterly cold with snow and icy blizzards— began to improve, and visibility got consequently better. Greenland Hill, Roeux, the Chemical Works and the Scarpe were clear targets on the left, while on the right Pelves Mill on the cross-roads, with the ruins of the little cottage beneath it, showed up clearly as a datum line for the enemy trench system south of the river. Jigsaw Wood, Hatchet Wood and Bois du Sars, all on the skyline, blocked further view, but sufficient was visible west of them to enable accurate registration to be carried out on all the enemy forward zone; his actual fire trench could always be observed from our own front line or even, in the case of the trenches near the river, from the commanding slopes of Orange Hill.

On Monday, April 23rd, a fresh attack was made by the 17th Division, with the 29th and 15th on the right and the 51st on the left, the objectives on the batteries' zone being Bayonet Trench northeast of Monchy, together with a small enemy salient which had been formed on this part of the front. Three attacks in all were made, and all failed; enfilade machine-gun fire from Roeux and from both sides of the river cut down our men, and eventually the operation had to be called off. On the 24th the attack was renewed and this time slight progress was made, but no advance of any account was effected and the losses amongst our troops were enormous. The battle was indeed becoming costly, and the gunners, as well as the infantry, were showing the effects of it. Every day the usual harassing fire took its toll of the detachments, and on the days when heavy bombardments were carried out on the battery positions (as on the 22nd when B/162 lost Major Benett-Stanford and Captain Body wounded, with two out of the three subalterns, Bostock and Neate, killed) numbers were cut down to an alarming minimum.

On April 28th the battle was again resumed on a grand scale. The 12th Division assaulted on the front of the batteries, this time with the 3rd Division on the right and the 34th on the left; at 4.25 A.M. the infantry attack was launched under cover of a very heavy artillery barrage, the objectives being those portions of Bayonet and Rifle trenches which still lay in the hands of the enemy. Three minutes after the attack began the enemy put down a light barrage of 10·5 cm. and 77 mm. shells, which became heavier on Bayonet Trench itself at about 7.30 A.M., but generally speaking the hostile artillery fire was slight. In the main the enemy appeared to depend upon his machine guns to ward off attacks, and in this he was fairly successful. Mist and smoke shell rendered observation very difficult, but by six o'clock the objective was reported to have been gained; from here, however, machine-gun fire began to tell and, although the right battalion of the brigade covered by the 33rd Divisional Artillery advanced according to plan, and was reported to have reached the second objective, the left battalion was held up by machine guns and could not advance.

At half-past six in the morning a smoke barrage was put down along the south bank of the Scarpe to try and help the left battalion, while at the same time the field howitzers turned on to the troublesome machine guns. All day long the batteries kept up a protective barrage in front of the infantry, increasing at times to intense rate when an enemy counter-attack showed signs of being launched. At 11.30 A.M. the infantry endeavoured to consolidate their positions under a now heavy enemy barrage which had been increasing in intensity upon Bayonet Trench since ten o'clock, but it was of no avail. Heavy machine-gun fire from across the river Scarpe prevented them from achieving anything, and not until nightfall was the position clear.

It was then found that Bayonet Trench had been captured in its entirety, but that only a portion of Rifle Trench had been wrested from the enemy; all along the infantry had been greatly impeded by machine-gun fire from which they suffered heavy casualties. From observation and reports received it would appear that the enemy had concentrated in considerable force upon this front, and it was probably due to the work of Forward Observing Officers from the batteries that the many hostile counter-attacks attempted had been smashed before they came to fruition. On the early morning of the 29th the infantry established a line of posts and generally consolidated the ground captured on the previous day, but no further gains were possible. A final effort at 3.0 A.M. on the 30th to capture the remainder of Rifle Trench from the enemy proved a failure, and the infantry, suffering heavy losses, were forced to return once more to their trenches.

Thus ended April, which had opened so brilliantly, and with the arrival of May a less cheering period was destined to begin. Thursday, May 3rd, in fact, marked the last great effort which was made to continue the advance along the whole of the front; on the 1st an unsuccessful attempt to capture the remainder of Rifle Trench had been tried, but this was purely a local operation, and on the 3rd all three Armies pulled themselves together and launched a combined assault stretching from Arleux-en-Gohelle on the left to east of Bullecourt on the right. On the immediate front of the batteries of the 33rd Divisional Artillery, with whom were also the 12th Divisional batteries and the VIth Corps Heavy Artillery, an intense barrage was put down on the enemy front line for three minutes before zero. At 3.45 A.M. the infantry assaulted, while the barrage crept on at the rate of thirty-three yards per minute; intense machine-gun fire was immediately encountered, together with a heavy barrage which fell upon infantry and gunners alike, but the front wave of assaulting infantry by keeping close up to our curtain-fire succeeded in reaching the line Pelves Mill-Gun Trench. Here the situation became very obscure; owing to the fact that zero hour had been fixed for an hour of darkness, all communication between the front and succeeding waves was lost, while a heavy machine-gun barrage put down by the enemy prevented our second wave from getting beyond Scabbard Trench. At ten o'clock a party of Germans entered Scabbard Trench and bombed our men out as far as the junction with New Trench, with the result that the infantry forming the first wave were left entirely cut off.

All this time the 18-pdrs. had been keeping up a protective barrage beyond the first objective, in the hopes of saving such of the leading troops as had got there. At 12.10 P.M. a new bombardment was organised and two hours later a fresh attack was launched, this time under a very novel barrage. The enemy, strongly dug in in Scabbard Trench, could not be reached by the flat trajectory of the 18-pdrs., and accordingly it was decided to organise a creeping barrage of 4·5 in. howitzers. For a quarter of an hour four batteries of field howitzers poured high explosive into Scabbard Trench, our own men lying not only close up to the trench but also all round it, and at 2.10 P.M. the howitzers lifted off and ceased firing, where-upon the infantry, keeping close to the barrage, rushed the trench. It was a desperate measure, this howitzer barrage, for it was like firing into the centre of a circle with our own men all round, and, with the infantry lying right up to and following so closely on the heels of the barrage, it seemed inevitable that a few rounds should fall short—and only a few short rounds of 4·5 in. H.E. are sufficient to do inestimable havoc and wreck the confidence of attacking troops. Like many desperate measures, however, it succeeded ; some fifty Germans, unable to stand the appalling weight of fire (about 80 rounds of H.E. per minute in a confined space), fled from Scabbard Trench and rushed down the bank running east towards Pelves Mill, while simultaneously a party of about one hundred of the enemy left the same bank and made for the cross-roads just west of the mill. Immediately they broke cover the 18-pdrs. switched on to the parties with excellent results, and two companies of the 17th Royal Sussex Regiment, profiting by the distraction, rushed Scabbard Trench in its entirety ; this they captured almost without casualties, and found seventy dead Germans, the victims of the howitzer bombardment.

The enemy now opened a furious bombardment upon Scabbard Trench, realising that it had at last fallen, and at 2.20 P.M. launched a heavy counter-attack which was beaten off after hand-to-hand fighting, in which we captured one officer, twenty-five men and two machine guns. All the afternoon the batteries were busy on various targets, especially upon enemy infantry who kept massing behind Keeling Copse and running in small batches to Cartridge Trench.

At the same time a good view of the hostile counter-attacks on Greenland Hill, north of the Scarpe, was obtained, and on several occasions the guns were switched round to the left and dealt smashing blows to the enemy every time he attempted to leave his trenches.

The total result of the battle was that on the extreme right the 5th Army advanced beyond Bullecourt, but was forced back again by the enemy who reoccupied the village ; around Cherisy all objectives were gained, but here again the enemy counter-attacked and drove out our troops ; on the immediate front of the batteries a partial success with enormous loss of life was obtained ; on the north of the river the attack on Roeux failed also, and only on the extreme left was any real success achieved. Here the 1st Army took Fresnoy and all the objectives north of Oppy. Oppy itself, however, proved too difficult for the attacking troops, nor were any of the objectives between it and the river captured. In short, the attack began well, almost brilliantly, but finished badly ; it was not a defeat—the operations north of Oppy saved it from being called that—but it was at least a partial failure which had cost many thousands of lives.

May, then, did not begin very well, and, after spending the whole of the 4th in consolidating the ground of the previous day's battle, a lull set in—a lull which was not broken until the 11th. At 7.30 P.M. on that day the 4th Division just north of the river carried out an attack upon Roeux Chemical Works and Cemetery, the 33rd Divisional Artillery supporting the operation on the flank. Covered by a barrage, the density of which was one 18-pdr. for every seven yards of front, the infantry rushed all the objectives and held them, together with 300 prisoners ; to this gain was added a further advance along the river's edge at 6.0 A.M. next morning, which was covered by a barrage put down on the north-western end of Roeux, and by midday on the 12th the infantry were secure in their newly-won positions. The ominous Chemical Works, from which such deadly machine-gun fire had been directed on our attacks south of the river, was now in our hands, and there seemed every chance of an advance being possible on the front of the batteries.

Orders for this advance were not long in coming. At 6.45 P.M. on that same evening (12th) the 12th Division, which was covered by the 33rd Divisional batteries, advanced to the assault on Devil's Trench, while the 3rd Division prolonged the attack to the right. After a three-minute bombardment with a density of one 18-pdr. to every ten yards of front, the 36th and 37th infantry brigades advanced upon the portion of Devil's Trench which ran northwards from Bit Lane to Harness Lane. Simultaneously with the attack, however, very heavy rifle and machine-gun fire was opened by the enemy from both flanks--Gun and Devil Trenches--which were held in force, and fifty yards short of the trench our infantry were stopped, unable to advance any farther.   Lieut. Wingfield, the forward observing officer of the 156th Brigade who was with the attacking company commander, got through to the guns and reported that the infantry intended to assault again at 10.45 P.M.   Accordingly, for fifteen minutes prior to that time the batteries put down a heavy barrage and then lifted on to the enemy support trenches.   Close on the heels of the barrage the infantry rose to the attack, but circumstances were against them ; darkness supervened everywhere, the infantry were scattered all over the place owing to the non-success of the first attempt, and Devil's Trench was only assaulted here and there.   By midnight it was reported that the remnants of the attacking company were back in their own original front line again.   The operation had failed completely.

The operations of May 3rd, costly enough by themselves, had now been followed by the two attacks on the 11th and 12th, and so heavy were the casualties amongst the infantry that, for a time at any rate, the infantry battle was broken off, and to the guns was given the task of wearing down the enemy and of destroying his morale.   This new period was ushered in on the 14th by a Chinese bombardment of the enemy trenches ; a bombardment, that is to say, which bore all the signs of a barrage covering assaulting troops but which, in reality, crept forward unfollowed by any infantry, and then dropped back suddenly on to the hostile fire-trench to catch such of the enemy as had manned the parapet to meet the expected assault.   In this case our guns pounded Devil's Trench for a short time, and then crept on by lifts of one hundred yards every minute. After three lifts the barrage suddenly dropped without warning on to the fire-trench again and blasted it with high explosives and shrapnel, while the Division on the left swept the area with enfilade machine-gun fire.   No movement was seen, but the enemy doubtless expected that another attack on Devil's Trench was being launched and would therefore have manned the parapet ; if he did so, his losses must have been severe.

Having thus attacked his forward infantry, the guns now turned their attention to enemy ration parties and back areas. Every night, for the past week or so, a part of the night firing pro-gramme (which was carried out every night by each battery mainly on back areas) had been to keep up intermittent shell fire upon the road running east from Pelves towards Hamblain. Aeroplane photographs now received, however, showed tracks running parallel to this road and about 150 yards south of it, tracks which became clearer every day. It was manifest that the enemy had given up using the road and was cutting across country; on the night of the 15th, therefore, the guns directed their fire in intermittent bursts on to the original road up till 9.0 P.M., and then at that hour, by which time all traffic would have been diverted on to the cross-country tracks, swept up and down those tracks with H.E. and shrapnel for ten minutes at an intense rate of fire. That this fire was effective in its object was clearly proved next day, when the enemy retaliated strongly upon our own lines of communication— sure sign that we had done something seriously to annoy him.

The batteries now began to have a bad time. Free from infantry attacks and suffering most of his casualties from the guns, the enemy turned the full fury of his attention upon the gunners. " B " and C/162 were engaged by a 5·9 in. high velocity gun, their positions being badly damaged; D/162 was registered by an enemy aeroplane which carried out an all-day bombardment upon it in co-operation with an 8 in. howitzer battery. Both brigades suffered severely from bombardment by 5·9 in. howitzers, while a couple of whizz-bang batteries devoted themselves to putting intermittent bursts and sniping rounds into all the battery positions, and especially those of the 156th Brigade, causing many casualties by the unexpectedness of their attacks. As a rule, in fact, these sudden bursts did far more damage to personnel than the long all-day bombardments, and it was just such a burst which killed Captain Heape of A/162 and so wounded Lieut. Tucker that he died next day—a loss grievously felt, for both officers were of the very finest type which the brigade contained. From day to day each battery in turn underwent a severe shelling, and the casualties in men and guns mounted, ever mounted.

On May 16th the lull in infantry fighting was broken, this time by the enemy. After bombarding our front trenches immediately north of the Scarpe, together with the village of Feuchy and the back areas in general, during the whole of the 15th, a big hostile attack was launched at 3.0 A.M. on the 16th and drove our troops out of Roeux Cemetery and Chemical Works. By 7.30 A.M. we had counter-attacked and recaptured the lost ground, and at 9.50 A.M. a hostile counter-attack was driven off. Shortly after ten o'clock our men were seen advancing north-west from the Chemical Works, but a furious hostile barrage was put down on them and they were forced to retire. All day long the batteries poured shell into Roeux and the adjoining trenches, and all day long fighting continued; by evening the situation had calmed down, and little change showed itself on the front as a result of the twenty-four hours' fighting. It was clear, however, that the enemy was not only going to offer a stubborn resistance but was even assuming an offensive attitude in places, and a bitter struggle was anticipated when orders were received for another attack on Devil's Trench.

On the 19th our troops were once again flung upon this deadly little objective—flung, as they had so often been before, on a narrow limited front with the knowledge that flank machine-gun fire must inevitably be met with.

Major Colfox (D/162) had, on the previous night, run a forward gun right up to Chinstrap Lane, twelve hundred yards west of Roeux, and had registered it over open sights in the early morning, in the hope that enfilade fire from here might assist the infantry in their oft-tried task. Under a heavy barrage the infantry rushed to grips with the enemy, but no sooner had our guns started than the enemy opened a heavy concentrated machine-gun fire all along the front, while his guns put down a dense barrage within thirty seconds of the beginning of the attack. A footing was gained in the part of Tool Trench still held by the enemy, but strong bombing attacks were delivered from both flanks, and our troops under the pressure of these attacks were forced to withdraw. Devil's Trench once more had proved a death-trap.

This venture was followed up at 11.30 P.M. on May 30th by an assault on Hook and Tool Trenches, but the attack only added one more item to the now growing list of local failures. Our troops were evidently seen leaving their trenches, and this enabled the enemy to open heavy machine-gun and artillery fire on them. In spite of this, and of the mud and water caused by a thunderstorm during the afternoon, the attacking troops reached their objectives, but so heavy had been the casualties suffered whilst crossing No Man's Land that the remnants were not strong enough to deal with the garrison of the trench. Most of the attackers were driven out by a counter-attack following immediately on the assault, but a party of the Manchester Regiment established itself in Hook Trench and managed to hold on till noon next day. The guns poured shell over their heads and put down barrage after barrage for their protection, but it was of no avail. Shortly after midday a superior force of the enemy counter-attacked with fury, and this gallant little party was overcome.

The advent of June brought with it a further succession of local attacks—efforts to straighten our line, to remove important points held by the enemy and generally to improve our tactical position. It was evident, from the non-success of the French offensive in the south, that no more operations on a large scale would be carried out here, but it was also clear that Higher Command had decided in its mind that our line must embrace certain tactical features now in the hands of the enemy, and to this end further local undertakings had to be effected. Following on two Chinese bombardments on June 3rd and 4th, in which the 33rd Divisional Artillery took part to the south of the river, the 9th Division carried out a short and successful attack around Greenland Hill on the night of the 5th, and consolidated all its gains. Soon afterwards, on the 13th, a very successful attack upon Hook and Long Trenches was made by the 76th Infantry Brigade. During the previous week a systematic bombardment had been carried out night and day upon the enemy defences to obliterate his trenches and to weaken his morale. Each day, however, there had been no firing between 5.0 A.M. and 9.0 A.M., and the enemy had grown accustomed to a period of quiet at this time. When, therefore, the infantry rushed across at 7.20 A.M., our barrage not starting till 7.21 by which time they were in the hostile trenches, they caught the enemy quite unprepared and showing little resistance. All gains were held and, under cover of a protective barrage, the ground was consolidated.

At 7.15 A.M. next day (14th) a further attack under cover of a barrage resulted in the capture of Infantry Hill by our troops, and the morale of the latter, somewhat shaken by the continued reverses at Roeux and Devil's Trench during the previous weeks, began now to rise again to the pitch of confidence and assuredness so badly needed. So greatly did it improve, in fact, that when the enemy counter-attacked at 2.15 A.M. on the 16th, in an endeavour to regain Infantry Hill, he was severely punished and beaten off — except for the loss of two southern posts in front of Long Trench — despite the fact that the attack had been delivered with a strength of some seven hundred bayonets under cover of an intense artillery bombardment. A second hostile attempt at 2.30 A.M. on the 17th, although preceded by a two-hour bombardment, only resulted in our losing a small portion of Long Trench, and it now seemed as though Infantry Hill were securely in our hands.

Just prior to these attacks the 33rd Divisional Artillery had received orders to move out to the wagon-lines and to take over part of the line further south. The enemy's attitude, however, appeared threatening, and accordingly the departure of the batteries was postponed until the activity had died down. By June 20th all appeared to be quiet, and at 6.0 P.M., after twelve weeks of continuous battle on this front, the march to the wagon-lines was effected. Taking their guns with them, the batteries topped the ridge west of

H

Battery Valley and marched back to the peace and rest of Arras once more.

The three months' fighting in this offensive had marked a brilliant chapter in the doings of the 33rd Divisional batteries. Under all conditions, in blizzards, in snow and mud, under intense shell-fire from the enemy they had maintained their reputation for straight shooting and complete reliability; moreover, and this was above all the most valued, they had won the entire confidence of the infantry. When the 3rd Division, which had carried out the operations of June 14th–19th under cover of the guns of 33rd Divisional Artillery, was withdrawn from the line, its G.O.C. Major-General Deverell wrote to General Stewart and asked that the personal thanks of the infantry might be conveyed to the batteries. "We wish them" he concluded in his letter, "all good fortune in the future and hope that we may again fight together with that close co-operation which has been so conspicuously marked whilst we have been together." High praise, that, and praise dearly won, for there were many gaps in the ranks as the brigades turned west-wards. On each and every battery the offensive had left a heavy mark, and the faces of new arrivals bore witness to the many blanks which had had to be filled, but the greatest loss which the Divisional Artillery as a whole had suffered was borne especially by the 162nd Brigade. On May 23rd Lieut.-Colonel O. M. Harris was carried away on a stretcher in the advanced stages of para-typhoid. To the officers and men of his brigade his name seemed inextricably interwoven with the brigade itself, for he had "made" it, working it up from its early raw stage at La Bassée to the fine fighting instrument it now was. With his going a certain gloom fell upon the brigade, for all ranks realised that they had lost not only a very gallant leader but a very true friend.

Before he left, however, Colonel Harris had one great satisfaction. Throughout the battle of Arras the 162nd Brigade had made it its object always to be the furthest forward, always to be the nearest to the infantry. Its batteries were the first across No Man's Land on April 9th, the first to advance as each enemy line fell, the closest up behind the infantry throughout the operations, and early in May this achievement was officially recognised. There came one day from Field-Marshal Sir Douglas Haig a message saying that a captured German 5·9 in. howitzer would be presented to the 162nd Brigade in recognition of the work it had carried out during the advance, and of the very fine manner in which it had on all occasions pushed up so close behind the infantry. Such a distinction has rarely, if ever before, been conferred upon a brigade of artillery, and to its commanding officer was due a full measure of praise in that he had worked it up to a pitch of efficiency which made such deeds possible.

    *   *   *   *   *   *

One night the brigades spent in their wagon-lines at Arras, and early on the morning of the 21st they hooked in and moved off through Beaurains down the long road which led to Bapaume, to pit their strength this time against the fortifications of the Hindenburg Line.

CHAPTER VII.

THE HINDENBURG LINE AND THE OPERATIONS ON THE COAST.
(JUNE—AUGUST 1917).

WHEN the batteries marched back to the wagon-lines on June 20th they knew that they were to set off next day to go into action immediately on another portion of the front, but their actual destination remained somewhat of a mystery. There was a rumour that they were going a considerable distance northwards, even to the Coast it was suggested, and therefore, when they set out in a southerly direction on the morning of the 21st, a certain amount of surprise prevailed amongst the rank and file. Southwards they headed, passing through Beaurains along the great road running down to Bapaume, and gradually they penetrated more and more deeply into the wilderness created by the enemy when he retreated to the Hindenburg Line in February and early March.

As events turned out, the march was to be a short one. After leaving the Bapaume road a few miles south of Arras, wagon-lines were established around Hamelincourt, Boyelles and Boiry St. Rictrude in the VII. Corps area, and one section per battery moved up into action the very same afternoon; the march had represented nothing more than a sideslip of some three miles to the right, but even this short distance brought the batteries into totally different surroundings. They were now moving through the country over which the enemy right had retired in his withdrawal earlier in the year, and on all sides they saw proof positive of the stories of destruction which had been related to them. Every tree, every bush, even the slender apple trees lay cut down and destroyed ; roads had been blown up, houses demolished, and the country had the appearance of a great wilderness with every natural feature shaved off as though by a giant razor. The Bapaume road, no longer a stately route bordered by trees, lay like a piece of tape across the naked ground ; houses gaped and tottered, blown up not by the shells of the pursuing army but by the prearranged handiwork of the retreating foe. It was a case of wanton destruction, wrath vented upon the country-side by a bitter and chagrined enemy, and, although it has been suggested that all this work was carried out in order to open the country for the great and last German drive westwards which was

ORDER OF BATTLE.

MAY—AUGUST 1917.

H.Q.R.A.

C.R.A.	Brigade Major.	Staff Captain.
Brig.-Gen. C. G. Stewart, C.M.G., D.S.O.	Major T. E. Durie, M.C.	Capt. W. E. Bownass, M.C.

156th Brigade.

Lieut.-Colonel B. A. B. Butler.
Adjutant : Capt. B. L. Oxley, M.C.
Capt. W. G. Sheeres.

"A" Battery.	"B" Battery.	"C" Battery.	"D" Battery.
Major H. McA. Richards, M.C.	Major M. A. Studd, M.C.	Major Barker, M.C.	Major W. A. T. Barstow, M.C.

162nd Brigade.

Lieut.-Colonel Conolly.
Adjutant : Capt. R. H. Pavitt.

"A" Battery.	"B" Battery.	"C" Battery.	"D" Battery.
Major G. Fetherston, M.C. Major W. G. Pringle.	Major H. C. Cory. Major Walker, D.S.O.	Major L. Hill.	Major W. P. Colfox.

destined to begin some nine months later, there can be little doubt but that it was merely a continuance of that policy of frightfulness and destruction which marked all his doings.

Despite this, very fair wagon-lines were obtainable around the ruins of the villages aforementioned, for the ground was dry and rolling and, there being no inhabitants in this area of desolation, there were no restrictions as to the setting up of horse-lines. Quickly the brigades settled down in their new surroundings, and as quickly the first sections moved up into action, to be followed next day by the remainder of the batteries.

Ever since May 12th General Stewart and his staff had been near Hamelincourt, controlling the artillery covering the infantry of the 33rd Division in the Bullecourt sector (at that time the 21st and 37th Divisional Artilleries, together with the 150th, 293rd and 79th Field Artillery Brigades), and on going into the line now the batteries came under the administration of the 50th Divisional Artillery. The 156th Brigade occupied the positions vacated by the 123rd Brigade of the 37th Division, situated east-south-east of Henin-sur-Cojeul and just west of the Hindenburg Line. The batteries of the 162nd Brigade were distributed at first amongst the 82nd, 83rd and 250th Brigade groups; ultimately, on the 23rd, they were placed under the control of the 250th (C and D/162) and the 251st (A and B/162) Brigade Groups, and supported the infantry from positions in Heninel (C/162) and east of Henin, all batteries except A/162 being just to the left of the 156th Brigade. The front covered by the brigades was roughly the line running southwards from Fontaine-lez-Croisilles nearly to Bullecourt.

This part of the front was of intense interest to the batteries. To begin with, they were in touch with the infantry of their own Division for the first time since February; the 162nd Brigade, it is true, was shooting over the trenches north of that part of the Hindenburg Line garrisoned by the 19th and 98th Infantry Brigades, but the 156th Brigade was actually covering the 33rd Divisional Infantry, and to the men there was a feeling almost of being home once more when they thus found themselves amongst their own. Added interest, moreover, was gained from the fact that the much-talked-of Hindenburg Line could here be examined, for the fall of Monchy had outflanked this part of the system, and the enemy with much reluctance but of dire necessity had had to retreat from it, leaving it to be occupied by our troops.

It was a mighty piece of fortification; in front of the fire-trench were three thick belts of wire thirty yards apart, each belt some fifteen yards deep; between the belts, which were so thick that hardly a mouse could get through them, lay concrete emplacements for machine guns or trench-mortars, reached from the front line by underground shafts. The fire-trench itself, about twelve feet in depth, contained concrete pill-boxes at every turn and on every tactical point, while the communication trenches running back to the support line were so wired as to form a defensive flank should any portion of the front be penetrated. On reaching the support line an exact replica of the fire-trench was met with ; three belts of wire and the accompanying pill-boxes and machine-gun emplacements lay in front of the trench, but this time a further feature was added. Throughout the entire length of the Hindenburg support, from Beaurains right down to Bullecourt, there ran an underground tunnel seven feet high, three and a half feet wide and thirty feet below the surface. Shafts ran down to it at intervals of twenty yards, and to all intents and purposes it formed a vast dug-out exactly under the parapet of the trench and running beneath it throughout all the miles of its length. Its existence could only be proved as far as Bullecourt, for from that point onwards it was held by the enemy, but doubtless it continued southwards with the Hindenburg Line itself since, offering as it did a perfect refuge for the garrison, it formed an integral part of the defences of this great system. For that portion of the passage which lay in British hands a " Town Major " even had been appointed, and from him could be obtained so many yards of the dug-out as the lawful habitation of the unit on the spot !

The batteries were not slow to get to work here. June 22nd and 23rd were spent in registration of the zone and in careful study of the front to be covered. On the 23rd the 156th Brigade bombarded Tunnel Trench at 11.35 A.M. and 7.30 P.M., and at midnight on the 23rd/24th supported an attack on it by the 19th Infantry Brigade from Lump Lane. The attack proved unsuccessful, and throughout the 24th the bombardment was continued, while the 162nd Brigade took up the running on the left in an attack on York, Bush and Wood Trenches. The 5th E. Yorkshire Regiment (50th Div.) carried out this assault at 12.30 A.M. on the 26th, and at first were successful. All the objectives except for the cross-roads north-west of Fontaine-lez-Croisilles were gained, thirty prisoners were captured and two hostile counter-attacks driven off. There followed, however, such a deluge of hostile shell fire that the newly-gained trenches were entirely demolished, and a large part of the ground gained had to be relinquished.

After this outburst the brigades settled themselves down to " artillery activity," searching for the opposing batteries and shelling all tracks and approaches to the enemy front line.   The two brigades each fired some six hundred rounds every twenty-four hours on targets of this nature, and by so doing aroused the ire of the enemy to no small extent.   Hostile counter-battery work increased rapidly in activity, but very few casualties were suffered.   A/162 (Major Pringle) were much damaged by hostile bombardments on the 22nd and 24th, while Major Richards' guns (A/156) on July 2nd were so heavily shelled that they had to shift their position, having lost three sergeants killed and a number of men wounded.   But if the batteries suffered in this manner, at least they gave as good as they took ; nightly activity was more than ever directed upon the hostile back areas and gun positions rather than upon the infantry, and to this was added a chemical shell bombardment carried on throughout the night of the 28th/29th which must have worried the enemy to a considerable extent, if the weight of his retaliation on the 29th were to be taken as a guide !

When the batteries came out of action prior to moving down to this part of the front a rumour was circulated, as already mentioned, that their destination was to be the Coast, and surprise prevailed that their route should take them southwards.   Battery commanders were told by their Group Commanders on arrival, however, that the Cherisy–Fontaine sector was nothing more than a sorting-area, and that they, like the batteries before them, would probably remain in action only some ten days or so before moving elsewhere.   Therefore, when orders were received on July 9th to move out of action in a couple of days' time, the news was not altogether unexpected.   The preceding period had been spent in the usual artillery activity with no infantry action of any sort, but unfortunately the enemy, by this continued harassing of his battery positions and roads, had been roused to an extreme pitch of retaliation.   He had of late taken to subjecting the valley from Henincl through St. Martin-sur-Cojeul down to Henin to a miniature shell storm, and as certain of the batteries had to utilise this route for their move out it seemed as though his efforts, hitherto fruitless, might meet for once with some success.

As matters turned out, however, the nightly searching took place some thirty minutes before the batteries moved, and the actual march away was carried out undisturbed on the night of July 11th/12th.   A/162, nevertheless, and one or two other batteries were very heavily shelled by 5·9 in. howitzers just as the teams and limbers arrived, and only by the greatest good fortune, coupled with some very marked gallantry amongst the men, did the guns get away without serious casualties.

On arrival at the wagon-lines it was found that no further destination had been determined, and that here for the present the batteries were to remain. There was no reason, indeed, for a move to any more distant area, for the horse-lines here were good and dry, tents had been pitched to shelter the men, harness " rooms " had been erected while the batteries were in action, and a very fair degree of comfort offered itself to all ranks. True, the horse-lines were in view of enemy territory at points, but they were a long way back—some five miles from the line—and no trouble from long-range fire was expected; on the other hand the uninhabited state of the area, due to the destructive march by the Germans early in the year, offered an excellent training ground for work of every description.

Refitting, overhauling and training began immediately after the arrival of the batteries at their horse-lines. From the 13th to the 15th a Divisional Artillery scheme with skeleton batteries was carried out around Adinfer Wood; this was followed by days of battery training, gun drill, driving and riding drill, battery staff work, training the detachments to cut gaps through wire entanglements and rush their guns over trenches, and every conceivable form of preparation for more open fighting.

All was not work, however; the weather was glorious and every opportunity was taken of giving the men a holiday, a rest from fighting and preparation for fighting, a chance of enjoying themselves. Five or six jumps were put up near each battery, and the respective wheelers knocked together gates for exhibition driving; the Divisional band came down and gave a concert one afternoon, while another half-day was spent in a cricket match between the two Brigades. Batteries arranged mule races for their own edification or ran off heats for the forthcoming sports, and altogether managed to make the time very pleasant.

As a final flourish, two days were allotted for a Horse Show and sports. On the 18th the Divisional Artillery Horse Show was held near Boiry St. Martin, and produced an excellent programme. Events were ushered in by the somewhat precipitous arrival on the course of a six-in-hand emanating from D/162; a six-in-hand which, although only hooked in to a G.S. wagon and consisting of horses quite unused to this form of equitation, was driven up the course by Major Colfox in true coaching style, the battery trumpeter rendering weird noises from the back, while General Stewart's A.D.C. took a prominent seat " to add tone to the picture ! " Followed a series of jumping, driving and " turnout " competitions, mule races and the like, till at last a very cheerful day and one producing some fine horses and horsemanship came to an end. Major Studd won the officers' jumping event. A/156 gathered up many of the other prizes, and the remainder were scattered amongst all the batteries.

Four days later a day was given up to Divisional Artillery Sports, the programme consisting not only of the usual flat race, jumping and obstacle items but also of one or two mounted events, and then the batteries packed their wagons, hooked in the teams and turned their backs sadly on this pleasant spot. They were off to the war once more, and rumour had at last been verified — the Coast was their destination.

The knowledge of this destination had been obtained by the batteries some time back. As early as July 4th General Stewart and his Brigade-Major (Major Durie), who had been relieved in the line by the C.R.A. of the 21st Divisional Artillery three days previously, set out for XV. Corps Headquarters to attend a conference, and did not return until the 8th. On the 13th orders had been received for one officer and fourteen men per battery to move ahead of the main body and report at headquarters of the 1st Division at Coxyde Bains, to prepare the positions which the guns were to take up, and with the name of the destination now disclosed an immediate rush had been made for maps to discover its locality. " Bains " certainly suggested the Coast, and surely enough it was ultimately found there — a small village some four miles west of Nieuport and right on the sea front. It was therefore with the knowledge of great events impending that the batteries marched off on July 23rd, glistening in the new paint and added burnish which eleven days in the rest area had made possible. Authieule and Amplier, both in the neighbourhood of Doullens, were their destinations that night, and these they reached in the evening after a march through very fine country under a glorious sky.

From 6.0 P.M. and throughout the night of Tuesday, the 24th, the batteries entrained at Doullens North and South and at Authieule. Eight horses in each van, guns and wagons lashed to long trucks by French porters, men crowded into big cattle trucks, they journeyed throughout the night and early morning past Hazebrouck and Bergues, and finally arrived in the forenoon of the 25th, the 156th Brigade at Adinkerke, the 162nd Brigade at Dunkirk. A rapid detrainment, water and feed for the horses and a hasty meal for the men, and the batteries set out in long columns for their wagon-lines. The 156th Brigade went right up to Coxyde Bains and established wagon-lines in the dunes behind the village ; the 162nd Brigade marched to Ghyvelde, a village two miles from the Belgian frontier and some distance behind the line, and sent up one section of horses from each battery to be attached to the 156th Brigade at Coxyde for use as a forward wagon-line.

The next morning battery and brigade commanders rode up to the line to reconnoitre the positions they were to occupy, and to inspect the work done by the advance parties, while on the 27th and 28th the guns of every battery were calibrated at the Coxyde Bains range, firing out to sea through electric screens, by which process the muzzle velocities of the guns were measured. On the night of the 28th/29th the 156th Brigade, with " A," " B " and C/162, moved up into action in the positions already prepared, and next night were followed by D/162. Considerable difficulty was experienced on both occasions owing to an enemy bombardment of the neighbourhood with gas shell throughout the night ; respirators were worn for two and a half hours and casualties were thereby averted, but the difficulty of finding the way in the darkness on an unknown road was naturally greatly increased.

On July 30th, when the batteries had opportunity to review their new positions, they found themselves in surroundings totally different from any yet experienced. On their left lay the sea, all around them was sand broken up by huge dunes, and practically nowhere could any shell holes be seen. This did not, unfortunately, mean that there was no hostile artillery activity ; on the contrary the enemy artillery, and in particular his high-velocity guns, showed the most amazing persistence in raking our battery positions. The reason for the absence of shell-holes was that the sand, continually kept shifting by the wind, silted up and filled in any hole within a few hours of its being made, leaving all the shell splinters lying on the surface like pebbles on a sandy beach. There arose from this the disadvantage of not being able to tell from the nature of the ground whether it was subject to enemy shelling or not, but on the other hand it offered real relief to eyes now physically wearied by the continual sight of torn and desolated country.

These coastal positions, indeed, offered many new and hitherto unexperienced features, but for every advantage there was at least one disadvantage. The sand, kept moving by the wind, removed the depressing sight of shell-holes ; but the same sand blew into men's eyes, blinding them, and jammed the guns at almost every other round fired. The view of Ostend—visible on a clear day from the Grand Dune—with the German destroyers occasionally entering and leaving its harbour, offered an object of great interest ; but the proximity of Ostend involved the presence of an infinite host of high velocity naval guns on land mountings, which blasted impartially infantry, batteries and roads right back to and beyond the wagon-lines. The sand was excellent in the wagon-lines for harness cleaning, and ensured dry standings for the horses; but it offered a constant threat to any animal which should eat of it, and necessitated the setting up of double picket-ropes for the horses, to prevent them from getting their heads down and contracting sand colic.

There was only one real consolation, and that was the presence of the sea. The sea, with its submerged wire entanglements, offered a zone free from the enemy; the sea occasionally provided the thrills of destroyers passing and of monitors bombarding Ostend and Westende. The sea, on a fine evening, somehow brought Home very near as it stretched in a glory of shimmering gold, unconcerned and utterly oblivious of warfare, back to and beyond the far horizon whither lay England. The land could be smashed, the land could be blasted and torn, but the sea remained ever the same, stronger and mightier than any war, the connecting link between Hell and the peace of an English home.

The batteries were very close to the sea, for they were on the extreme left of the whole of the line. Headquarters of the 162nd Brigade were established in the West Sand Dunes about 700 yards south of Groenendyk Plage. " A " and B/162 lay some 150 yards in rear of headquarters; D/162 was almost on the beach, for it took up a position in the East Dunes 150 yards from the water's edge, with C/162 not far off in the West Dunes about three hundred yards from the shore; both these batteries lay in front of headquarters and south of the Groenendyk Plage–Nieuport Bains road. The 156th Brigade was farther inland but still quite close to the coast, B/156, the southernmost battery, being 300 yards south of the Yser. Both brigades, since they were situated on the extreme left of the line, covered the left or Nieuport Bains sector, which ran from the Coast along the south side of the Yser and along New Trench to Barnes Bridge. In addition to the 33rd Divisional Artillery, the infantry of the 66th Division, who held this front with one infantry brigade (two battalions in the line), were also covered by the 66th Divisional Artillery and three Army Field Artillery Brigades, the whole being under the command of Brigadier-General D. B. Stewart, C.R.A. 66th Division.

It may seem strange that such a great mass of guns should cover a one-brigade front, and in the ordinary course of trench fighting this weight of artillery would far have out-reached requirements. The coastal zone, however, was not an ordinary part of the line; there was a great deal of mystery hanging around it, a great deal of " hush-hush " talk and, to give a hint as to the truth of this talk, a vast concentration of artillery. Ever since the batteries had detrained at Adinkerke and Dunkirk the men at the wagon-lines had seen, day after day and hour after hour, heavily laden trains pull in, disgorge batteries and battalions, shunt out and be replaced by more trains. Every day fresh batteries marched up the pavé road long the Nieuport canal to occupy positions amongst the sandhills ; every day an inspection of the dunes around Nieuport discovered fresh batteries congregated in every hollow, in every depression of the ground, until there seemed to be no room for more.

It was, indeed, a mighty concentration ; close up to Nieuport the field guns lay in tier upon tier; behind them the six-inch howitzers occupied every possible position and many that were almost impossible ; eight-inch, sixty-pounders and 9·2 in. jostled each other for room further back, while over their heads rushed the shells of the long-range guns in action near Coxyde Bains. Clearly an offensive was impending, but how and where ? The area immediately in front of the 66th Division was flooded and impassable, and on the left lay the sea. Was it from there that the blow was to fall, or was the right to attack and, piercing the German lines, force the enemy troops facing Nieuport to retire ? Rumour held orgy.

Meantime the batteries of the 33rd Divisional Artillery to all outward appearances cared for none of these things. They were in action, there was certain destructive work to be done, and the enemy was making the doing of it very uncomfortable. From Dune 18 and the neighbouring O.P.'s targets were registered and bombarded, destructive and harassing fire was maintained on selected " sore " spots, and the front was kept in continual turmoil. On August 2nd the 49th Division on the right carried out a daylight raid with the assistance of the batteries, and on the night of the 7th/8th the guns supported two raids on the Lombardzyde and St. Georges sectors, both of which were successful. There followed, on the night after this raid, a projector gas attack which was launched on the enemy in the Nieuport Bains sector in conjunction with a barrage fired by all batteries, and it is scarcely surprising to record that the enemy's temper now became extremely frayed. Every battery was shelled by high-velocity guns, 5·9 in. howitzers and innumerable gas shells ; the roads and approaches—especially the Coast road—were under continual bombardment, and the strain upon the detachments grew increasingly heavy. 162nd Brigade wagon-lines, in order to cope with the ever-increasing demand for ammunition, had moved up on July 31st to St. Idesbalde, and the 156th Brigade, which on August 1st had sent its horses back to La

Panne, now, on the 5th, brought them up to Coxyde Bains once more.

The night of the 15th/16th saw another projector gas attack on the Nieuport Bains sector, during which the batteries fired on the areas around Golf Road and Polder Trench, and which was followed by increased enemy artillery activity. Nieuport and the batteries around it, Pelican Ridge and the roads running inland from the coast were all raked by enemy fire which increased in violence on the 18th, when a practice barrage on the right divisional front was carried out. There followed four more days of practice barrages and then, on the night of the 24th/25th, the 19th Infantry Brigade, supported by the guns, attacked and captured Geleide Post. It was only a small operation, however, and the batteries covering it merely fired on their S.O.S. lines ; moreover it was a short-lived success, for the following night the enemy won it back again.

For four weeks now the batteries had carried out continual bombardments of the enemy ; practice barrages had been fired, and an immense concentration of artillery had gathered together. An attack was clearly impending and it was evident that the enemy realised the fact, for his guns had shown the very greatest activity for some weeks ; they were forever bombarding battery positions, roads and communications, usually with high-velocity naval guns on land mountings, but also with 5·9 in. and 8 in. howitzers, while of late a 17 in. howitzer had been in the habit of blasting the field batteries around Nieuport. Therefore the news came like a bombshell when, on the night of August 27th/28th, the batteries were ordered to withdraw to their wagon-lines. It seemed incredible that this great concentration of artillery should be broken up without being used for any offensive operations, and at first it was thought that the 33rd Divisional Artillery might be an isolated case. But no ! Every day battery after battery — some heavy, some of field guns — pulled out from the sand dunes and headed for the rest area, their work over, their object unfulfilled. The mighty hosts of batteries, which for weeks now had been lying in every hollow and valley amongst the dunes, melted away and disappeared without ever learning the object of their coming.

Many and varied have been the reasons put forward for the breaking off of this attack. Some say that the advance of the enemy at Lombardzyde early in July put a check to our plans ; some attribute it to the long spell of wet weather and to the non-success of the great attacks at Ypres on July 31st and August 16th, while many assert, not without truth, that the enemy obtained our entire operation orders for the battle and took counter-preparations accordingly. Undoubtedly an attack had been planned, and an attack on some entirely novel lines. The 1st Division had, for weeks past, been kept isolated from all other troops while it practised unusual offensive operations. Some of the batteries had received orders that on a certain date they were to embark on a certain ship at a certain port — all at present described in code — and the general belief was that an offensive by land was to be launched in conjunction with an attack somewhere near Ostend from the sea. Imagination, running riot, spread the report that large rafts were to be towed inshore on which there would be field-batteries firing as they floated in, while other rafts were to carry infantry and tanks. The whole idea sounded fantastic and a desperate adventure in view of the manner in which the Belgian coast bristled with enemy guns and submerged wire-entanglements ; and, with the memory of Gallipoli fresh in the minds of all, it is surprising how any such operation could have been considered worth the gamble and the inevitable cost.

Whatever had been planned, however, nothing was carried out. The batteries were left to reorganise in their wagon-lines for two days — a period which the enemy utilised by bombarding with long-range high-velocity guns the horse-lines of both brigades, and especially those of the D.A.C. which suffered severe casualties — and on Saturday, September 1st, under sudden orders they marched out, battery by battery, on a three-day trek which brought them in glorious weather through Ghyvelde and Cassel to the back areas of the Ypres Salient. At Reninghelst and at Dickebusch their march terminated, and wagon-lines were there established while parties went up to the line to prepare positions for the guns to occupy. At last, after nearly two years' fighting, they were to experience the desolation and horror of the Salient, the deadliest portion of the whole line for gunners, and were to take part in the autumn battles for the Passchendaele Ridge ; had they known it, few of the men who, early in September, marched up past Dickebusch and Shrapnel Corner to the battery positions beyond Zillebeke Lake were ever destined to return, while the majority of those who did came down on stretchers, the wreckage of modern war.

CHAPTER VIII.

THE AUTUMN BATTLES OF YPRES AND PASSCHENDAELE.
(SEPTEMBER—NOVEMBER 1917.)

In and around the Salient of Ypres there are to be found the graves of more gunners than in any portion of the line, and even those graves represent a mere particle only of the many thousands to whom Ypres brought death. That much discussed, much described and oft-portrayed area will never and can never be properly comprehended by any man who has not fought there, for, before the real meaning of the Salient can be understood, the picture of destruction which it offered must be accompanied by the realisation of the dread, the feeling of utter desolation and misery, the terrible haunting horror which seized all men as they stepped out through the Lille or Menin Gates with their faces set towards the east. No man, be he ever so brave, was without fear in that place, while the majority were in constant terror, a terror so rending, so utterly shattering that death came often as a merciful release. Yet of that fear no man need be ashamed; it was a terror entirely within and invisible, and to outward appearances there were no signs thereof; in the which there is not shame but honour.

The 33rd Divisional Artillery had yet to undergo these trials, but their beginning was not long delayed. On the night of September 5th/6th, twenty-four hours after the conclusion of the march, one section of each of the 18-pdr. batteries of the 156th Brigade went into action and relieved portions of the 11th, 12th and A/298 batteries; "A" and B/156 occupied positions south-west of Fosse Wood, C/156 lay north of Maple Copse, and on the two succeeding nights, one section at a time, the remainder of the batteries came up. The 162nd Brigade was not so rushed as it had no "opposite numbers" to relieve, but on the other hand the batteries had to prepare the positions they were to inhabit, and this, in view of the appalling state of the ground, was extremely difficult. To begin with, the finding of any patch of ground which guns could possibly reach, and from which they would be able to fire more than two or three rounds without sinking into the mud, proved an arduous task, while the work of

ORDER OF BATTLE.

SEPTEMBER—NOVEMBER 1917.

H.Q.R.A.

C.R.A.	Brigade Major.	Staff Captain.
Brig.-Gen. C. G. Stewart, C.M.G., D.S.O.	Major T. E. Durie, M.C.	Capt. W. E. Bownass, M.C.

156th Brigade.

Lieut.-Colonel B. A. B. Butler.
Adjutant : Capt. W. G. Sheeres.
Capt. H. W. Smail.

"A" Battery.	"B" Battery.	"C" Battery.	"D" Battery.
Major H. McA. Richards, M.C.	Major M. A. Studd, M.C.	Major Barker, M.C.	Major W. A. T. Barstow, M.C. (*wounded*). Capt. W. G. Sheeres, M.C.

162nd Brigade.

Lieut.-Colonel E. J. Skinner, D.S.O.
Adjutant : Capt. R. H. Pavitt.

"A" Battery.	"B" Battery.	"C" Battery.	"D" Battery.
Major W. G. Pringle.	Major Walker, D.S.O. (*gassed in September*). Major H. C. Cory, M.C.	Major L. Hill, M.C.	Major W. P. Colfox, M.C. (*wounded*). Major Beerbohm (*killed*). Major F. L. Lee.

I

preparing platforms and shelters on the positions, when chosen, involved not only great labour but a still greater patience.

The enemy, fully alive to the indications of a renewed offensive on our part, swept the whole of the battery positions with shell storms of increasing density, inflicting casualties amongst the working parties and wrecking the work they had done, so that at times it appeared as though nothing would be ready for the remaining guns of the division when they were ordered up into action.   No sooner was one platform in a position prepared, with a few sandbags thrown up around it for the protection of the detachments, than a 5·9 in. shell would blow the whole thing to pieces, and the work had to be begun all over again.   Day after day the working parties, reinforced by men from the D.A.C. and from the Trench Mortar batteries, toiled unceasingly not only at their own positions but at the two positions they had been ordered to prepare for the 23rd Divisional Artillery, for they saw, after a very few hours of the Salient, that without protection of some sort or other no detachment could possibly survive a single barrage.

At length, after eight days' work, some reward for the labours of the working parties showed itself, and it was well that this was so for now the remaining batteries were ordered to move up into action. On the night of the 13th/14th " A," " B " and C/162 took up the positions marked out for them, to be followed on the next night by D/162, and by the early morning of Saturday the 15th the whole of the Divisional Artillery was in action and registered on the zones to be covered.

Already severe casualties had been suffered by the 156th Brigade south-east of Zillebeke, who since September 5th had been in action under the 24th Divisional Artillery, while the 162nd Brigade working parties had also borne the weight of the hostile fire.   From the 15th onwards, however, conditions became far more severe, for on that day began the organised bombardment by our guns prior to the forthcoming attack, and the resulting increase of counter-battery work by the enemy.   On September 13th the 156th was put under the control of the 23rd Divisional Artillery on the relief by the latter of the 24th, and with A/103 formed part of the right group under Lieut.-Colonel B. A. B. Butler (O.C. 156th Brigade) whose headquarters were at Tor Top.   On its arrival in the line on the 14th the 162nd Brigade was also controlled by the 23rd Divisional Artillery, but, with the exception of C/162 which was placed in the right group, the batteries went to form part of the left group, commanded by Lieut.-Colonel Groves (O.C. 103rd Brigade) whose own batteries less A/103 made up the rest of the group.   " A," " B " and D/162 lay on the northern,

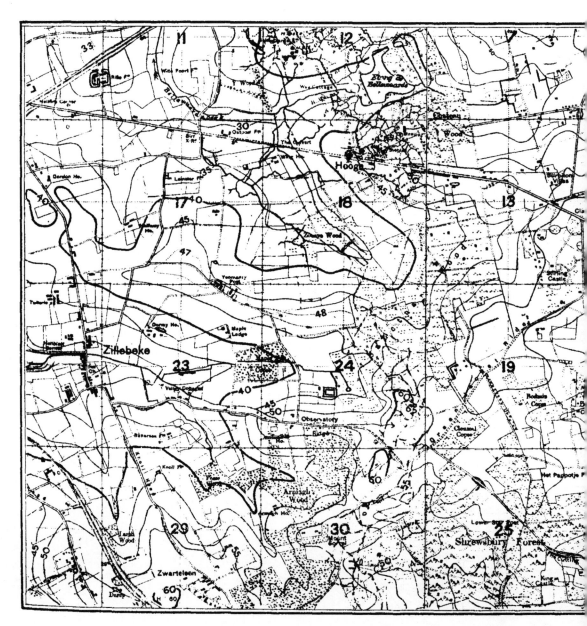

Scale 1:20,000.

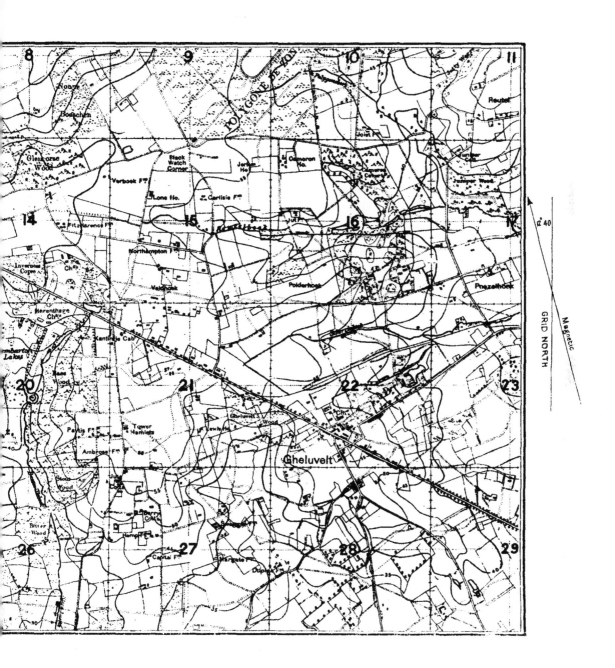

southern and western edges of Maple Copse (due east of Zillebeke) while C/162 was in action just south of Fosse Wood; the positions of the 156th Brigade have already been noted.

It will be remembered that throughout July and August, 1917, a succession of big attacks was carried out by the British troops in the Ypres Sector, with the object of driving the enemy back from the semi-circle of low-lying hills which overlooked our trenches in the Salient. The proposed coastal operations of the foregoing chapter had, indeed, been planned in connection with the Ypres offensive, and with the breaking off of the former the batteries were sent down to take part in further undertakings against the Passchendaele–Gheluvelt ridge. The ill-omened autumn offensive against the Passchendaele ridge was, in fact, about to begin, and the first battle of the series was fixed for September 20th. For this, the limits of the zone covered by the Divisional Artillery were Clapham Junction on the north and Dumbarton Lakes on the south, the 162nd taking the left portion of the zone, that is from the northern limit for 700 yards southwards to Polderhoek Château, the 156th the right portion of the zone from Dumbarton Lakes 700 yards northwards; the middle gap was covered by the centre group of which the 33rd Divisional Artillery formed no part. It had been extraordinarily hard to find any marked feature upon which to range the guns, but Gheluvelt Mill, situated as it was upon a small mound, offered a tolerably clear feature for registration purposes, and this was utilised by the majority of the battery commanders prior to the barrages which now began.

The whole barrage table for the forthcoming attack had, by the 15th, been issued to the batteries, and the practice barrages which now began to be carried out consisted sometimes of portions of this table, sometimes of the complete barrage fired in its entirety. As a rule these " rehearsals " were fired at half the rate which would be used on the day of the attack, but the same proportions of shrapnel, H.E. and smoke shell were adhered to, and therefore if only a part even of the barrage were fired—such as the portion behind which the infantry would advance from the first to the second objective— the curtain of fire as it appeared on the ground would offer an exact model of the real attack barrage, except for a certain diminution of density. This fact was important, for it was realised that the bad state of the ground to be attacked over would force the infantry to advance very slowly, and that therefore a great deal depended upon the barrage to keep enemy machine-gun fire down until our infantry could get to grips with their assailants. Every day one and some-times two practice barrages were fired, and on each occasion one officer of considerable experience was sent up from every artillery group to observe the effect thereof.   In particular, reports were rendered dealing with the density of the barrage, whether all batteries opened fire simultaneously, whether there were any gaps or rounds falling short, whether the average height of the shrapnel bursts was correct and whether the barrage crept forward uniformly.   After every barrage these reports were examined and collected, and before the next practice was carried out the necessary alterations had been made.

The first practice barrage began at 4.0 P.M. on September 15th and was carried out along the whole Corps front ; followed certain minor adjustments, and at 5.30 A.M. on the 16th it was fired again. At 10.0 A.M. on the same day an "Army barrage," *i.e.*, a barrage on the whole of the Army front, was fired, to be followed on the afternoon of the 17th by another Corps barrage.   On September 18th the last two Army barrages were fired, one at 6.0 A.M. and one at 8.30 P.M., and at 11.0 A.M. on the 19th the Corps had its last rehearsal.   It was a relief when these practices were over ; they invariably called down heavy retaliation from the enemy who, as soon as he saw an infantry attack was not pending, turned the full blast of his guns on to our batteries.   It was impossible to cease firing and put the detachments under cover, for this action would have resulted in gaps appearing in the barrage and confusing the observers who, unaware of what was happening, would have reported that the barrage was uneven and full of "holes."   The programme had to be carried out from start to finish whatever the enemy did, and if the batteries lost heavily in these days it was all that was to be expected of the Salient.   Lose heavily they did, both in officers and men, and as the latter stood around their guns in the small hours of the 20th, ready to begin this time the real barrage covering the assault, there was not one detachment which had not already been seriously depleted in numbers, which had not been compelled to call up considerable reinforcements from the wagon-lines.

It was on September 18th that the orders had been received which fixed the 20th as the day of attack, and on the last two nights, the 18th/19th and 19th/20th, the howitzers of both brigades busied themselves with prolonged gas bombardments of the enemy batteries. The only hope of salvation for the guns lay in silencing some of those batteries, and they knew that their chances of surviving the long all-day barrage which they were to carry out on the day of the attack rested almost entirely on the efforts of the two preceding nights, and on the work of the heavy artillery which, by intense counter-battery work on the 20th, would try to keep down the enemy fire.

Twenty minutes to six in the morning of Thursday, the 20th, had been fixed for the delivery of the assault, and some thirty minutes before this the detachments of all batteries manned their guns and stood by, ready for the signal to go.   Very feverish were those last few minutes of waiting, for nearly every battery was being heavily shelled, and it was probable that, as soon as the attack was launched, the enemy guns which were causing all the trouble would come under the counter-fire of our own " heavies," and would at any rate diminish the now alarmingly heavy fire which they were directing upon the wretched detachments.

With terrible slowness and deliberation the minutes passed; 5·9 in. and 4·2 in. shell were crashing every moment into the battery positions, ammunition was exploding, men were being knocked out and a number of direct hits were destroying the guns, killing and wounding every single man of the detachments.   In some of the batteries a few more minutes of this would have put every gun out of action, but mercifully zero hour was at last reached, a sheet of flame lit up the entire countryside and with a great roar the barrage began. The batteries of the 33rd Division poured forth a curtain of fire in front of the advancing infantry, the heavy artillery bombarded the enemy batteries and roads, and, whatever happened all round them, whatever bombardment they suffered, the detachments were now fully occupied and took heed of nothing but their work.   The assault had begun !

The infantry who were even now advancing under cover of the guns of, amongst others, the 156th and 162nd Brigades were, as already stated, troops of the 23rd Division.   On the right the attack was continued by the 41st Division, on the left by the 2nd Australian Division, and together the long line advanced slowly through the mud towards the enemy trenches.   The ground was very bad ; it was estimated that the infantry advancing across No Man's Land could not cover one hundred yards in less than six minutes, and accordingly the barrage was so timed as to move forward twenty-five yards every minute and a half.   Even at this slow pace the infantry were hard put to keep up with it, while the work of the gunners was rendered exceedingly heavy ; for the ultimate objectives were fairly deep within the enemy lines, and with the barrage moving so slowly the infantry were not due to reach their farthest goal till a late hour, while an intense rate of fire had to be maintained over their heads the whole time.   Moreover, there was not one battery which by now had not had some of its guns knocked out, and the speed of the remainder had, of necessity, to be increased in order to keep up the full volume of fire.

From 5.40 A.M. onwards the batteries roared forth at intense rate ; slowly the barrage crept on ahead of the infantry till it reached and covered the first objective ; halted there for fifty minutes while the assaulting troops reorganised themselves, and at 7.8 A.M. moved off to the second objective, now at the slower rate of one hundred yards in eight minutes.   At 7.40 A.M. the second objective was reached and covered, and for two hours and thirteen minutes a protective barrage was maintained what time both infantry brigades in the forward line brought up their reserve battalions for the attack on the 3rd and last objective.   At 9.53 A.M. the last phase of the attack began and, moving forward now at only ten yards per minute, the barrage started to creep towards the third objective, reached it at twenty-five minutes past ten and, passing over it, put up a protective curtain of fire beyond while the infantry established themselves in the newly won trenches.   This protective barrage, covering as it did the ultimate objective of the day's fighting, had to be maintained until well on in the afternoon ; since it was fired at a slower rate, however, it now became possible to relieve some of the detachments at the guns and to set about clearing up the battery positions.

As already described, nearly all the batteries were heavily shelled just before the launching of the attack early in the morning.   Shortly after the earlier phases of the barrage this hostile bombardment had eased off under the counter-battery work of our own heavy artillery, but throughout the morning—and, in fact, during the whole of that day and night—every one of the battery positions was searched and swept at intervals by 5·9 in. and 4·2 in. howitzers, the resulting damage to personnel and equipment being very great.   With gun muzzles pointed now to a high elevation, small detachments maintained a protective barrage at a slow rate of fire while the remainder of the men—after eating a hasty meal—began to repair and reorganise the positions.

Yawning holes gaped everywhere ; guns had been knocked out and had to be dragged from the pits on to the road ; ammunition, buried or scattered by hostile fire, was dug up ; the dead were removed and placed away near the road, whither presently a wagon would come for them, while the gun pits themselves required to be rebuilt so as to be fit for the new guns which the wagon-lines had already been ordered to bring up.   It was gloomy work, this, and was rendered all the more depressing by the certain knowledge that presently the enemy would open fire and would wreak the same havoc all over again, but the outstanding necessity presented itself of keeping every gun and every battery fully ready at a moment's notice to support the infantry and prepared to open fire on any target within range.

All this time news at the batteries had been scarce.   A Captain from the right and left artillery groups had been attached to the two infantry brigades (68th and 69th) covered by the guns, and, in addition, subalterns from the same artillery groups had accompanied the two assaulting battalions in the attack on the third objective. Their duty, however, was to report straight to Group headquarters, and therefore it was left to the batteries only to surmise from the continuity of the progress of the barrage that the attack must have, at any rate at first, succeeded. The primary objective—the " Red Line "—ran from Fitzclarence Farm through Herenthage Château to the eastern edge of Dumbarton Wood, while the second objective—the " Blue Line "—extended from a point midway between Black Watch Corner and Cameron House down east of Veldhoek to the eastern edge of Bass Wood, and, as the weight of artillery forming the barrage on the divisional front alone consisted of 84 18-pdrs., 30 4·5 in. howitzers and 42 heavier guns and howitzers, not counting the batteries detailed for special work, it was hoped that these two objectives at least might be overrun with comparative ease. It was in the advance to the " Green Line," the final objective of the day's battle, which ran from Carlisle Farm due south for eleven hundred yards, bending back slightly to the west of Gheluvelt Wood but embracing Tower Hamlets, that trouble might be forthcoming, for by then the enemy should have recovered from his first surprise and might offer very considerable resistance.

At last news was received. A short message stated that all objectives had been taken but that very heavy fighting had occurred in the advance upon the last objective, and only the excellence of the creeping barrage had made success possible. The official report written later by the 23rd Division stated : " The barrages were very punctual and effective. Prisoners seemed dazed and utterly demoralised. The creeping barrage from the second to the third objective and the protective barrage beyond the latter are deserving of special mention. Replies to S.O.S. were both prompt and effective, rapidly dispersing any attempts at concentration or counter-attack. This instilled great confidence into our infantry." These last remarks were not received till a later date ; at the time there came only the bare news that all objectives had been taken and that a large part of the success gained was owed to the excellence of the barrage. It was good to learn that the day was won, that success had been achieved, and it offered some slight comfort to know that the service of the guns, which had involved such heavy losses amongst the detachments, had been of avail. Only on the right had non-success been met with, and there the left brigade of the 41st Division had been unable to advance beyond the second objective. The troops covered by the 33rd Divisional Artillery, however, threw out a protective flank ; the S.O.S. barrage was so arranged as especially to protect the right of the 23rd Division which was in the air except for the thin defensive flank already referred to, and gunners and infantry set themselves to watch for the inevitable counter-attacks.

All through the afternoon the batteries had been busy breaking up concentrations of the enemy, and hitherto had been successful in keeping them at bay. The valley of the Reutelbeek and the area around Reutel Village offered some cover, and continued calls from the infantry kept the guns at work on these areas. A determined counter-attack launched shortly after 7.0 P.M. was beaten off under our artillery fire ; all night intermittent bursts from every battery swept the enemy hollows and approaches, and at 4.30 A.M. on the 21st a special barrage was fired with the object of breaking up any enemy operation which might have been planned for daybreak. By these means, and by continuing these methods throughout the day of the 21st, the infantry were able to maintain all their gains, and by the evening of the 21st were assured of their position. Two furious counter-attacks by the enemy, delivered after an artillery bombardment lasting one and a half hours in each case, were broken up at 3.0 P.M. and at 7.0 P.M. by our artillery fire, and gunners and infantry alike now set themselves to try and repair the wreckage of their positions before offensive operations should break out anew.

The heavy firing which preceded the attack, the all-day barrage which had been maintained on the 20th and the wastage of ammunition incurred through enemy shells blowing up the dumps around the guns necessitated very heavy work all through the 21st and 22nd in bringing up ammunition from the wagon-lines. The lines of the 162nd Brigade were a great deal too far back for carrying out so much gun-line work, and, as early as the 15th, forward wagon-lines composed of one section per battery had at first been maintained on the eastern outskirts of Dickebusch ; later, after being heavily shelled on the night following the attack, they had been moved across the road to the neighbourhood of Dickebusch church. From here, and from the 156th Brigade lines a little farther back, parties of pack horses came up on the 21st to carry ammunition from the nearest dumps to the battery positions, for it was impossible in the majority of cases to bring ammunition wagons and teams anywhere near the guns. Light railway tracks had been run as far forward as possible, and, from the termini at Valley Cottages, Verbrandenmolen and other points which the little petrol-driven trucks were able to reach about once in four days, the pack animals carried the ammunition to the batteries. During the whole of the two days following the attack this transport of ammunition was carried out, although continually interrupted by hostile shell storms which inflicted many casualties amongst men and horses, and by the 23rd not only were dumps at the guns completely up to strength again, but further new guns had come up from the Corps gun " pool " on the Reninghelst–Steenvoorde Road, and had in the majority of cases replaced all the guns knocked out during the previous week's fighting.

It was well that the guns had succeeded in replenishing their ammunition on the 21st and 22nd, for on the 23rd began preparations for a fresh attack. Throughout the two preceding days the enemy had pounded and smashed every battery position in the attempt to prevent as far as possible any further operations, but as fast as the guns were damaged repairs were executed, and at seven o'clock in the morning of the 23rd every battery was able to take part in the Corps practice barrage which had been fixed for that hour. Like its predecessors it was fired at a reduced rate to that at which the real attack barrage was to be fired, and like its predecessors it called down severe hostile retaliation. C/162 (Major Hill) was so heavily shelled that it was compelled to move out to a fresh position three hundred yards to the left flank, and every battery received the usual searching which now had come to be regarded as inevitable, while the rest of the day saw shell storms of increasing violence delivered upon every area where any of our batteries were to be found.

On the night of September 24th/25th the infantry of the 33rd Division relieved the 23rd Division, and General Stewart, moving up to Burgomaster Farm in Dickebusch, assumed command of the artillery covering the front. The whole of the 25th marked a day of intense activity amongst the guns. At 5.40 A.M., while the infantry relief was still in progress, a strong counter-attack was launched by the enemy, preceded by a heavy barrage. For one and a half hours our batteries maintained a rapid rate of fire on their S.O.S. lines, but were unable to prevent the right of the 100th Infantry Brigade astride the Menin Road and the whole of the 98th Brigade from being driven back to the support line. At 11.35 A.M. the S.O.S. signal was again sent up by the 100th Brigade, and again the guns burst forth in their support—this time with success.

At 2.15 P.M. a Corps practice barrage was fired, and at 3.30 P.M., before the practice was over, devastating bombardment by guns of all calibres was opened upon our battery positions. For upwards of half an hour this bombardment continued, inflicting considerable damage upon the battery positions, and then for a short time the weary detachments had a rest. Not for long, however ! At 5.30 P.M. the storm broke out afresh, this time upon gunners and infantry alike, and once again, now under heavy shell fire, the batteries responded to the S.O.S. signal sent up an hour later by the left brigade and by the Australians further to the left.   This counter-attack was also repulsed, and by midnight it was found that the right brigade held their line intact except for a small portion of trench north of Menin Road, but that the left brigade north of the Reutelbeek had been beaten back three hundred yards, though possibly some posts were still held 150 yards in front.

Such a day as the 25th was not very favourable for preceding an attack, yet when Wednesday, the 26th, dawned it found the infantry of the 33rd Division assembling for the assault which had been fixed for 5.50 A.M.   It will be remembered that just prior to the attack on the 20th the field batteries were all subjected to an intense bombardment, while the infantry were allowed to assemble in the front line almost untouched.   Now the positions were reversed ; at 5.0 A.M. the enemy put down an intense barrage on the infantry, just as the latter were forming up for the attack, and inflicted very heavy casualties upon them.   For fifty minutes the hostile bombardment tore them and shook them, and it was in greatly diminished numbers that the infantry advanced across No Man's Land when, at 5.50 A.M., the guns blazed out in the assault barrage.

For this attack one hundred and two 18-pdrs., thirty-six 4·5 in. howitzers and a large number of heavy guns were covering the divisional front, which stretched from the southern edge of the Polygon de Zonnebeke on the north to a point three hundred yards short of Gheluvelt on the south.   Dumps of eight hundred and thirty rounds per 18-pdr. gun and seven hundred and fifty rounds per 4·5 in. howitzer were maintained at the guns for, as previously, the barrage was to move at the very slow rate of one hundred yards in six minutes to the first objective, and one hundred yards in eight minutes to the final line to be taken.   Moreover, a protective barrage was to be maintained beyond the final objective for half an hour after its capture (8.40 A.M.), and from then until 2.15 P.M. was to continue at a reduced rate searching all the ground beyond the infantry to a depth of one thousand yards.   From this it will be seen that allowance had to be made for a very heavy expenditure of ammunition.

At 5.50 A.M. the infantry went over the top, and at 7.45 A.M. came the first news.   A captain from the right and left artillery groups (between which two groups the 33rd Divisional Artillery was split up) had been attached to the headquarters of the two infantry brigades delivering the attack, while a subaltern from each group accompanied the battalions assaulting the final objective, and from them came the information.   The 39th Division on the right and the 5th Australian Division on the left had captured the Red Line—the first objective—but the 33rd Division had been held up. The first objective on the front of the latter ran from Joist Farm past Jut Farm and through Polderhoek to the northern edge of Gheluvelt Wood, and had proved too strong for the troops who, during the previous twenty-four hours, had been fighting hand to hand in numberless counter-attacks and had endured the most intense bombardments. At 8.40 A.M. the trench which had been lost in the previous day's fighting just north of the Menin Road was recaptured, and at 11.55 A.M., after calling back the barrage, a fresh attack under the creeping fire of the batteries was launched upon the first objective. For twenty minutes the guns carried out this new programme, but at 12.15 P.M. a message was received asking the batteries to keep up a protective barrage beyond the Red Line until further notice, as a heavy barrage was being maintained by the enemy upon our assaulting troops. This protective barrage was continued for upwards of an hour, which fact indicated that no further progress had been made by the infantry, and throughout the afternoon intermittent fire was directed upon the enemy beyond the first objective until such time as orders should be received for a fresh attack.

In the middle of the afternoon a severe enemy shell storm descended upon all the batteries and inflicted serious casualties. At the same time a heavy bombardment of our infantry was reported, and at 5.0 P.M. our guns, themselves heavily shelled by the enemy, opened fire on their S.O.S. lines until 6.30 P.M. when they slowed down. At 6.40 P.M. the S.O.S. signal was again sent up, and again for one and a quarter hours the batteries put down a barrage. Scarcely had they stopped than the enemy launched yet another counter-attack, and not till nine o'clock at night did the gun detachments cease the barrage firing which they had begun shortly before 6.0 A.M. that morning. With the arrival of night matters became quieter and no further operations were attempted. From information received it was gathered that the infantry of the 33rd Division held the original line from which they had been driven on the preceding day, and had established advanced posts in the first objective although not occupying it in force. The casualties were reported to have been terribly heavy.

On the morning of the 27th a resumption of the advance was carried out. Ammunition was running low but, with pack horses hard at work bringing up fresh supplies, the batteries kept a covering fire over the infantry, and by 9.45 A.M. the latter had established themselves in force in the first objective of the previous day's fighting and had pushed out posts beyond. At midday the left brigade were very heavily shelled and asked for covering fire from the batteries, and half an hour later the 5th Australian Division on the left reported that they could see the enemy massing in Polderhoek Château Wood. On hearing this the guns of the 156th and 162nd Brigades were immediately turned on to this area, searching and sweeping it for upwards of three-quarters of an hour, and the threatened counter-attack was broken up. At 2.15 P.M., however, it developed again, and for an hour the guns of the 162nd Brigade maintained a medium rate of fire on their S.O.S. lines, at the end of which time all was reported quiet.

So the day wore on; the guns in continual action, the detachments, depleted by hostile shell fire and weary almost to death, seizing what opportunities they could of getting a few moments' rest. At a quarter to seven in the evening the never-ending S.O.S. call was sent out again, and for another hour the batteries fired on the lines indicated, breaking up the attempted counter-attack and assisting our troops to advance slightly upon the Blue Line— the final objective of the previous day's battle—towards which they had been working gradually the whole day long. When this barrage was finished night firing began and was continued throughout the night, two calls for support from the infantry being responded to at 1.15 A.M. and 5.10 A.M. respectively, and at twenty minutes past five on the morning of the 28th such gunners as still survived pulled themselves together to fire a Corps practice barrage.

This practice barrage had a threefold object. In addition to further shattering the enemy's defences and upsetting his morale, it was so timed as to coincide with any enemy counter-attack which might have been fixed for dawn, and which would therefore be dispersed by the fire of our guns before it could come to a head. Moreover, it also helped our front line troops under cover of its fire further to improve their position, and so well did it succeed in this respect that, at 8.0 A.M., the infantry reported that they had consolidated their front only one hundred yards short of the Blue Line. This operation, apart from an Army barrage at 5.15 A.M. on the 29th which coincided with and broke up a pending enemy counter-attack, proved the last combined operation between infantry and gunners to take place in the month of September; with the two brigades now engaged in the usual harassing fire which was the order of the day on this front, we must turn our attention to the life of the batteries and, leaving their tactical operations alone for a few moments, see how they had fared during the previous four days' battle.

The losses amongst the detachments had been cruel. In all

the fighting a very heavy portion of the enemy's fire had been directed in counter-battery work upon the gun positions, and the batteries, being almost continually engaged with S.O.S. calls and unable to take any form of cover, had been shot down time and again. Moreover, the work had been desperate ; with weakened detachments an incessant fire had had to be kept up almost without a break, and such intervals as offered themselves were necessarily utilised in rebuilding damaged gun platforms and in restocking with ammunition. The men were in an advanced stage of fatigue, and as yet no signs were forthcoming of any possibility of a rest. On September 27th B/162 (Major Cory) was relieved by B/102 and marched down to St. Hubertshoek, near Hallebast Corner, whither the 162nd Brigade wagon-lines had moved on September 25th, and here this one battery remained in rest until October 7th, but for the remainder there was no relief. With men from the D.A.C. and from the Trench Mortar batteries the guns were kept in action, but this course involved the use of many unskilled numbers, and few detachments had more than one man who could safely be trusted to lay the piece in a barrage.

On September 28th two moves took place which brought home to the batteries the fact that, for the present at any rate, they were not to be relieved. On that day General Stewart and his Staff, on the relief of the 33rd Division infantry by the 23rd Division, handed over control of the artillery to the incoming C.R.A. and moved out to rest at Boeschepe, where the headquarter staff remained until the batteries themselves at a later date were ultimately relieved. Simultaneously, Lieut.-Colonel E. J. Skinner, commanding the 162nd Brigade, came up and took over the control of the Left Group from Lieut.-Colonel Groves (103rd Brigade) and set up his headquarters first at Dormy House but later, on October 1st, at Bedford House, one thousand yards south of Shrapnel Corner. The zone covered by the two brigades was very slightly altered and now ran from Gheluvelt on the Ypres–Menin road to a point about 1,700 yards northwards, but the battery positions remained the same, and October came in to find them preparing for offensive operations again.

On October 1st an Army practice barrage had been fixed to begin at 5.15 A.M., and, just as the gunners were assembling to fire the opening rounds, a furious shell-storm was opened by the enemy upon our own front line and the whole area up to one thousand yards in rear of it. It was manifest, from hostile aeroplane activity and the weight of artillery fire which was being brought to bear, that a big counter-attack was impending, and the Army barrage accordingly came down at a very opportune moment. At 5.50 A.M., while it was at its height, the enemy were seen advancing in a series of waves upon our front line, and with that action there began a day of the most intense fighting. All communications with the front line were cut, not even pigeons succeeded in finding a way through the dense hostile barrage, and until the evening every battery was kept in almost continuous action answering the numerous S.O.S. rockets which appeared, and replying to the enemy bombardment which, even without the evidence of rockets, called by its weight for active reply. Not until midnight did the situation ease, and then it was found that the infantry had maintained their whole front except for the left which had been bent back very slightly. To the extraordinary heroism of the infantry the G.O.C. 23rd Division ascribed the defeat of the hostile attack—and with this the gunners very heartily agreed—but he added in his report that the field batteries had maintained such splendid protective fire that the enemy had, on frequent occasions, been broken up before they could get to grips with the garrison of our front line.

Although the Army barrage on October 1st had coincided with and had helped to defeat an enemy counter-attack, its primary object was to prepare for a renewed offensive on our part, and this offensive now took definite shape. After firing another practice barrage on October 2nd and maintaining throughout the 2nd and 3rd a destructive fire upon the enemy system—the while long strings of pack horses refilled the ever-diminishing dumps of ammunition around the guns—the batteries in the early morning of October 4th set range-drum and dial sight to the opening elevation of yet another barrage, this time no practice but as a definite and vital protection to infantry moving forward to the assault. Despite the rain and the ever deepening mud the offensive was ordered to be continued.

At 6.0 A.M. on Thursday, October 4th, on the zone covered by the 33rd Divisional Artillery the infantry of the 5th Division advanced to the attack, supported by one hundred and eight 18-pdrs., thirty-six 4·5 in. howitzers, sixteen 6 in. howitzers and an assortment of heavier howitzers and 60-pdrs. Their right lay upon the northern edge of Gheluvelt Wood and their left upon Juniper Cottages, and, with the barrage moving ahead of them at the rate of one hundred yards in six minutes, they essayed the capture of the high ground south-west of Reutel together with the eastern slopes of the Polderhoek spur. The actual line of their one and final objective ran from a point 500 yards south of Reutel, past the south-west corner of Juniper Wood and east of Polderhoek Château to the northern edge of Gheluvelt Wood, the holding of which line would cover the communications of the 21st Division across Polygon Beek on the left in their attempt to capture Reutel; the objective of the 5th Division, in fact, was the southward continuation of the first objective of the 21st Division, and formed the right flank of an attack which, further north, was intended to penetrate deeply into the enemy lines. On the right of the troops covered by the 33rd Divisional Artillery the infantry of the 37th Division were to advance their left slightly to conform with the line of attack.

Throughout the night of the 3rd/4th the enemy had carried out an intense bombardment of our front line system and had, from time to time, swept the battery positions with shell-storms from 5·9 in. and 4·2 in. howitzers. To this hostile bombardment the batteries had, at the request of the infantry, energetically replied at intervals during the night, but the opening rounds of the barrage at six o'clock in the morning smashed their way into the beginnings of an enemy counter-attack which was concentrating on the front of our own attack. Fortunately the barrage dropped before the enemy concentration was complete, and the fire of our guns at zero broke up the enemy attempt before it could come to a head. Notwithstanding this, however, very considerable opposition was met with, and only on those parts of the front where the infantry managed to keep right close under the barrage fire of the batteries was complete success achieved.

The barrage, as already stated, had been arranged to move forward at the rate of sixteen yards per minute until it should reach a line two hundred yards beyond the objective. Here it was to halt, fire a round of smoke shell from every alternate gun as a warning that the protective line had been reached, and be maintained at a slow rate to cover the infantry while they were digging in. In addition, moreover, to this standing barrage, it was arranged that every now and then the batteries should search by short lifts for one thousand yards beyond the line of the protective barrage ; while at 8.10 A.M., by which time the objective of the 5th Division should have been fully secured, the barrage was to move on towards Gheluvelt in conformation with the fire covering the 21st Division further north in their advance on the second objective, thereby suggesting a resumption of the advance on the 5th Division front. In point of fact, however, no further advance beyond the first objective on the front covered by the 33rd Divisional Artillery was intended ; the batteries, when they reached the extreme limit of their range, were to drop back to the protective barrage line again, their work of drawing attention away from the 21st Divisional front being finished.

As events turned out, the operations of the 5th Division were not entirely successful. The 13th Infantry Brigade, under the guns of Lieut.-Colonel Butler's Group (the right group), reached the final objective with the right battalion in the afternoon, after being held up for a time by a strong point north of Lewis House.   The left battalion of the same brigade, however, encountered strong opposition at Polderhoek Château and was unable to keep up with the barrage. Survivors of the assaulting troops actually reached Polderhoek Château and even penetrated beyond it, but after severe hand to hand fighting a line was taken up two hundred yards west of the Château.   The left infantry brigade (95th), covered by the guns of Lieut.-Colonel Skinner's Group, was also unable in places to keep up with the barrage.   The right battalion found that the ground between the Reutelbeek and the company on the southern edge of Cameron Covert was so sodden as to be absolutely impassable ;   a detour to the right and left was accordingly made, and a line consolidated in the 13th Brigade area and between Cameron Covert and the stream.   The left battalion of this brigade at the same time did actually reach its final objective, but so heavy was the hostile fire coming from the high ground around Poezelhoek that the position became untenable, and a line was taken up in the area of the 21st Division on the left, running from Reutel westward and facing south, while the 21st Division formed a defensive flank by continuing this line to Cameron Covert.

By three o'clock in the afternoon the right brigade disentangled the muddle and formed a general line running from the northern edge of Gheluvelt Wood north-north-east to the Scherriabeek and then on to a point fifty yards short of Polderhoek Château ;   here there was a gap of some 150 yards, and the line then continued due north for another hundred yards, to be carried on northwards through Polderhoek Wood to Cameron Covert by the left brigade. It was well that even this rough line was organised, for throughout the afternoon infantry and gunners alike were hotly engaged by the enemy in numerous counter-attacks.   In all, five attacks were launched by the enemy on the right brigade front during the afternoon, and three more in the evening, and in each case every gun which could be brought to bear was switched round to help the exhausted infantry. After the most severe fighting, and after continuous firing by the batteries throughout the remainder of the day, the infantry were able to report that all gains were held ;   rifle and artillery fire had smashed every enemy attempt to advance, and our new line was securely held.   During the night of October 4th/5th the left battalion of the left brigade, under cover of the guns, withdrew from the 21st Divisional area and took up a line through the middle of Cameron Covert, and so on the morning of the 5th the line stood solid.   On this part of the front the objective had not been captured except upon the extreme right, and the casualties had been tremendous. Further to the left, however, success had been met with, and Reutel Village, Abraham Heights and Gravenstafel were now in our hands.

It may be complained that this chapter has dealt too fully with the infantry operations, and has not sufficiently recorded the daily life of the batteries and their experiences during the attacks. The answer to this complaint is, briefly, that the batteries had no daily life but rather a daily death, while their experiences—day in, day out—were invariably the same.   Morning, noon and night the men were splashing about in mud, trying to keep their ammunition clean and their guns serviceable ; daily they were shelled, sometimes with long deliberate bombardments, sometimes in hurricane shell-storms which descended upon them for forty minutes or so two or three times a day.   They were always wet, always cold ; they continually saw the guns and ammunition, which they had spent hours in cleaning and preparing, blown to bits in the passing of a second ; they helped to bring up more guns, more ammunition, and saw, in the serving of these new guns, their mates blown to pieces, shattered, torn.   They grew to believe that relief would never come, that for all time they must exist in the grim shadows of Maple Copse, of Fosse Wood and of Armagh Wood.   They felt, as they saw the shells crashing down all around them, that they were forgotten by God and man.   There *is* no daily history of the batteries to record save the success or failure of the operations in which they took part, and for the supporting of which they paid this heavy price.   There lies the true history of the batteries, and that it is which in these pages must be recorded.

From October 5th there ensued a pause during which the batteries strained every nerve to get up more ammunition from the dumps, to clear up their shell-wrecked positions and to sort out the gun line personnel into some sort of workable detachments.   B/162 came up into action again from the wagon-lines on the 7th and took over its old position from B/242, and for a few days such registration and reconstruction of positions was carried out as was possible, having regard for the heavy enemy fire which continually swept the entire area in which the batteries were located.   Only for a short time was there a lull, however, for a fresh attack had been ordered to be carried out on October 9th.

On Tuesday, the 9th, the 5th Division attempted to complete the capture of the Polderhoek ridge and, by extending its left to Polygon Beek, to form connection with the 17th Division.   For this purpose the weight of artillery, the pace of the creeping barrage and the formation of the standing barrage were to be identical with those of the 4th, but the objective in this case was to include the whole of Polderhoek Château and Wood together with Cameron Covert, and was to bend back to the then front line at Joist Farm on the north. The 15th Infantry Brigade was responsible for the attack on the right, while on the left the 95th Infantry Brigade was ordered to pivot on a stationary left flank and, clearing all the ground east of Cameron Covert to as far south as the Reutelbeek and as far eastwards as the line of the objective, was to form the connection between the left of the 15th Brigade and the right of the 17th Division.

Zero hour was shortly after 6.0 A.M., and three minutes after the beginning of the barrage the infantry advanced to the assault. The ground, already a sea of mud, was churned up yet more by the intensity of the barrage, and the troops forming the extreme right of the 5th Division, by their efforts to avoid portions of ground which were utterly impassable, lost direction and moved towards the south-east. The mistake was presently discovered, but too late to catch up the barrage, and a line was taken up a little in advance of the previous front line immediately north of the Scherriabeek. Simultaneously the left and centre companies of the right battalion advanced on their proper course, but came under intense fire from Gheluvelt and Polderhoek Château, and only one platoon—themselves all wounded—reached the Château; ultimately, owing to heavy casualties, they withdrew to their original front line. Loss of direction was responsible also for the failure of the left battalion of this brigade to reach its objective. Moving too much towards the right it came under heavy fire from some houses north of the Château and, suffering many casualties, was held up. By ten o'clock in the morning, despite the fiercest efforts by the batteries to beat down the opposition, the whole brigade was back in its old line. The left brigade, having no forward movement on the right to which to conform, did not advance at all.

The state of the ground was now becoming appalling, and, with two successive attacks rendered failures by the mud, a lull set in on this part of the front—a lull during which each of the batteries in turn managed to seize a few days' rest at the wagon-lines. The news that these short rests were to be granted was received with mixed feelings; clearly, if it was thought necessary to send each battery in turn for a short spell at the wagon-lines, the brigades were not destined to move right out of the line yet awhile, but on the other hand this new plan did assure a short interruption of the nerve-racking conditions of the gun line, and for this reason at any rate it was welcome. On October 13th Lieut.-Colonel Butler and Lieut.-Colonel Skinner handed over the control of their groups to the commanding officers of the 27th and 103rd Brigades respectively and, accompanied by the personnel of one battery from each brigade (A/156 and D/162), moved out to the wagon-lines. On the 17th these two batteries moved back into action again after a four-day rest, and on the 18th three more batteries moved out. Each battery in turn had four days at the wagon-lines of comparative rest and quiet, and then moved up into action again, and by the 24th all the batteries except C/162 were back in the line once more, slightly refreshed, slightly reorganised, but still suffering greatly from an almost complete lack of trained men. C/162 (Major Hill) had been left at the wagon-lines owing to the fact that the severe casualties sustained by the battery just prior to moving out had rendered it unfit to go back into action again.

On October 24th 162nd Brigade Headquarters moved back into the line also, and took over command of " C " Group at Bedford House under the 7th Divisional Artillery. This group consisted of " A " and D/162, " B " and C/156, and also of the 46th, 47th and 112th Australian batteries. The front covered by the group and held by the infantry of the 7th Division was, at the same time, changed from north of Gheluvelt to just south of it, as the batteries could reach this new zone at a slightly shorter range; with the new front allotted and registered, orders were received for this group and also for the 156th Brigade to cover an attack by the 7th Division to be launched on the 21st. It seemed madness for any such attack to be contemplated, for the weather had been wet and stormy since October 9th and the ground was even more impassable, even more treacherous than it had been earlier in the month. The only hope of salvation for the infantry lay in the putting down by the batteries of such a curtain of fire as would completely cover the assaulting troops while they waded through the mud, and this the batteries now prepared to do. D/162 (Major Lee), its position at Maple Copse being almost completely untenable owing to the searching fire which the enemy continually directed upon it, moved eight hundred yards northwards on the 24th to a position just west of Zouave Wood. D/156 (Major Barstow) moved forward to the middle of what had been Sanctuary Wood, dropping the trails just off the road under the shelter of the slopes in the western half of the wood, and at dawn on Friday, the 26th, all batteries manned their guns to support this, as it seemed to them, desperate venture.

The actual front of the attack by the 7th Division, which the guns of the 33rd Divisional Artillery were to cover, included Gheluvelt and the ground for six hundred yards north and south of it, and the assault was supported by one hundred and forty-four 18-pdrs., forty-eight 4·5 in. howitzers, thirty-two six-inch and twenty heavier howitzers. Two objectives were fixed, the first including the whole of Gheluvelt except the extreme eastern outskirts and running down south-west to Berry Cottages, while the final objective reached from the lake north-west of Gheluvelt down to Reigate farm, running one hundred yards east of Gheluvelt Village, the object of the operation being to capture Gheluvelt and some ground along the Zandvoorde Spur, and so to secure the hold on Tower Hamlets. " C " Group covered the 20th Infantry Brigade on the left, while " A " and D/156 with B/162 were acting under the orders of Lieut.-Colonel Marriott, commanding " B " Group, and covered the 91st Infantry Brigade on the right.

At 5.40 A.M. the barrage began, the nearest fringe of it dropping one hundred and fifty yards in front of the infantry as they formed up for the attack. There it remained for six minutes, and then started gradually to creep forward at the rate of twelve yards per minute ; after traversing two hundred yards at this pace the speed of advance was slackened down to ten yards per minute for another two hundred yards, and then, at a uniform pace of seven yards per minute, it moved on to the protective line beyond the first objective. Here it remained from 7.4 A.M. until 7.50 A.M. to give the infantry time to reorganise and prepare for the next attack ; at 7.50 A.M. it moved forward again, after four minutes' intense fire to warn the assaulting troops that the time to advance had come, and so forward at the same slow rate to the protective line beyond the final objective ; this it reached at 8.46 A.M. and there remained as a protective barrage to allow the infantry to consolidate the ground won.

Thus moved the barrage, but what of the infantry who should have been close behind it ? Already attention has been called to the bog-like nature of the ground across which they were to attack, and, even had it not, the extraordinarily slow rate of the barrage—twelve yards per minute—should be sufficient evidence of the opinion formed by the Higher Command of the sort of conditions with which the infantry would have to contend. As events turned out it was this very mud which denied success to our troops. Enemy artillery fire on the forward system had been light up till zero, and not for seven minutes after our barrage dropped did the enemy put down any sort of reply with his guns. The cause of the infantry's undoing was the machine-guns which played upon them and swept them while they struggled helplessly in the mud—machine-guns safely ensconced in concrete pill-boxes while our men were in the mud up to their waists. By twenty minutes to eight the 91st Brigade was held up at Lewis House and forced back to its original line ; at half-past eight elements of the 20th Brigade had reached Gheluvelt, but were stopped by the enemy pill-boxes and ultimately had to come back.   Throughout the morning the gunners maintained a protective barrage beyond the infantry to try and assist them in their now almost hopeless task, but at 2.35 P.M. the barrage was called off and the battle ceased.

All along the line of the 7th Division, and further to the right, the assaulting troops had been beaten back to their original positions and in some cases even west thereof.   Machine-gun fire from Lewis House and Berry Cottages had stopped the 91st Infantry Brigade, while the men of the 20th Brigade had been beaten by the mud itself.   They had fought their way right through to Gheluvelt but, on reaching it, had been unable to ward off counter-attacks as they were up to their waists in mud and every rifle was clogged and smothered with the same substance.   A message sent that afternoon to headquarters urged that the advanced battalions should instantly be relieved " owing to heavy officer casualties, disorganisation and the condition of the rifles," and that sentence in itself very aptly summed up the conditions.   Disorganisation there had been, and very considerable at that, but such was the condition of the ground that nothing else could have been expected.   Thus the day ended in failure on this particular portion of the front ; under normal circumstances, and with anything like firm ground over which to attack, success might well have been achieved, but the weather conditions stepped in and tilted the balance in favour of the enemy with overwhelming effect.

This was the last infantry operation in which the 33rd Divisional Artillery took part.   On October 28th " A " and C/156 moved out to the wagon-lines ; three days later they were followed by D/156, which had been very heavily gas shelled on the night of the 29th/30th.   B/156 was relieved on November 2nd, and next day the whole of the 162nd Brigade withdrew from the line and marched back to Dickebusch, this time with the promise before them of a real period of rest in the back areas.

The losses of the batteries in this autumn fighting had been appalling.   For fifty-one days they had been in continuous action under the worst of conditions, covering attack after attack and undergoing interminable shell fire from enemy guns of every calibre. The smallest possible personnel was kept at each position, and seldom did the total strength at the gun line of any one battery exceed thirty-six officers and men.   Yet the battle casualties of the 162nd Brigade numbered three hundred and fifteen for this period, while those of the 156th Brigade were almost as great.   A/156, a six-gun battery, had twenty-six guns disabled during the time it was in the line, while D/162, which had suffered the loss of one hundred and six casualties including six officers, had had nineteen guns put out of action by the enemy. The batteries had, in fact, been practically wiped out, and it was a mere remnant of their former selves which reached the wagon-lines. They had marched up to the Salient a fine fighting weapon, the outcome of many months' training and experience, hardened and versed in all the methods of war. They came away from that murderous spot smashed, depleted, worn out, their work accomplished but at a tremendous cost. Ypres was no longer to them a legendary spot, but a plain, ghastly reality, a grim and deadly place where the batteries learnt, as they had never learnt before, the full horror of war. In trench fighting it is the infantry who look more closely into the depths of Hell than do any other branches of the Service; but at Ypres the field guns share this deadly privilege, and the price of it is high, higher than can be bought with anything save human life itself. The 33rd Divisional Artillery had shared that privilege, had paid that price, and the account thereof may be seen to-day in the cemeteries which cluster round Reninghelst, Dickebusch and La Clytte, in the nameless graves lying amid the shell holes of Maple Copse, Sanctuary Wood and Armagh Wood.

CHAPTER IX.

AFTER the tremendous fighting of the autumn offensive at Ypres and the smashing casualties which were suffered therein by the batteries, a full month in the rest area was required to bring the 33rd Divisional Artillery back to anything like its normal pitch of efficiency once more. Every detachment in every battery had to be reorganised and built up on the foundation of the few remaining gunners who had survived the two months' battle; raw recruits from England needed instruction and drilling, gaps in the non-commissioned ranks awaited filling, newly-joined officers were watched and tested. From highest to lowest the personnel of the two brigades were busily engaged in the tremendous work of smartening up and training, of teaching and of learning, of overhauling equipment and of filling up stores, of removing all traces of the scorching fires through which the batteries had recently passed. By November 3rd both brigades had completed the withdrawal to the wagon-lines at Dickebusch; on the 4th the 156th Brigade marched to the training area around La Nieppe, to be followed the next day by the 162nd Brigade which moved into billets in Bavinchove, Zuytpanne and Trois Rois, all in the neighbourhood of Cassel. Here for a week they remained, at first resting and refitting, then beginning the more elementary forms of training and gradually bringing the batteries back to something approaching a state of efficiency once more.

On November 12th a move was made to the Bouvelinghem area, still further from the line. The 156th Brigade found billets in Bas Loquin and Warlez, the 162nd in Alquines, Le Buisson and Haute Planque. Billets were none too good and horse lines had to be set up in the open, but the surrounding country was more suitable for the advanced training which now became possible, and in real earnest did the instruction and drilling of the batteries set in. Gun drill and driving drill became a daily affair, while battery staff work and manœuvring in the open were added to the curriculum. Training of every description, combined with sports, races and concerts, kept the men busy and contented, with the result that efficiency and smartness appeared once more and the havoc of the autumn became almost completely effaced. As the month wore on and time for a return into action drew near the condition of the batteries grew daily better, and by the end of November it could fairly be said that both brigades had very nearly reached their old high standard once more.

It had been generally understood that a bare four weeks of rest could be hoped for, and that the end of the month would see a return into action. On November 22nd Brigadier-General Stewart and his staff had moved up to the Menin Gate at Ypres to take over command of the artillery covering the infantry of the 33rd Division, then holding the line at Passchendaele, and daily the order was expected for the batteries to follow. Semi-officially it had been stated that the brigades would be in action by December 3rd, but night set in on November 30th without any warning order having been received, and the line was distant a full three days' march. It was difficult to believe that, with so much time to spare for the issuing of warning orders, any sudden move could be contemplated, yet that was actually what took place. At five o'clock on the evening of Saturday, December 1st, orders were received for the batteries to march at 8.0 A.M. on the following morning and, moreover, to be in action by the evening of December 3rd.

Such haste, such rushing and such short notice seemed strange, in view of the fact that for over a week the batteries might have had the preliminary notice ; yet fourteen hours, and fourteen hours of darkness at that, was all the warning that was received, and far into the night the detachments laboured by the light of lanterns, packing the vehicles and getting ready to move at daybreak. To reach the line in two days meant a very considerable march table for each day, and Zermezeele had accordingly been fixed as the billeting area of the batteries for the night of December 2nd/3rd. Late in that evening and in darkness the brigades, after a long day of trekking, laboured in to the lines allotted to them and hastily settled for the night, as an early start was ordered to be made on the following day.

At daybreak on December 3rd the march was resumed, and now further rush tactics were adopted. The personnel of one section per battery was conveyed to Ypres by motor lorry while the remainder of the batteries continued the march by road, for it was intended to take over a portion of the battery positions that very night in the line, so that on the following morning the 33rd Divisional Artillery would be able to assume responsibility for the artillery support of the zone without further delay. By midday

ORDER OF BATTLE.

DECEMBER 1917—MARCH 1918.

H.Q.R.A.

C.R.A.	**Brigade Major.**	**Staff Captain.**
Brig.-Gen. C. G. Stewart, C.M.G., D.S.O.	Major T. E. Durie, D.S.O., M.C.	Capt. W. E. Bownass, M.C.

156th Brigade.
Lieut.-Colonel B. A. B. Butler, D.S.O.
Adjutant : Capt. H. W. Smail, M.C.

" A " Battery.	**" B " Battery.**	**" C " Battery.**	**" D " Battery.**
Major F. B. Carrell.	Major M. A. Studd, M.C. Capt. S. G. Taylor.	Major Barker, D.S.O., M.C.	Major D. Jones, M.C.

162nd Brigade.
Lieut.-Colonel E. J. Skinner, D.S.O.
Adjutant : Capt. R. H. Pavitt.

" A " Battery.	**" B " Battery.**	**" C " Battery.**	**" D " Battery.**
Major W. G. Pringle, M.C. Major G. Fetherston, M.C.	Major H. C. Cory, M.C.	Major M. M. I. Body, M.C.	Major F. L. Lee, M.C.

these advance parties had " debussed " at Potijze Château, where
guides were waiting for them, and by three o'clock in the afternoon
control of one section per battery had been taken over, while every
battery commander was busying himself in learning from his
" opposite number " the zone to be covered and the general character-
istics of the battery position itself.   Thus the programme had been
adhered to, and by the evening of the 3rd a portion of the relief was
carried out ; just forty-eight hours after the receipt of the warning
order, and thirty-six hours since the beginning of the march from
a training area so far distant as to be within ten miles of Boulogne,
two guns per battery of both brigades were in action once more.

While all this had been going on at the gun line, the remainder
of the brigades had marched to the wagon-lines which they were to
occupy during such time as the batteries were in action—the 156th
Brigade taking over an area 1,200 yards south-east of Vlamertinghe,
where permanent huts and stables were being built on either side
of the road, while to the 162nd Brigade had been allotted an open area
half a mile west of Ypres, between Goldfish Château and Belgian
Battery Corner.   These lines were reached late on the evening of the
3rd and were extremely difficult to get into, in the case of the 162nd
Brigade, owing to the fact that the approaches from the road were
rendered quite impassable by mud.   A most uncomfortable night
was spent on the side of the road, and not until daylight came was
there any chance of getting horses and men into their permanent
" billets "—mud lines and tents in the month of December !   Longer
notice, less rushing and a spreading of the march over three days
would have meant much to both horses and men, yet the programme
had been organised and ordered by some Higher Command which
was for ever impressing upon Divisional Artilleries the importance
of the care of horses and the need of avoiding any unnecessary
overwork or strain !

On Tuesday, December 4th, the remaining two sections per battery
marched up to the gun line, led by guides from the advance parties,
and completed the relief of the outgoing units, the 26th and 311th
Army Field Artillery Brigades.   The 156th Brigade together with
D/162 formed No. 1 Group of the artillery covering the divisional
front and was placed under the command of 158th Brigade Head-
quarters, while Lieut.-Colonel Skinner (162nd Brigade) commanded
No. 2 Group which comprised the 18-pdr. batteries of his own brigade.
This was, however, only a temporary arrangement, for on December
17th Lieut.-Colonel Butler (156th Brigade) took over command of
No. 1 Group which was enlarged to contain the whole of the 33rd
Divisional Artillery, while Colonel Skinner and his headquarters

Magnetic

GRID NORTH

Scale 1:20,000.

moved out to the wagon-line, leaving the 186th Brigade to form No. 2 Group.

As matters now stood, the whole of the 33rd Division was concentrated together, the artillery covering for once its own infantry on the Passchendaele Ridge–Crest Farm–Meetcheele Line. The batteries of the 156th Brigade all lay along the Langemarck–Zonnebeke road north-west of Zonnebeke, between Windmill Cabaret and Kansas Cross, and covered the right of the zone, while the 162nd Brigade supported the left zone from positions around Gravenstafel. " A " and B/156, however, moved their guns to the vicinity of Otto Farm on the 12th and 14th respectively.

Infantry action was at a standstill, for the mud and general condition of the ground precluded movement of any sort; in few places, indeed, was there any fire-trench at all, fortified shell-holes linked together in groups and half-full of water offering the only possible cover to the front-line troops. The forward system was almost completely cut off by a vast sea of mud which extended back to and beyond the battery positions and was traversed at intervals by narrow duck-board tracks, the sole means of communication from front to rear. Any smashing of those tracks, any detour from them to avoid shell-fire meant hours of struggling through the slime, while the wretched men who got wounded while crossing the morass were, as likely as not, engulfed in the mud and never seen again.

Infantry operations, it has been said, were at a standstill, but the same could by no means be recorded of the artillery. From dawn till dusk the enemy was for ever pounding away at our lines, raking battery positions from end to end and destroying the wooden roads which offered the only possible route for the supply of ammunition and rations. Gravenstafel, Kansas Cross and the road right back to Wieltje were in a continual state of eruption, while devastating shell-storms daily descended upon the battery area between Gravenstafel and Zonnebeke. It was a grievous time for the gunners; dug-outs were impossible, as water was met only eighteen inches below the surface, and pill-boxes were few and far between. Even the latter, with their doors facing towards the east, were by no means sure refuges, and it was while actually standing inside such an one that Captain Gallie, who had distinguished himself so wonderfully in the autumn fighting, was killed on December 14th. The only way to minimise casualties was to scatter a number of little shelters all around the battery positions and, by keeping the men thus separated, to reduce the damage which one direct hit alone could do. Yet even so the strain of being eternally wet and cold, of being for ever soaked with mud and under continuous shell-fire was tremendous, and, as far as was possible, detachments at the guns were relieved every four days.

There was, indeed, little for the men to do except to keep the gun-pits and ammunition serviceable, and to try to keep themselves alive. Firing was reduced to the minimum of registration, calibration and response to infantry calls, for it needed a full day's work by every man to keep the guns clean, to rebuild the gun-pits after their daily destruction by hostile shell-fire and to keep dry the ammunition which, even when it was not blown up by enemy bombardment, used to sink of its own accord in that bottomless mud which rendered almost any form of foundation useless. Moreover, every round fired necessitated the bringing up of fresh supplies from the wagon-lines, and this was work not lightly to be undertaken. As late as September 1920 the road from Wieltje to Gravenstafel was still but a faint track of ploughed-up earth winding across the shell holes and literally paved with the skeletons of horses and, in some cases, of men; it was one of the main arteries—and there were but few in that wilderness of mud—from the wagon-lines to the batteries, and, to the terrible cost of the drivers and teams, well the enemy knew it.

Thus, from December 4th, the batteries just barely existed; they had had a month's rest in the back area and knew that, for gunners, this would be considered sufficient to keep them going for a long time to come—hopes of relief, therefore, were not even entertained. At intervals the guns were registered on the Gasometers east of Passchendaele; at intervals they bombarded enemy positions around Moorslede, but mostly the detachments contented themselves with preparing for emergencies by keeping the guns as serviceable as was possible. It was a nightmare existence from which all ranks hoped that they might one day awaken, but the awakening was not yet expected.

It seemed, therefore, scarcely credible to the 162nd Brigade when, on December 19th, orders were received to march out next day to the wagon-lines. Foul as were the conditions in the line, a mere seventeen days of continuous action was never regarded by Higher Authority as sufficient to entitle a battery to a rest, and neither officers nor men had in their wildest dreams hoped to spend Christmas out of the line; yet such was now to be the case. On Thursday, December 20th, all batteries of the brigade had reached their wagon-lines in safety, and on December 23rd they marched back to Divisional reserve in a camp on the Poperinghe–Busseboom road, leaving their less fortunate comrades of the 156th Brigade to carry on the war in their absence. Less fortunate the latter certainly were, for they were destined to spend Christmas in action, but on the other hand the positions they were occupying were not so bad as those of the 162nd Brigade, nor had they been subjected to such violent shell-storms.

December 23rd to the 26th were spent by the 162nd Brigade in overhauling kit and equipment, in helping to build permanent standings in the camp they were occupying, and in celebrating the unexpected luxury of a Christmas in rest. On Christmas night a dinner for the officers was given at " Skindles " in Poperinghe, while on Boxing Night the batteries organised dinners for their men. On this day, also, the 156th Brigade was relieved by the 48th Army Field Artillery Brigade and came down to the wagon-lines, with the result that the whole of the 33rd Divisional Artillery was able to see out in peace the old year which held for it such mighty, such proud and such undying memories.

In peace the old year went out, but by no means in idleness. On Boxing Day orders had come for the preparation of ten reserve battery positions to cover the Army defence zone and to be occupied in the event of a German offensive on the Ypres sector, and every day before dawn working parties from each battery set out in motor lorries to Potijze Château, between which spot and Oxford Road the proposed positions lay. From December 26th to January 7th the work was carried out during every hour of daylight, for orders, inspired possibly by the fears of a German Spring offensive, were imperative that the work should be pushed on as hard as possible.

On January 7th the work ceased temporarily and one section per battery of each brigade went into the line again, relieving the 250th and 251st Brigades of the 50th Divisional Artillery. January 8th saw the relief complete, and once more the brigades were back in action, the 162nd occupying the same positions around Gravenstafel, the 156th remaining as before round Windmill Cabaret, Otto Farm (the pill-box where Captain Gallie of A/156 was killed) and Van Issacker's Farm, but with two guns of B/156 (Major Studd) and two 4·5 in. howitzers of D/156 (Major Jones) in forward positions for use as anti-tank guns. The front to be covered remained unchanged, while the " grouping " of the batteries showed but little alteration—Lieut.-Colonel B. A. B. Butler commanding No. 1 Group which consisted of the whole of the 156th Brigade and B/119, while No. 2 group (162nd Brigade) was controlled by Major N. G. Jervis from a pill-box east of Frezenburg. Lieut.-Colonel E. J. Skinner commanded the whole of the 33rd Divisional Artillery group which was made up of the 156th, 162nd and 119th Brigades.

The organisation and allocation of the brigades were therefore but little changed since the previous tour of duty in the line before Christmas, but a great difference showed itself in the attitude of the enemy. Hostile artillery activity had died down in an extraordinary way, and comparative quiet reigned in the battery area after the shell-storms of the earlier period. Roads were only occasionally searched, battery positions were subjected merely to a few sniping rounds or at most to short neutralising bursts of fire, and the long concentrated bombardments which previously had been the order of the day were now exceptional events. "Quiet day," "light shelling of tracks," "intermittent bursts of fire on Zonnebeke Road and Windmill Cabaret" appear frequently in the official diaries of that period, and only on two days—January 13th and 20th—did the hostile artillery show any marked activity. On those two days the Zonnebeke–Windmill Cabaret area and the Crest Farm–Meetcheele line were bombarded respectively, the latter very heavily indeed, but these two outbursts marked isolated exceptions to the quietness which had now set in and were not of long duration.

On January 29th, after a most uneventful period in the line, one section per battery of each brigade was relieved by the 50th Divisional Artillery and marched again to the wagon-lines. Next day the relief was completed and the batteries marched to the Oudezeele area, the gun line parties handing over their guns in action and moving by lorry to the first night's halting place, there to join up with the wagon-line personnel who had marched by road in the ordinary way. The next day saw a continuation of the move to Zudrove and Le Bas, and on February 1st the ultimate rest billets were reached in Thiembronne, Merck St. Lievin and Bout de la Ville. Here the batteries carried out the usual overhauling and training, rejoicing at the quite phenomenal number of "rests" which they had of late been enjoying.

It was, indeed, most unusual for artillery to reach the rest area so often as had the 156th and 162nd Brigades of late. Gunners were usually kept in the line almost continuously, staying on after the infantry of their division had been relieved and covering the incoming troops. A scheme was now in practice by which the whole of the 33rd Division—infantry and gunners alike—held the line together and went into rest together, the 50th Division acting as their "opposite number," and by this scheme the two brigades were benefiting. It could not last for long—it was too good for that; but while it lasted it was wondrously pleasant!

There came an interruption in the ordinary routine of training on February 12th; the 18-pdr. batteries of the 156th Brigade were ordered to march to Tilques, there to have their guns calibrated by the Sound-ranging Section, after which they were attached to the 98th Infantry Brigade for tactical exercises. On the 14th the 18-pdrs. of 162nd Brigade were also calibrated, so that, by the 15th, all guns were ready for the return into action which had been ordered for February 22nd. Before this march took place, however, C/162 (Major Hill) was detached from the Divisional Artillery for special duties. On February 18th it marched to Tilques to join the 2nd Army Artillery School as a training battery, and there it was left when once more the move to the line was made.

On February 19th the 156th Brigade moved to the Elnes area and on the 20th to La Nieppe, the 162nd Brigade reaching Renescure on the same day. On the 21st advance parties from each brigade moved by rail to Vlamertinghe to take over the wagon-lines of the 50th Divisional Artillery, while the batteries continued their march to Zermezeele and Rietveld—D/162, which had gone round by Tilques to calibrate its guns, rejoining the rest of the brigade on this day. February 22nd saw the arrival of the batteries at their wagon-lines east and south-east of Vlamertinghe, the same which they had occupied on the return to action in early January; A/162, however, remained near Goldfish Château, and B/156 went to Ypres Asylum. On the 22nd also lorries took one section per battery direct to the forward area, the 156th Brigade this time relieving No. 2 Group (251st Brigade), the 162nd Brigade No. 1 Group (250th Brigade).

The relief was complete by Saturday, February 23rd, and on the next day 33rd Divisional Artillery Headquarters took over the control, at Menin Gate, of the artillery covering the infantry of the 33rd Division on a two thousand yard front opposite Passchendaele and due west of Moorslede. On this occasion the 162nd Brigade took over the positions previously held by the 156th along the Lange-marck–Zonnebeke road, "A" and D/162 (Major Fetherston and Major Lee) at Windmill Cabaret, some six hundred yards north-west of Zonnebeke, B/162 (Major Cory) about two thousand yards also to the north-west of the village, while Brigade headquarters were situate in a pill-box one thousand yards north-east of Frezenburg. The 156th Brigade positions, with the exception of Major Carrell's battery (A/156) which remained at Otto Farm, were those which had previously been held by the 162nd Brigade at Gravenstafel.

The policy adopted by the batteries on their return into action now was to remain quiet, only registration and calibration being carried out. The enemy on the whole were also inactive until the end of the month; one or two attempts were made to rush our advanced posts, and a large raid was executed—unsuccessfully, however—upon the division on the right. Apart from this, and from a certain amount of activity with high-velocity guns upon our back areas, the enemy attitude was very similar to ours.

March saw a change in the general policy of the Germans holding this part of the line. An ever-increasing volume of artillery fire began to be directed upon our battery positions, while high-velocity guns were continually searching the roads and back areas. On the 2nd nearly all our batteries were heavily shelled, while severe bombardments were carried out upon both flanks of the division ; on the 3rd enemy aeroplanes were very active and continued so for several days, especially on the 7th when low-flying machines appeared everywhere. On the 6th a big shoot was carried out on the Windmill Cabaret area N.W. of Zonnebeke, and on the 9th the batteries of the 33rd Divisional Artillery were bombarded with gas shell. The front was indeed gradually boiling up to a state of high enemy activity, and, with the fine weather which supervened and the knowledge that an enemy offensive was almost inevitably coming on some part of the front, the plan of action to deal with such an emergency was continually tested. On March 10th in the early morning all batteries fired " counter-preparation," a slow barrage which was to be used in the event of an enemy attack being expected. On this and the succeeding days fire was also directed upon special targets, upon machine guns, dug-outs and likely places for the concentration of hostile troops, while all batteries constantly practised the drill of pulling their guns out of the pits at short notice and of engaging targets on the flanks and at short ranges.

On the 14th a heavy German raid was repulsed, a prisoner who had been taken beforehand having given information concerning it, and on the 17th all batteries again fired in response to an S.O.S. call at 4.40 A.M., but in this case no infantry action took place. All this time the enemy long-range guns were for ever bombarding Ypres, Wieltje, St. Jean, Potijze and every road leading up from the back area, as many as one thousand high-velocity shells being poured into the neighbourhood of Ypres each day. At the same time battery positions, and especially the area between " Seine " and Abraham Heights, were continually shelled, gas at night being the usual practice.

Thursday, March 21st, 1918, was a comparatively quiet day in the Ypres sector. The batteries had not been worried much, and for their own part had not done more than to direct bursts of fire upon enemy dug-outs and machine guns which were annoying the infantry. About 1.0 P.M., just as the detachments were sitting down to their midday meal, came the first message, telephoned up from Divisional Headquarters, of the beginning of the great German offensive in the south. Little news was given beyond the fact that the attack had been launched and that our troops, after giving up the advanced system, " were holding the enemy on the main Army Defence Line." Every few hours further messages came in, admitting certain losses of ground but stating that the enemy was being held in the main, and that the day was going in our favour. Such reports were certainly encouraging to the men, and in no way gave any suggestion of defeat ; bit by bit, however, names of villages which had been captured by the enemy began to appear, and reference to a map disclosed the disquieting fact that a deep penetration into our lines had been made, a penetration which must necessarily become deeper still owing to the loss of certain tactical points. Information was very sparse and rumours immediately became rife everywhere, so that a fair idea of the situation could hardly be obtained. It was, indeed, of little use to worry ; the batteries had their own share of the front to look after and knew that, sooner or later, they would be plunged into the battle themselves—" sufficient unto the day . . . . " then, for in France it was not good to worry about troubles before they came.

On March 25th the front covered by the 33rd Divisional Artillery was extended some five hundred yards further to the south, S.O.S. lines being rearranged accordingly, and on March 28th/29th one section each of " B," " C " and D/156 moved out to alternate positions S.E. of Kansas Cross, S.E. of Bostin Farm and east of Kansas Cross respectively. During the preceding weeks the enemy had been constantly shelling the Abraham Heights area with gas and had rendered it quite untenable, B/156 having as many as forty gas casualties in one week ; the change of position described above had therefore become an urgent necessity. Although the enemy artillery activity had died down since the 21st it was still fairly vigorous, especially upon roads, back areas and wagon-lines—the latter suffering considerably.

A further extension of the brigade zones to the south was made on March 29th, and on the same day another section of " B," " C," and D/156 moved back to the alternative positions described above. Next day Major Hill's battery (C/162), which had left Tilques on the 27th and had marched up via Godewaersvelde to wagon-lines at Goldfish Château, sent one section into action at Bostin Farm, one thousand yards west of Zonnebeke Church, to be joined by the rest of the battery on the night of March 31st/April 1st ; by the end of March, therefore, the 33rd Division had its guns well distributed in depth, and could be certain of giving adequate protection to the infantry even should the latter be forced back behind the line of forward guns.

L

Thus the batteries remained for the first week of April. March had made its exit with a heavy enemy bombardment on the evening of the 31st upon the forward, battery and back areas, with a heavy gas concentration upon the Frezenburg line, to all of which the batteries had at infantry request responded. April came in, bringing with it little news save an ever-increasing expectation of attack on the Divisional sector, and so the first week passed while everybody held his breath, as it were, in anticipation.

On Sunday, April 7th, portions of the 156th and 162nd Brigades were relieved by the 28th Army Field Artillery Brigade (Colonel Paynter) and marched out to their wagon-lines near Vlamertinghe. On the 8th the relief was completed and the batteries were all resting in the wagon-lines, hourly expecting orders to move down south to the aid of the hard-pressed 5th Army, for thither they all believed they were to go, nor is it too much to say that considerable despondency was felt in both Brigades at not being engaged in the battle then in progress. Before any such orders were issued, however, an enemy offensive was suddenly launched upon them from much nearer at hand, and, although the 162nd Brigade marched to the Peselhoek-Poperinghe area on April 9th, there was to be neither for them nor for the 156th Brigade any rest. The Germans were about to start their great attack in the north which grew into a drive for the coast, and every man, every gun, every available round of ammunition was needed in the great struggle shortly to begin.

CHAPTER X.

PART I.

THE GERMAN OFFENSIVE IN FLANDERS.
(APRIL—MAY 1918.)

EARLY on the morning of Tuesday, April 9th, there came to the batteries, as they lay resting in their wagon-lines, the sound of tremendous shelling to the south, a continuous thunder which was maintained throughout the whole of that and the succeeding day (April 10th), giving rise to considerable speculation and rumour. Clearly a great weight of artillery was at work and almost certainly an attack was, if not already begun, at least imminent, but what was happening and why did not the batteries move up to take part in the battle ? Of news or orders there were none, and not for many hours did the men learn of the mighty German thrust which even then was in progress, the thrust which, starting between Givenchy and Bois Grenier on the 9th, spread northwards to Messines on the 10th and marked the beginning of the greatest battle yet seen on the Flanders front.

At last, on the afternoon of April 10th, news came to the 156th Brigade that the Germans had attacked and advanced on a long front between Ploegsteert Wood and Givenchy ; that they had taken Armentières and had advanced well in the direction of Bailleul, though Neuve Église was still ours, and that the batteries were to move up into action immediately to stop this onslaught. At 5.0 P.M. the march began, and the brigade set out for its rendezvous, a point about one mile west-north-west of Neuve Église, which it reached in pitch darkness after many weary hours on roads greatly congested by traffic and by refugees who, in the last stage of exhaustion, had scarcely strength to get out of the way of our troops. Here the situation was found to be very obscure ; nobody knew where the infantry were, but warnings were received that parties of Germans were believed to be little more than a mile to the south, and at any moment the guns might be called upon to open fire. Consequently the horses remained fully harnessed up all night and practically alongside the guns, the latter having their trails dropped in a position ready to fire, Lewis guns and guards were posted in every battery position, and so the brigade stood awaiting information which would clear up a little the prevailing chaos.

ɩ At three o'clock on the morning of Thursday, the 11th, the expected orders arrived, and at half-past four began the march to Vierstraat, where positions had been allotted to the brigade. By ten o'clock Lieut.-Colonel Butler had completed his reconnaissance of Vierstraat cross-roads, by half-past ten the four battery commanders were engaged upon the same work, and midday saw the batteries in action bombarding the enemy who had by then reached a line running just east of Wytschaete and curving away thence towards the north-east. The battery positions lay around Vierstraat and between that village and Kemmel, and from observation stations north-east of Wytschaete the S.O.S. lines of the guns were quickly registered.

Meanwhile the 162nd Brigade, farther back in the Poperinghe rest area, had also received urgent orders to move into action. On the morning of April 10th the batteries had paraded for a drill order of the whole brigade and had moved off to some open country near by to begin the exercise. While this was actually in progress a dispatch rider arrived and brought the parade to an abrupt conclusion, for he carried with him orders for the brigade to join the 19th Division at Dranoutre immediately and to move into action without a moment's delay. Leaving Captain Pavitt (the Adjutant) to collect the batteries and lead them to the rendezvous, Lieut.-Colonel Skinner (O.C. 162nd Brigade) set off by motor with his orderly officer to report for orders to the C.R.A. 19th Division near Neuve Église. Owing to various difficulties on the way these orders were not received until 2.0 P.M., but their effect was that Colonel Skinner should bring his batteries into action immediately near Spanbroekmolen. As no horses were available, the reconnaissance of these positions had to be carried out on foot and took a long time, but when the positions were finally chosen the orderly officer (Lieut. Bartholomew) was sent back to Dranoutre to await the arrival of the batteries and to guide them to their positions.

Meantime Colonel Skinner set out to find the infantry Brigadier in that part of the line, so that he might inform him of his plans. This was a long and tedious business in an unknown place in a now dark and rainy night, and, on finding the Brigadier, Colonel Skinner to his disgust, if not surprise, was told that the positions he had chosen had, since he had left them, practically fallen into the hands of the enemy. There was only one thing to do, and that quickly. Setting out as fast as possible, he covered the four miles to Dranoutre in pitch darkness and, arriving there at the same time as the batteries,

ORDER OF BATTLE.

April—August 1918.

H.Q.R.A.

C.R.A.	Brigade Major.	Staff Captain.
Brig.-Gen. C. G. Stewart, C.M.G., D.S.O.	Major T. E. Durie, D.S.O., M.C.	Capt. W. E. Bownass, M.C.
Brig.-Gen. G. H. W. Nicholson, C.M.G.	Major W. A. T. Barstow, D.S.O., M.C.	

156th Brigade.

Lieut.-Colonel B. A. B. Butler, D.S.O.
Adjutant: Capt. H. W. Smail, M.C.

"A" Battery.	"B" Battery.	"C" Battery.	"D" Battery.
Major F. B. Carrell.	Major M. A. Studd, D.S.O., M.C. Capt. S. G. Taylor, M.C. Major W. G. Sheeres, M.C.	Major Barker, D.S.O., M.C.	Major D. Jones, M.C.

162nd Brigade.

Lieut.-Colonel E. J. Skinner, D.S.O. (*wounded*).
Lieut.-Colonel Ramsden.
Lieut.-Colonel W. R. Warren, D.S.O.
Adjutant: Capt. R. H. Pavitt, M.C.

"A" Battery.	"B" Battery.	"C" Battery.	"D" Battery.
Major G. Fetherston, D.S.O., M.C.	Major H. C. Cory, M.C.	Major M. M. I. Body, M.C.	Major F. L. Lee, M.C. Major R. D. Russell, M.C.

he stopped them and held a consultation with the C.R.A. of the 19th Division, who had just been shelled out of his headquarters. After a short discussion regarding the general situation which, as can be judged by the foregoing narrative, was very obscure, the batteries marched at once into action between Rossignol Wood and Parrot Camp (North of Kemmel Village), and by 3.0 A.M. on Thursday, April 11th, were in action, Brigade Headquarters being at Parrot Camp. Thus they found themselves after a seventeen-mile march along roads congested with troops, transport, refugees and cattle, a march which had been preceded by over an hour's work on drill order the previous morning ; unfavourable conditions, those, to usher in one of the greatest battles yet fought.

From April 11th onwards the batteries were under the administration of the 19th Division. Brig.-Gen. Stewart and his staff had, on April 9th, handed over control of the artillery in the Passchendaele sector to Colonel Paterson (119th Brigade R.F.A.), but had marched straight to Dranoutre, and on the 11th remained with headquarters of the 33rd Division. On that fateful day General Stewart commanded a composite infantry brigade until the early morning of the 12th, when he took over command of the artillery covering the infantry of the 33rd Division on the Meteren front, south of the 156th and 162nd Brigades. The latter were therefore left with the C.R.A. 19th Division.

During this period from the 11th onwards both brigades underwent the severest trials. Great demands were made upon them ; the batteries were required to shoot on a big area whenever an enemy attack showed signs of developing, yet never did the guns fail to carry out their work. Attempts were daily made to man O.P.'s on Kemmel Hill, but although the gallantry of observing officers and signallers always enabled communication to be established, the heavy and continuous fire which the enemy brought to bear upon the hill rendered it impossible for that communication to be maintained. In the case of the 156th Brigade observation was usually carried out from a point north-east of Wytschaete, while the batteries of the 162nd Brigade were able to obtain a very good view of the enemy from the ridge just in front of the guns.

From the moment that the batteries dropped into action they were shelled almost continuously, but no infantry actions developed. This was in a large part due probably to the efforts of the batteries, by which every sign of concentration was smashed at the outset. Especially was this the case on the 12th, when small bodies of the enemy were continually advancing in the open, but were as continually broken up by the fire of the guns. Every suspicion of move-

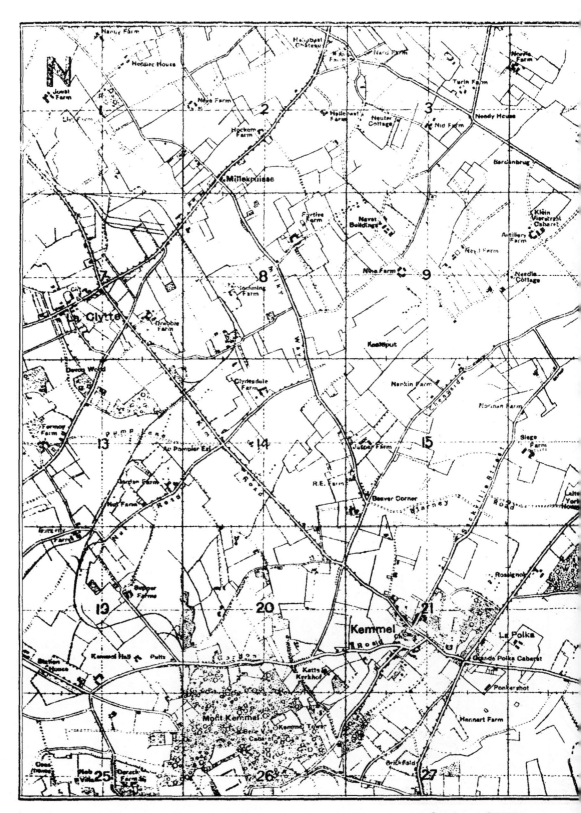

Scale, 1:20,000.

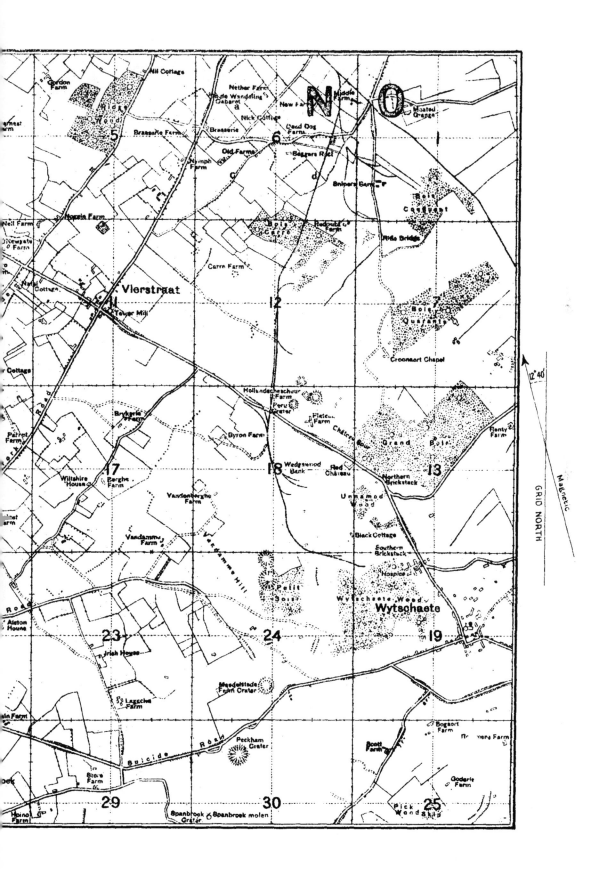

ment was shelled and, whether movement was visible or not, harassing fire was maintained night and day. On the 15th information was received that our line was to be withdrawn to Vierstraat–Lindenhoek, but in the evening this retirement was cancelled, and the fatal morning of April 16th dawned to find the batteries still occupying the same positions.

A dense fog hung over the ground on Wednesday, 16th April, blotting out all vision and deadening sound. There was no suggestion of an enemy attack on the front covered by the batteries, no preliminary bombardment—other than the continuous shelling which had characterised every day since the offensive began—no S.O.S. signals, yet early in the morning of that day the enemy made a heavy attack from the south and, advancing his line in a north-westerly direction, captured Wytschaete Ridge, Wytschaete Village and Wood, together with the Hospice and Peckham. Apparently the Germans, making use of the thick fog, advanced without an artillery barrage, and the same fog hid the infantry S.O.S. signals. The first intimation of an attack was obtained by the Forward Observing officer of the 156th Brigade, who from his O.P. three hundred yards north-east of Wytschaete suddenly saw Germans twenty-five yards away. He opened rifle fire upon these at point-blank range, but needless to say was unable to stop them. He then tried to get away in order to warn the neighbouring batteries, but was shot in the stomach and later died of his wounds. The batteries, however, were by now fully roused and were pouring gun fire into the advancing troops to try and check their onslaught. Those of the 156th Brigade were just able to remain in their positions, and, as soon as dawn broke, set up O.P.'s on the ridge of the Kemmel–Vierstraat road, the original O.P.'s being by then in enemy hands. From this ridge observed fire was directed all day upon Wytschaete Village and Ridge, and great havoc was wrought amongst the Germans as they advanced in the open.

Meanwhile the 162nd Brigade was also enduring a deluge of shell similar to that which was descending upon the 156th but, being further to the right, was in more imminent danger of being captured, since the enemy advance was, as already described, taking the form of a north-westerly sweep from the south. Shorter and shorter grew the ranges of the guns, until at last the necessity of a retirement became imperative ; reluctantly the withdrawal began, one section per battery at a time. In this operation conspicuous gallantry was shown by all ranks, for the gun positions were being torn and swept by a veritable tornado of shell which rendered the approach of the teams well-nigh impossible. As an instance of this, the retirement of a section of A/162 under Lieut. J. R. B. Turner may well be quoted ; such heavy fire was directed upon his guns that the teams could not get near them, and guns and wagons had to be man-handled out of action.   Under a hail of shell each gun in turn was saved, every temporary lull being taken advantage of for a team to dash in, limber up and get clear, and ultimately the section was successfully withdrawn.   Similar deeds were enacted in every battery, and ultimately the whole brigade was withdrawn, the leading sections coming into action in fresh positions and covering the withdrawal of the remainder by their fire.   By this means every gun was saved, while the continuity of the barrage covering our own infantry was never broken—a most gallant performance by the personnel of the batteries, and a fine example of the tactical handling of a brigade of artillery.

After the first rush the enemy advance slowed down and ultimately stopped, there being no further attack on the evening of the 16th nor on the night of the 16th/17th.   Lieut. Bruce and Lieut. McDonald of the 156th Brigade went forward to Byron Farm and got good information regarding the position of the infantry, and during the whole of the night the batteries kept up a slow harassing fire upon all likely places where the enemy might concentrate for a further assault.   162nd Brigade Headquarters, which had been set up in the ruins of a small cottage a short distance in front of the new positions occupied by the batteries, was heavily shelled, although hitherto the spot had been more or less immune ; after losing the wireless operator and several men, together with a great deal of stores destroyed, it moved out and was established at dawn with D/162.

Thursday, April 17th, brought with it a heavy enemy bombardment of all the battery positions.   The 162nd Brigade, as a result of its retirement on the previous day, lay east of the Millekruisse–Hallebast road, between the road and Kemmel-Beek ; Major Cory's battery (B/162) was on the left, nearest Hallebast Corner, with C/162 (Major Body) next on the right.   A/162 (Major Fetherston) lay further to the right still, and then came Major Lee's guns (D/162) on the Millekruisse–Kemmel road.   The 156th Brigade was still hanging on to the original positions held prior to the enemy attack on the previous day, but the flashes of the more forward batteries must have been clearly visible to the enemy on Wytschaete Ridge, and the guns came in for a heavy gruelling.   This did not prevent them, however, from giving the utmost support to a counter-attack launched by our infantry upon Wytschaete at 7.30 P.M., in which the guns of the 162nd Brigade also took a large share.   The counter-attack was unsuccessful, and, with the enemy still on Wytschaete Ridge, the necessity of a withdrawal of a portion of the 156th Brigade to a more covered position became apparent. Next day (April 18th) a reconnaissance was carried out and positions were chosen some one thousand yards further west, behind the road known as Cheapside which ran parallel with and about eleven hundred yards west of the Kemmel–Vierstraat road. On the 19th these positions were occupied by two batteries and the guns were registered from just in front, the whole Brigade except for Major Carrell's battery (A/156) being now clustered around Lieut.-Colonel Butler's headquarters in a line five hundred yards in length. A/156 lay further to the north-east, little more than a quarter of a mile from Ridge Wood.

From April 17th until the 25th the enemy did not make any considerable advance, and, although the batteries were daily shelled, a fair amount of opportunity offered itself for strengthening the gun line. A certain readjusting of positions also took place about this time. D/162 sent forward a section under Lieut. Bennet and Lieut. Garrod to a position two hundred yards south of Siege Farm, near the old position which had been held prior to the loss of the Wytshcaete Ridge, and from which some excellent harassing fire was carried out. On the 22nd Major Studd (B/156), with only four serviceable guns left, moved two of them some three hundred yards further south on the Kemmel–Ridge Wood road, and to this latter position was added on the 23rd a third gun, received that morning from the I.O.M. On April 24th A/156, who had been very heavily shelled on the previous day, moved two guns to a position three hundred yards north of Siege Farm ; the remainder were to have moved thither on the morning of the 25th, but the events of that day, as will presently be shown, put an end to any such ideas. About the 23rd also Major Jones (D/156) put one 4·5 in. howitzer two hundred yards to the north of the A/156 " Siege Farm " section. Thus the batteries were more split up, each brigade having a main line of guns with detached sections thrown out slightly in front, from which latter the majority of the firing was done.

Before the further operations on this front are described a word must here be spoken of the battery wagon-lines. As a rule the wagon-lines were looked upon as comparatively safe—a " cushy " job for those whose lot it was to live there—but the wagon-lines during the German advance were far from restful. True, they did not suffer the dense barrages which the gun line had to face ; but they were constantly shelled by high-velocity guns at long range, a most disconcerting performance which meant that day and night, at odd intervals, a shell would crash into the crowded horse-lines or work havoc amongst the men's bivouacs, and even occasional shells are

terribly upsetting when they burst amongst a mass of horses.   In
addition, enemy aeroplanes came nightly and scattered bombs along
the length and breadth of the lines, while daily the weary drivers
and teams had to make their way up to the batteries with ammunition, usually being shelled all along the road.   The consequent strain
upon horses and men may well be imagined.

Throughout this period the wagon-lines were kept in two portions
—a forward wagon-line, in which were kept the gun teams and such
wagons as were necessary to the batteries in a move of any emergency,
and rear wagon-lines where lived the main body of drivers and teams.
From April 12th until the loss of Kemmel on April 25th the forward
wagon-lines of both brigades were situated between Hallebast Corner
and Vierstraat, the rear wagon-lines of the 156th Brigade being in the
Reninghelst-Ouderdom area, while those of the 162nd Brigade lay
at first at Canada Corner, north of Locre, moving on the 17th to the
area between Reninghelst and Busseboom.   There they were all
kept continually moving, sometimes in Reninghelst, sometimes nearer
Busseboom, every spot they inhabited being shelled by the enemy
and, after a very short period, rendered uninhabitable.   In both rear
and advanced wagon-lines the casualties amongst horses and men
mounted rapidly, but it is safe to say that the " emergency " teams at
Hallebast Corner had far the worst time.

To return to the tactical situation, however.   On April 19th
both brigades had been put under the command of the C.R.A. 9th
Division, but on the 22nd the French 28th Division came up into
the line and the French Artillery Commander took over control of
the 162nd Brigade.   Headquarters of the latter moved over to
Scherpenberg to be near the French commander, but the distance
from there to the batteries was too great for any efficient control to
be carried on, and permission was obtained by Lieut.-Colonel Skinner
to move his headquarters back to Millckruisse so as to be near the
batteries, and also near the commander of a " groupe " of French
artillery which had just come up and lay in action to the east of
and near the village.   Lieut. Norton (C/162), who could speak
French fluently, was left as liaison officer with the " C.R.A." of the
French division.

The disposition of the two brigades on April 24th, therefore,
was as follows.   The batteries of the 156th were grouped together
about 1,800 yards due north of Kemmel, with an advanced section
of 18-pdrs. (A/156) and one advanced 4·5 in. howitzer (D/156)
near Siege Farm and about 600 yards in front of the main line of
guns.   Lieut.-Colonel Butler's headquarters were right amongst his
guns, between " C " and B/156, but the remaining two sections of

A/156 were some 1,200 yards to the north-east and were so far away that, when the battle began on April 25th, it was found impossible to exercise command over them.

The 162nd Brigade also lay together between the Millekruisse-Hallebast road and the Kemmel-Beek, and therefore slightly in rear of the 156th Brigade.   Lieut.-Colonel Skinner's headquarters were in Millekruisse, and in this case one advanced section of 4·5 in. howitzers (D/162) was thrown forward in a position just west of Rossignol Wood.

As far as communications were concerned, a party of scouts was kept on the top of Mount Kemmel in visual signalling with the guns, while O.P.'s were manned at Desinet Farm, at Vierstraat Cross-roads and elsewhere, whence good observation of Wytschaete Valley and Wood and all the country to Spanbroekmolen was obtainable ; these O.P.'s were also in visual communication with the guns, but the fog and smoke during the battle of the 25th rendered all their work impossible.   Each brigade had, in addition, a liaison officer with the infantry battalion in the line, and therefore the system of communication between infantry and artillery, and the observation kept upon the enemy by the guns, was as good as could be hoped for.   Buried cables, however, were scarce, and it needed but a few well-placed shells to cut off all connection of this kind.

April 24th was an unusually quiet day, though prior to this date the enemy counter-batteries had been very active, each of our batteries being carefully and accurately registered.   This may have been done by sound-rangers, but stringent precautions to avoid being located by them were taken, and the universal opinion, which was reported by Colonel Butler to Corps Headquarters, was that the location of the batteries was being carried out by expert observers in the German balloons.   These had come very close to the line and numbers of them were constantly in the air, entirely unmolested either by the Flying Corps or by the R.G.A.   April 24th, therefore, gave little hint of what was coming, unless the exceptional activity of the German anti-aircraft guns were taken as a sign.   The quietness, however, was soon to be broken ; at 1.0 A.M. on Friday the 25th a few of the batteries were warned that an enemy attack might be expected at dawn, but the remainder were completely unaware that any untoward events were impending until suddenly, at 2.0 A.M., there descended upon them with a roar and a crash the most appalling barrage that they had ever yet undergone.

With a fairly extensive experience of shelling, it was acknowledged by all ranks that never before had such a bombardment been endured.   In the battery positions it was hell, the gunners working their pieces in a perfect hailstorm of shell fire, while, to add to this tremendous test of endurance, a large proportion of the barrage consisted of gas shell which necessitated the wearing of gas helmets by all ranks.   How any of the guns or gunners survived that terrible morning remains to this day a mystery, yet survive it they did and to most excellent effect.   The barrage which enveloped the guns was also beating down upon the front line system, and the batteries, in order to show the infantry that they were not forgotten, opened fire on their S.O.S. lines.   It was soon very clear, however, that an attack was imminent, and accordingly "counter-preparation" was begun and continued for several hours.

From 2.0 A.M. until 5.30 A.M. the barrage did not relax, but from 4.30 A.M. onwards high explosive gradually superseded gas shell until the bombardment became one almost entirely of high explosive. Although this change did even more to wreck the battery positions than had the chemical shell, it at least dispersed the gas and enabled the men ultimately to remove their respirators ; they were by now almost dropping with the physical exhaustion of firing their guns at top speed in gas helmets, combined with the nervous strain of this terrific bombardment, and a breath of fresh air came to them as a blessed relief.

At 5.30 A.M. a considerable bombardment was maintained on the battery positions, but the full fury of the barrage dropped back on to the infantry and, after resting on the trenches for about forty-five minutes, began to creep forward towards the batteries once more.   Under cover of this creeping barrage the enemy infantry advanced to the assault, and as it rolled up inexorably towards the guns again—who all this time were being pounded and smashed by the enemy artillery—the Germans advanced swiftly over the front line and began to approach the battery area.   Thick fog enveloped their movements, practically every telephone wire was cut and, as the same fog prevented any visual signalling at all, the situation became extremely obscure.   With a visibility of only fifty yards it was impossible for battery commanders to know when the enemy might not be right up to and amongst the guns.

At 6.10 A.M. the infantry got through their last message to the guns ; on a buried cable to 156th Brigade Headquarters the company commander of a front-line company stated that he was still being shelled, but that the Germans had so far made no movement.   Shortly afterwards the cable was destroyed and a terrible silence, as far as information was concerned, set in.   It would appear that, very shortly after the despatch of that last message, the enemy assault was delivered.

At about 7.0 A.M. Lieut.-Colonel MacCullock of the 9th K.O.Y.L.I. rode up to the battery positions. His battalion had been lying in support in the valley of the Kemmel-Beek, where it had been heavily gas shelled, and he now decided to move up to a line of disused trenches on the forward slopes of Hill 44, just in front of the guns. While his men were settling down into position, Colonel MacCullock rode up along the main road to find out what was happening towards Wytschaete, and, penetrating as far as the Grand Bois, he discovered that this was still in our hands, whereupon he returned to complete his dispositions for the defence of Hill 44. While this was still in progress, Lieut. Phipps (156th Brigade) returned from Desinet Farm at about 7.50 A.M. and reported that the enemy's rifle fire had got very near. Owing to the fog he had been unable to see any Germans, but there was no doubt but that they were rapidly approaching; he further added that there were practically no French troops to be seen in that area. Even while he was making his report some French infantry retired through the line of guns, shouting that the enemy were in Kemmel village and were coming on fast. It was therefore clear that there now remained no infantry between the guns and the enemy except for the K.O.Y.L.I. whose right flank terminated in front of B/156, there being from there southwards an ominous gap.

At 8.45 A.M. patrols sent out reported that there were no British troops to be seen on the other side of the Kemmel–Vierstraat road, and following almost immediately upon this news small parties of Germans were seen coming across the road. These were immediately engaged by such of the guns as were still serviceable, but by 10 A.M. the enemy had pushed across the road and, although he did not appear to have made much progress in the visible ground near Godizonne Farm, had got beyond Siege Farm further to the south and was within five hundred yards of the batteries.

Shortly before this last period a decision had had to be come to as to the withdrawal of the guns. The only infantry in the neighbourhood were the 9th K.O.Y.L.I. and some stragglers of the late front-line battalion whom Major Barker (C/156) had collected to form an escort to his guns; the line held by these troops ran about one hundred yards in front of the batteries, but stopped on the right at Hill 44, and south of this point no troops were to be seen at all. Northwards the left of the K.O.Y.L.I. was continued by some other infantry, but the whole line was terribly thin and could not hope to stop a determined rush by the enemy. Lieut.-Colonel Butler and Lieut.-Colonel Skinner were therefore faced with this problem:— Hill 44, a slight rise in the ground on the Ridge-Wood–Kemmel road, had a surprisingly good command over the country from Dickebusch Lake round by the west to the northern slopes of Mount Kemmel; it was, therefore, very important to hold it. For this purpose the only infantry available were the 9th K.O.Y.L.I., but they were in the best of spirits. On the other hand, reconnaissance showed that, whereas the Germans were only using volatile gas on Hill 44, they were using mustard gas some 700 yards to the rear, and the natural deduction was that Hill 44 was part of the enemy objective. If, therefore, the enemy gained the hill he would capture the guns *en bloc*, and there would be no further obstacle to impede his progress. It was accordingly decided to withdraw, one by one, a proportion of those guns which were still undamaged, but to keep the remainder in action in their present positions until the retired guns, from a line further back, could open a full volume of covering fire upon the enemy opposite Hill 44.

Hitherto the tactical continuity of the narrative has been maintained in order to relate, as clearly as possible, the true story of the attack by which the Germans captured Kemmel Hill, but now a digression must be made so as to follow closely the action of the batteries in their withdrawal. To do this, the story of each Brigade will be taken separately, beginning with the 156th.

At 9.0 A.M., shortly after the first crossing of the Kemmel–Vierstraat road by the Germans, the order to prepare for a withdrawal was issued from Lieut.-Colonel Butler's headquarters. Since as early as 6.0 A.M. A/156 had in its main position only one gun capable of firing, and by 8.45 A.M. this gun also had been silenced; therefore, on receipt of Colonel Butler's message, the battery withdrew from its main position and moved to a fresh line in the direction of Ouderdom. Shortly afterwards a section of Major Barker's battery (C/156) was also withdrawn.

By 11 A.M. practically all the ammunition in B/156 southern position had been expended, and moreover the guns were unable, owing to trees, to fire at ranges of less than 1,200 yards. Major Studd therefore removed the breech-blocks and dial sights from these guns and, sending back a portion of his detachments to the wagon-lines to hurry up the teams which had already been sent for, concentrated his efforts on the two guns which he had kept in a position 300 yards further north. Of these two guns, one was taken away by a team belonging to C/156 to a previously reconnoitred spot north of La Clytte; the other was run forward by hand, with the assistance of nine men of the K.O.Y.L.I., for a distance of some one hundred yards to the crest of the hill, whence Major Studd and his four remaining gunners engaged the enemy over open sights at a range of 300 yards.

By 11.15 A.M. the remaining two sections of C/156 were in full view of the enemy, some five hundred yards away, and, as their ammunition was running out, a withdrawal to a line north of La Clytte was decided upon.   From a position of assembly two hundred yards to the rear the limbers were brought up, one at a time ; the first gun got away without being fired upon ; the second and third escaped under heavy rifle fire, but the lead driver of the fourth gun took it through a patch of soft ground which made the pace so slow that all the horses and one of the drivers were shot, and the gun had to be abandoned for the time.   The withdrawal of this battery was rendered very difficult by the fact that there were only one sergeant and six men still unwounded ; all the officers and the remaining other ranks had been either killed or disabled, though Major Barker continued to command his battery despite his wound.   They had put up a most brilliant fight, and the gallantry of all ranks was unsurpassable, typical of every battery on this grim morning.

There remained now only the advanced section of A/156, D/156, and the single gun of B/156.   The advanced section of A/156 (Lieut. Blackwell in charge) for a long time had been firing upon the enemy at point-blank range ; early in the morning teams were sent up to try and save these two guns, but the rapid advance of the enemy had not been realised and, fight to the last though they did with the enemy all around them, the guns together with their teams were captured. The advanced gun of D/156 near by had been knocked out earlier in the day and had to be abandoned, after the withdrawal of dial sights and breech-blocks.   D/156 main position had also to be abandoned temporarily.

Thus, by 11.0 A.M. the only gun in action in the forward positions was the solitary 18-pdr. manned by Major Studd and his four men. This little party was now joined by Colonel Butler who, by his quiet bearing and confidence, greatly inspired both gunners and infantry. He collected and controlled a party of machine gunners whose officer had just been killed, and for some time remained with Major Studd's gun, the capture of which was only prevented by the thin line of K.O.Y.L.I. in front.   Machine guns and a 5·9 in. howitzer worried this party considerably, but steady harassing fire was kept upon the enemy and prevented them from making any further advance.

At about 11.30 A.M. this single gun was switched round through 180° to fire on some Germans who were making for La Clytte, almost directly in rear.   At first about twenty of the enemy were visible who, on being fired at, ran back one hundred yards into some scrub. This movement, however, caused some three hundred of the enemy to get up and bunch round their officers.   Major Studd turned his gun on these and obtained a number of bursts right amongst them, with the result that they ran back five hundred yards into a patch of dead ground.

So the morning wore on, the enemy making no considerable advance since he had established himself well across the Kemmel–Vierstraat road. By 1.0 P.M. the ammunition of B/156 solitary gun had all been expended ; as its presence was drawing fire upon the K.O.Y.L.I., it was run back behind the slope, and Major Studd, removing breech-block and dial sight, set out with his four men to find out what had happened to the remainder of his battery.

Thus, at 1.0 P.M., the last gun of the 156th Brigade ceased to operate in the forward positions ; all the remainder had either got away or been silenced by 11.0 A.M., and it only remained to remove those which had had to be abandoned. At 5.0 P.M. in the evening Captain S. G. Taylor took up teams and attempted to save the guns of B/156, but was only able to reach the single gun in the northern position as it was impossible in the darkness to tell where the enemy was. During the night of 25th/26th and the morning of the 26th the howitzers of D/156 (less the advanced one, which had been hit) were removed from under the enemy's nose, as was also the one gun of C/156 which had been abandoned, and on the morning of the 26th also Captain Taylor brought up his teams and saved the three guns of B/156 in broad daylight with the enemy only four hundred yards away —a very fine performance.

So ended the doings of the 156th Brigade on April 25th ; three guns had fallen into the hands of the enemy, but all the remainder, although a few had temporarily to be abandoned, were saved ; in every case the guns had been fought to the last, tremendous casualties being inflicted upon the enemy. Let us now turn to the 162nd Brigade and follow their doings also on this memorable day.

The four batteries of the 162nd Brigade had, in common with all the other guns, been enveloped in the tremendous barrage which the enemy put down at two o'clock in the morning. In spite of this terrific storm of shell —the intensity of which may be judged from the fact that Lieut. Squire of B/162 was killed by the concussion of the bursting shell all around him, his body being otherwise unwounded —the detachments under their battery officers' control maintained a steady rate of fire upon the enemy. All communication between " A," " B " and C/162 and Brigade headquarters completely broke down, and runners were either killed or prevented by wounds from reaching their destination ; to quote the words of one who was a witness of the batteries' deeds : —"Standing on the fringe of that barrage was hell enough for me ; to think of Fetherston, Body, Lee and Cory (the four battery commanders) and all the others walking about in their batteries in the thick of it—I don't know how they ever got out." Casualties came thick and fast amongst the detachments, guns were disabled or completely knocked out, yet the fire of the guns never faltered, and all through the morning they offered a determined opposition to the enemy advance.

The first guns to move back were, of course, the forward section of D/162 at Rossignol Wood. By great good fortune the wire between this forward section and the main battery position remained intact, as did also the wire from there on to Lieut.-Colonel Skinner's headquarters, and the most useful information was thereby transmitted to the Divisional Commander. At about 8.0 A.M., the enemy being then almost on top of the two forward guns, orders were sent to Major Lee to withdraw this section, and teams were immediately sent forward under Lieut. Escott to carry this into effect. Making their way through the barrage, the little party reached the forward section just as the latter, who had been firing at intense rate the whole morning, had expended practically all the ammunition. In front the enemy were only three hundred yards away ; on either flank they had worked right round until they had almost closed in on the guns, yet the withdrawal was carried out successfully under heavy rifle, machine-gun and shell fire, the gunners with their officers walking beside the guns. It is impossible to say too much for such a fine feat; the section, under two young officers (Lieut. Bennet and Lieut. Garrod, and later Lieut. Escott who was in charge of the teams), had been in a very exposed and advanced position; it came under the most intense fire both prior to and during the retirement, every horse in both teams—there were no wagons—was hit, yet the guns were saved without the loss of a single small store, and all the wounded were brought safely away. In recognition of this performance every driver of both teams was awarded the Military Medal.

Shortly after the return of this advanced section to the main line of guns, the withdrawal of the latter to previously reconnoitred positions began. The batteries had now been firing for many hours in the face of a perfect hail of shell, and, great as had been the tenacity and determination shown by officers and men in keeping up a vigorous rate of fire upon the enemy in spite of terrific retaliation, still greater tenacity and courage was shown in the carrying out of the retirement. For some time past not a single runner had succeeded in making the double journey from Brigade Headquarters to the batteries and back, each man in turn falling a victim to the intensity of the enemy barrage, but finally Lieut. Stanley-Clarke of B/162, with much good

M

fortune and considerable gallantry, succeeded in conveying to the guns the order to withdraw.

Gun by gun the retirement began, each battery retaining a proportion of its guns in the forward position until the remainder had got safely away. It was a performance on the part of the officers, gunners and drivers which has never been surpassed ; while other brigades were being forced to abandon their guns, the 162nd Brigade retained practically its full tactical powers. Only three guns, two of C/162 and one of A/162, could not be removed until nightfall and were then got away with the enemy only a few hundred yards distant, but not one single gun was lost to the Germans by the 162nd Brigade on April 25th, and in this achievement they stood practically alone. Many of the neighbouring batteries of other Divisions had earlier been silenced or had been forced to abandon their guns, and too much praise cannot be given to the officers and men of this Brigade who, in the face of overwhelming short-range fire, continued to serve their guns long after they might reasonably have been expected to retire, and even then withdrew them in an orderly manner.

On the withdrawal of the batteries being completed, Brigade Headquarters moved back to a prearranged rendezvous on the Reninghelst–Ouderdom road. No horses or transport could come up to assist in this, and the entire equipment had to be carried by the Headquarters' staff under the direction of Captain Pavitt (the Adjutant). A number of casualties were suffered during the march from shell-fire and from low-flying aeroplanes, but ultimately the new control-post was reached and command of the batteries was carried out from there.

Thus has been described in detail the story of the two brigades and the part they played in one of the great battles which threatened the Channel ports. Before we return to the main narrative again and describe the doings of the rest of that day, a word must be said of the officers and men who put up such a wonderful fight. Names have already been mentioned in connection with deeds of especial gallantry, and yet with hesitation has this been done, for how can one name in one battery be singled out from amongst the others when all behaved in such a magnificent way ? Every officer, every man on that day showed such gallantry as can never be surpassed, and proud should be he who can say, " I served with the 33rd Divisional Artillery on April 25th, 1918 ! "

Yet two names must be mentioned, for without them this narrative would be incomplete. Through all the trials and horrors of the day, through all the great strain of the whole of this period every battery was inspired and encouraged by the presence of the two Brigade Commanders, Lieut.-Colonel B. A. B. Butler and Lieut.-Colonel E. J. Skinner. When times were grim and depressing, when the enemy seemed to be pushing remorselessly on, when the brigades, with their backs to the wall, appeared to be forgotten by God and man, there was ever the presence of those two to cheer up and hearten the weary spirits of their officers and men. With the control of the artillery continually passing from one Division to another, even from one nation to another, but little was done for the gunners who were left to look after themselves. Orders from above were few and far between, and in many cases came too late to be of any use ; communications from Division and Corps were seldom received, and it remained with the two Brigade Commanders to discuss between themselves the situation as it appeared to them, and to issue orders to the batteries accordingly. The battery commanders and their officers and men—wonderfully gallant fellows all—had behind them the moral support of their Brigade Commanders, but Lieut.-Colonel Butler and Lieut.-Colonel Skinner had no such comforting support from above. Yet they were for ever calm, confident and cheerful, and bore the tremendous strain of acting on their own initiative in a way which the batteries strove hard to repay. Colonel Skinner was wounded on May 10th and taken away in an ambulance ; Colonel Butler met a soldier's death in the final British advance in the autumn, but the names of both will ever bring to the minds of those who served under them a sense of deep gratitude and a happy memory of a very highly valued friendship.

The main narrative of the battle was broken off at the point where, at 10.0 A.M., the Germans had established themselves firmly across the Kemmel–Vierstraat road and had pushed on past Siege Farm towards the battery positions. It was about this time— shortly before it, to be exact—that the withdrawal of the 156th Brigade had begun, and it was about now that the culminating point of the battle was reached. Having got past Siege Farm, the enemy advance seemed to slow down as though requiring a breathing space, and for this the fire of the guns and of the 9th K.O.Y.L.I. who were still on Hill 44 was largely responsible. At 11.30 A.M., as already recounted, a strong attempt was made by some five hundred of the enemy to work round by the south to La Clytte so as to cut off the retreat of our troops, but this manœuvre was defeated, and Colonel MacCullock, taking the initiative, decided to counter-attack without delay. As many guns as could be collected were warned of the plan but, just as the 9th K.O.Y.L.I. prepared to launch their assault, a counter-attack was delivered by fresh British troops from the direction of La Clytte, with the result that Colonel Mac-Cullock considered that any movement on his part was unnecessary.

A condition of stalemate now ensued. Whenever the enemy showed himself he was fired on, while he on his part began sniping very actively. Artillery fire was slow, taking the form of occasional rounds thrown about promiscuously and varied by five-minute barrages. The roads, however, were kept under constant fire by enemy high-velocity guns, while counter-battery work on both sides was maintained. About 3.30 P.M. one section of A/162, still in action near Millekruisse, fired at the request of the infantry on some Germans who were collected in huts on the far side of Cheapside, and shortly afterwards our infantry reinforcements arrived.

The situation now seemed well in hand, and during that night and the following day no further enemy advance took place. The 162nd Brigade, having succeeded in withdrawing all its guns except three, was able to come into action again immediately, and indeed some of its guns were in their fresh positions before the withdrawal of the remainder had begun. Therefore in a very short time they were all bombarding the enemy from a line east of the Zevecoten–Ouderdom road and, under the orders of the 9th Division, were covering an infantry brigade of the 49th Division along the La Clytte–Millekruisse road. The 156th Brigade had fewer serviceable guns and did not come into action again as a unit until next day, when positions were taken up one mile north of La Clytte and were occupied until the 28th. On the night of the 28th/29th the 156th Brigade pulled out and began to march to the Winnezeele rest area; the German attack on the 29th, about to be described, delayed this march for a few hours, but ultimately Winnezeele was reached. Next morning (30th) this brigade was again called up into action, but only for a few hours, and ultimately returned to Winnezeele with the prospect of a few days of rest ahead.

From April 26th to 28th the whole of the battery area was heavily shelled by the enemy, while the roads and wagon-lines were searched by high-velocity guns. The wagon-lines, indeed, came in for a very bad time and, after being shelled out of different camps, came ultimately to rest about one mile west-south-west of Poperinghe, with forward wagon-lines between Ouderdom and Reninghelst. On the 26th Lieut.-Colonel Skinner's headquarters were shelled out and forced to move to Reninghelst, and on the 27th the whole of the 162nd Brigade changed positions; " A," " B " and " C " batteries occupied an area near Goed Moet Mill, east-north-east of Ouderdom, " D " battery moved 600 yards north of Ouderdom, while Brigade headquarters went to De Drie Goen Farm.

On Tuesday, April 29th, even while the relief of the 156th Brigade was still in progress, the combined effort of both brigades was called upon to resist yet another German attack, for at 5.0 A.M. the enemy assaulted with eleven divisions in mass formation, the density being from six to eight bayonets to the yard. It was again the same story, from the batteries point of view, of terrific shelling resolutely borne, but this time there was the satisfaction of knowing that the work of the guns had been successful. The attack, after getting up to within one hundred yards of the line held by the 49th Division, was repulsed, as was also a second assault at 6.0 A.M. ; the German effort to turn the Ridge Wood flank proved a costly failure, and the enemy dead lay in rows in front of our line.

The fight of April 29th was the last big episode of the German offensive in Flanders. From that date onwards there were a number of local actions but no large-scale attacks, nor was any serious penetration made by the enemy. From May 1st until the 7th the 162nd Brigade continued to bombard the enemy and to be heavily shelled in return. On the 6th Brigadier-General Stewart and his Staff took over from the C.R.A. 9th Division the control of the artillery covering the front, which extended from Kruisstraathoek cross-roads on the north to just south of Vierstraat. This artillery consisted of the 50th, 51st and 122nd Brigades (9th Division), the 149th Brigade (30th Division) and the 162nd Brigade. On the 7th/8th, however, one section of the 162nd Brigade was relieved by the 121st and marched into rest at Winnezeele, while at the same time the 156th Brigade came up from the back area and took over the positions of the 149th Brigade, in the very area where the wagon-lines had been when the batteries were in action at Passchendaele five short weeks earlier.

April 29th had been the last large-scale operation which the enemy undertook on the Lys front, but Thursday, May 8th, saw a most determined local action, in which the 156th Brigade and the two sections per battery of the 162nd Brigade still in the line took an active part. At 3.0 A.M. on the morning of the 8th the enemy put down a very heavy barrage on the battery and back areas, to which was added, at 5.0. A.M., a severe bombardment on the front system. All the morning until 11.0 A.M. this barrage continued, and under cover of it the Germans attacked. The right brigade front was penetrated, but the left brigade formed a defensive flank from Hallebast Corner to the southern end of Dickebusch Lake. All day long the batteries fired on their S.O.S. lines, a steady rate being maintained until 6.15 P.M., when a quarter of an hour's intense bombardment was followed by a counter-attack on the part of the

19th Infantry Brigade. By this counter-attack all objectives were regained except on the extreme left where the situation remained obscure, and, after a night of intermittent harassing fire with counter-preparation fired at 3.30 A.M. in the morning (9th), the remainder of the 162nd Brigade withdrew from the line and marched to Winnezeele for a short period of rest.

SPECIAL ORDER OF THE DAY

BY

FIELD-MARSHAL SIR DOUGLAS HAIG, K.T., G.C.B., G.C.V.O., K.C.I.E., COMMANDER-IN-CHIEF, BRITISH ARMIES IN FRANCE.

I wish to convey to all ranks of the Royal Regiment of Artillery my deep appreciation of the splendid service rendered by them in all stages of the Somme and Lys battles since the opening of the enemy's attack.

The difficult conditions imposed by a defensive fight against greatly superior numbers have been faced with the same skill, courage and devotion to duty which characterised the work of all branches of the Artillery throughout the offensive battles of 1917. With less constant and loyal co-operation on the part of both field, heavy and siege batteries, the great bravery and determination of the infantry could scarcely have availed to hold up the enemy's advance. The infantry are the first to admit the inestimable value of the artillery support so readily given to them on all occasions.

The knowledge possessed by each arm, doubly confirmed by the severe tests already passed through successfully, that it can rely with absolute confidence upon the most whole-hearted and self-sacrificing co-operation of the other is the greatest possible assurance that all further assaults of the enemy will be met and defeated. I thank the Artillery for what it has already done, and count without fear of disappointment upon the maintenance of the same gallant spirit and high standard of achievement in the future.

(Signed)   D. HAIG, F.-M.,
British Armies in France.

General Headquarters.
May 9th, 1918.

CHAPTER X.

PART II.

HOLDING THE ENEMY IN THE NORTH.

(MAY—AUGUST 1918.)

FOLLOWING on the two checks which had been administered to the Germans on April 29th and May 8th, there now set in a period of holding the line and of taking every possible step to prevent the enemy from renewing the offensive. From May 9th until the 12th counter-preparation was fired morning and evening, and to the weight of artillery employed in this was added, on the 10th, three groups of the French 47th Regiment of Artillery together with the 107th French heavy battery. On the same day also the 44th French Regiment relieved the 19th Infantry Brigade.

On May 12th the 162nd Brigade, after a very short three days' rest, moved into action in the II. Corps area and relieved the 17th Brigade R.F.A. in the vicinity of Salvation Corner, Ypres. A/162 relieved the 18th Battery, " B " the 26th, " C " the 92nd and " D " relieved D/17, and here they remained under the command of the C.R.A. 29th Division until the 17th. On Friday, the 17th, after an uneventful period they were themselves relieved by the 187th Brigade (41st Divisional Artillery) and moved to their wagon-lines one and three-quarter miles E.N.E. of Poperinghe, continuing the march next day to wagon-lines in fields one mile north-east of Hout-kerque. Previous to this the 156th Brigade had come out of action on the 12th and had marched on the 15th to Clifford Rest Camp, near Proven; the whole of the 33rd Divisional Artillery, therefore, was now concentrated in II. Corps Reserve.

From May 18th to the 31st a period of rest and training—very badly needed by all ranks—was enjoyed. The two brigades were attached to the 49th Division, and were detailed to support with the latter the right flank of the Belgian Army in case of enemy attack. This involved a certain amount of reconnaissance of various battery positions to cover the different lines of defence, but apart from this there was little to do, and the blessed absence of shell-fire and of constant expectation of attack came as a tremendous relief.

On the 20th General Sir Herbert Plumer inspected the 33rd Division, in the following week all guns were recalibrated at Tilques, and on the 29th, as a final distraction, the 162nd Brigade held mounted and dismounted sports at D/162 wagon-lines. A final distraction it was, for on May 31st orders were received for the two brigades to relieve the 245th and 246th Brigades (49th Divisional Artillery) in the Ypres sector, and on June 1st the march began.

The relief was spread over two days, but the morning of Tuesday, June 3rd, found the whole of the 33rd Divisional Artillery in action just south of Ypres—an area which the men were beginning to regard with an air of regular proprietorship. Both brigades occupied positions midway between Vlamertinghe and Ypres ; with main wagon-lines just east and north-east of Poperinghe, and forward wagon-lines in the vicinity and north-west of Vlamertinghe, the batteries settled down to cover the right brigade of the 6th Division opposite Voormezeele.

From June 3rd to the 7th the time was passed in harassing the enemy, while he in return kept up a heavy shelling of the battery positions and roads. On Saturday the 8th, at 4.57 A.M., the French 46th Regiment on the right attacked Ridge and Scottish Woods under cover of a barrage, in which the 33rd Divisional Artillery took part, and captured both places, but counter-attacks at noon left Ridge Wood in enemy hands again. On the 8th also the 33rd Division relieved the 6th Division, and the two brigades found themselves covering their own infantry once more.

During the rest of June little of any importance took place. On the 10th Major Lee's battery (D/162) moved its position some 500 yards further south to some old horse standings, and during the whole of this period considerable counter-battery work was carried on by both brigades with excellent effect. On June 13th the French attacked and captured Ridge Wood for the second time, but again lost it in a counter-attack during the afternoon. On the 20th two raids were carried out, one by the 1st Middlesex on Lankhof Château, just north of Voormezeele, at 12.15 A.M., the other by the 2nd Worcesters at the same hour on Manor Farm, south of Zillebeke. The latter was completely successful, but in the Middlesex raid the British covering party met a German covering party in No Man's Land at three minutes before "zero." Fierce hand-to-hand fighting ensued and the British covering party, reinforced by the raiders who were forming up at the time, drove the enemy back to his trenches. No identifications were, however, obtained.

Following this raid there was but little hostile retaliation. The enemy activity had died down considerably of late, although from the 17th to the 19th heavy area shell-storms occurred once more upon the guns, and indeed it seemed that the enemy was devoting all his attention to the battery and back areas.   This, in fact, was hardly surprising.   The chief work of the 156th and 162nd Brigades at the time was the bombardment of enemy roads and battery positions, and in the latter considerable success had attended their efforts.   Many explosions were caused amongst the enemy batteries which were the targets, and it was only natural—a compliment, in fact, to the accuracy of the British guns—that the Germans should turn the chief blast of their hatred upon the originators of this trouble.

Thus the month passed out uneventfully but uncomfortably, and July came in to continue the conditions which had been prevailing.   On June 30th a slight change in the disposition of the brigades had been made, for on that day the 11th Army Field Artillery Brigade withdrew from the line and the 156th Brigade was left to cover the entire front of the left infantry brigade, the 162nd looking after the right.   To simplify this " A," " B " and D/156 took over the positions of the 83rd, 85th and D/11 batteries respectively, and July found them in action in the Canal sector.   The policy of the batteries remained the same—harassing fire on roads and tracks, constant counter-battery work and occasional responses to infantry calls, while the enemy continued the practice of frequent shell-storms on the batteries, with high-velocity guns looking after the roads and back areas.   In particular the forward gun positions at Groenen Jager and the area around Vlamertinghe and Goldfish Château received exceptionally heavy bombardment.

At the end of the first week certain alterations of the front covered by the batteries were made; the infantry of the 33rd Division handed over to the division on their left the front from Zillebeke Lake to the Ypres–Comines Canal and, sideslipping to the right, took over from the 6th Division on the right (who had relieved the French 46th Division on June 26th) the front to as far south as the Vijverhoek–Eizenwalle railway.   No infantry operations took place, however, until the 14th.

On Monday, July 14th, at 6.0 A.M. the right battalion, right brigade of the 33rd Division (1st Middlesex), together with the 18th Infantry Brigade of the 6th Division on the right, attacked under cover of the guns to recapture the original front line east of Ridge Wood and from there to Voormezeele, and succeeded in every detail.   The enemy barrage was not really strong, and only for short periods was it heavy.   At first it was confined to the forward area but later in the day spread to the batteries, and during the afternoon the latter came in for a fairly severe gruelling. All gains were held, and the Forward Observing Officers dealt very effectively with small parties of the enemy who kept dribbling up as though concentrating for a counter-attack. No such concentration, however, was permitted by the guns to be carried out. Counter-preparation was fired daily, morning and evening, and so the British troops were able to boast of a successful advance on their part on the scene of the late German offensive ; the strategic initiative was once more in our hands.

Following on this attack, hostile artillery activity greatly increased. All battery positions were heavily shelled, Goldfish Château and Vlamertinghe being bombarded with great severity, and C/162 forward section had both its guns knocked out by direct hits. It was a typical period of trench warfare, when the artilleries of both sides sought each other out and pounded away at the opposing positions, keeping the while a watchful and active eye on the doings of the infantry.

It was therefore a most suitable time for " new hands " to come and learn the ropes, and fortunately come they did. On July 14th five American artillery officers were posted to each brigade, to see what active service was like and to learn British methods. They were the advance party of a division shortly to come into the line, and for several days they remained with the batteries before they returned to their own units, there to expound to the latter the information and experience they had gained. On July 25th a battalion of the 30th American Division took over part of the front of the right infantry brigade, 33rd Division, and thus the United States of America began to take a part in the war in the north.

The only striking feature which presented itself during the month of July on this sector was the constant fear of a renewed enemy offensive. The German reserves, even as late as July 20th, numbered some thirty-five divisions opposite this part of the front alone, and, with the presence of such an enemy concentration, it was only natural that there should be continued warnings and alarms of impending attacks. On July 21st the wagon-lines of all batteries were ordered to " stand by " throughout the night, with teams fully harnessed up ; on July 24th a message was received at 1 A.M. that the enemy would attack at dawn. Again on the 26th the battery wagon-lines were rudely disturbed by a warning that an enemy assault was hourly awaited, and once again the drivers stood by their teams expecting at each moment to hear the distant crash of the opening barrage. As a result of these rumours every battery was called upon to reconnoitre tiers of positions to be occupied in case of a successful enemy attack, but such an event never took place, and the month drew to a close with no untoward affair to mark its going.

Thus July passed out as its predecessor had gone—uneventfully, but with considerable liveliness. With its going, however, the Division lost Brigadier-General Stewart, who on July 29th handed over the command of the Divisional Artillery to Brigadier-General G. H. W. Nicholson. General Stewart had been with the Divisional Artillery for many months, first as Colonel, later as Brigadier, and, although the exigencies of war often took him away from the brigades to other sections of the front where the infantry of the Division was being covered by artillery not of its own, his presence was familiar and welcome to all ranks. His departure was a cause of great regret to his many friends, but he left behind him a unit of which any Commander might justly be proud.

August 1918, a month of great deeds amongst the troops farther south, brought little change of conditions in Flanders, and the holding of the line continued as before. On the 2nd the 156th and 162nd Brigades assisted in a raid which gained identification of the 8th German Division in this sector; the 8th Division, however, seemed to be following a policy exactly similar to its predecessors, and life in the batteries continued as before, with rather an unusual interlude on the 6th, when His Majesty the King inspected selected officers from the 33rd Divisional Artillery at Lovie Château.

On August 7th the rear position of A/162 (Major Fetherston) was moved to a point 500 yards north-east of Goldfish Château, midway between Vlamertinghe and Ypres, and on the 10th C/162 took a similar step. At this time two more American officers, Captain Westfeldt and Captain Fields, were attached to the 156th and 162nd Brigades respectively, while forty-eight hour visits of infantry officers to the batteries also began—a most welcome interruption to the monotony of these days, and a very interesting diversion for all concerned.

On Saturday, August 17th, the 119th and 120th Infantry Regiments of the 30th American Division relieved the infantry of the 33rd Division in the line, and the 156th and 162nd Brigades found themselves under the control of an American C.R.A. for the first time. It was a novel experience; the 33rd Divisional Artillery had at different times covered nearly half the British divisions in France; it had worked alongside the Belgians, and had supported and been controlled by the French on various occasions. Now the guns found themselves co-operating with the United States Army whose troops they covered for the remainder of the month.

On August 28th came a sudden change. After a period of artillery duels, of enemy bombardments on certain areas and of vigorous counter-battery work by both sides, there appeared the advance parties of the 330th and 331st Brigades (66th Divisional Artillery) who came to relieve sections of the 33rd Divisional Artillery. One section per battery moved out to the wagon-lines on Wednesday the 28th, and on the 29th/30th the relief was completed, the 156th Brigade marching back to wagon-lines in the Haandehote area, the 162nd to a camp near Houtkerque. By August 30th the concentration of the 33rd Divisional Artillery in the back area was complete, and on the evening of that day there came the warning order to prepare to entrain for the 3rd Army.

On August 31st-September 1st the brigades entrained—the 156th at Proven, the 162nd at Heidebeke and Waayenburg—and left for ever the dismal surroundings of the Ypres sector, where they had been for twelve long months. Down in the south, whither they were now going, the British offensive was in full swing; finished for ever was the stagnation of trench warfare. The batteries, after manfully holding the gate of the north, were about to be thrown into the great advance in the south which thrust the enemy back on to his own frontier, and were to take part in that wonderful pursuit which ended in victory for the Allied arms, bringing to a close the world-wide struggle of over four weary years.

CHAPTER XI.

BEFORE the doings of the 33rd Divisional Artillery in the 3rd Army advance are followed, it will be wise to review the tactical situation on this part of the front from the opening of the British offensive on August 8th up to the point where the 156th and 162nd Brigades joined in the battle. Accordingly, the movements of the batteries in question must be left for a moment while the broad aspect of these operations is considered.

On August 8th Rawlinson's (4th) Army had opened the offensive with a brilliant victory between the Ancre and the Avre, and on the 21st Byng (3rd Army) extended the zone of attack northwards to beyond Albert. A succession of attacks from August 23rd onwards pushed the enemy back over the old Somme battlefields until, on the 31st, our troops had forced the crossing of the Somme at Clery and entered Peronne next day.

By September 6th, after constant attacks, Rawlinson's Army had penetrated seven miles to the east of Peronne, while Byng had reached the western edge of Havrincourt Wood. On the 7th the greater part of the wood was in our hands, and three days later the 3rd Army was beyond our original front line of March 21st. The result of these operations was that the Germans were forced back to the Siegfried line—a great defensive zone seven miles in depth and many times stronger than the Hindenburg line—with a few strong positions still held in front thereof, and, before the grand assault on the Siegfried line could take place, it was necessary that these few strong positions should be captured. To achieve this, Byng struck on September 12th with the IV. and V. Corps between Trescault and Havrincourt, capturing both villages and clearing the ground for the coming battle. On the 13th he made a further advance on the 3rd Army front between Havrincourt and Gouzeaucourt, and there now only remained the capture of certain strategical features, marked down for assault on the 18th, before the 3rd Army front would be ready to take part in Foch's supreme effort against the Siegfried line.

ORDER OF BATTLE.

SEPTEMBER—NOVEMBER 1918.

H.Q.R.A.

C.R.A.	Brigade Major.	Staff Captain.
Brig.-Gen. G. H. W. Nicholson, C.M.G.	Major W. A. T. Barstow, D.S.O., M.C.	Capt. W. E. Bownass, M.C.
	Capt. S. D. Graham.	
	Major C. E. Boyce, D.S.O.	

156th Brigade.

Lieut.-Colonel B. A. B. Butler, D.S.O. (*killed*).
Major W. G. Sheeres, M.C.
Adjutant: Capt. H. W. Smail, M.C.

"A" Battery.	"B" Battery.	"C" Battery.	"D" Battery.
Major F. B. Carrell.	Major W. G. Sheeres, M.C.	Major Barker. D.S.O., M.C.	Major D. Jones, M.C.
Major K. W. Milne, M.C.		(*till end of September*). Capt. L. Vestey.	

162nd Brigade.

Lieut.-Colonel W. R. Warren, D.S.O.
Adjutant: Capt. D. Strachan.

"A" Battery.	"B" Battery.	"C" Battery.	"D" Battery.
Major G. Fetherston, D.S.O., M.C.	Major H. C. Cory, M.C.	Major J. R. Barnes, M.C.	Major R. D. Russell, M.C.
Major S. G. Taylor, M.C.	Major Vaughan-Hughes, M.C.		

Thus matters stood when, on September 16th/17th, the 156th and 162nd Brigades moved into action. They had not gone into the line directly on arrival in the Army area but, on detraining at Petit Houvain, Frevent and Bouquemaison, had marched to billets around Rebreuviette and Roziere on the main Frevent–Avesnes-le-Comte road, where they remained for thirteen days. This period was spent in training, in the carrying out of tactical schemes and in general practising of open warfare, and on September 14th/15th the march into action began. Great secrecy was being maintained regarding the concentration of troops on any part of the front, for the element of surprise was proving a tremendous factor in the success of every attack; the march of the batteries up to the Line was therefore conducted by night, the brigades leaving their billets at evening on the 14th and, after an all-night march through Bouquemaison and Doullens, arriving at Acheux (156th) and Louvencourt (162nd) at 5 A.M. on the 15th. Next night the performance was repeated and, passing through Albert and Le Sars, the batteries reached Le Transloy in the early morning of the 16th. From here positions were reconnoitred in the V. Corps area around Heudecourt to support the 17th Division in an attack on the Gouzeaucourt–Peizière line, and wagon-lines were established on the afternoon of the same day in the neighbourhood of Bus.

On the night of the 16th/17th the batteries advanced into action north of Heudecourt in a tremendous thunderstorm; officers and men, after the long marches of the preceding nights, were completely exhausted and, as soon as the guns were unlimbered, literally dropped where they stood while awaiting daylight. They were all worn out with bodily fatigue and ached for rest, and a few hours they now obtained before, on the 17th, a rapid but accurate registration was carried out. There was little time for this latter to be achieved as the attack had been fixed for the next day, but twelve hours of daylight sufficed for the essential preparations to be made, and by nightfall on the 17th the batteries were ready to fulfil their part of the programme in the coming battle, despite the fact that the barrage table was not received until 11.0 P.M.

On September 18th at 5.20 A.M. the assault was delivered in heavy rain along the whole Corps front, the 156th and 162nd Brigades covering the infantry of the 17th Division, with the 38th Division on the left and the 21st on the right. The division on the left was held up, but the 17th, after fierce fighting, gained their objectives and consolidated a line north and east of Gauche Wood. Many prisoners and guns were captured, and during the whole afternoon the batteries of the 33rd Divisional Artillery were busy engaging numerous moving

Magnetic.

GRID NORTH

Scale 1: 40,000.

targets and silencing hostile machine-guns and trench mortars. Two counter-attacks were broken up by the fire of the guns, and at nine o'clock at night a further creeping barrage was put down under cover of which the 17th Division pushed north and consolidated a line just north of St. Quentin Redoubt.

After three days of active artillery fire, during which the infantry of the 33rd Division (which had relieved the 21st on the 20th) slightly advanced its line, the batteries of the 156th and 162nd Brigades began to move up. On the night of the 21st the wagon-lines had been brought to the Equancourt area, and on the 23rd the guns themselves advanced, 156th Brigade to an area about 1,700 yards north of Peizière, 162nd Brigade to new positions about 2,000 yards S.S.E. This move was not carried out without loss, for the advanced guns moving up in the afternoon were subjected to the most intense shell-fire, but ultimately all guns reached the new line and from there the harassing of the enemy was continued.

It was on this day (23rd), or rather on the night of 23rd/24th, that a serious calamity befell the 162nd Brigade. An intense enemy gas bombardment put the whole of the Headquarters staff and "B" battery out of action, reducing the personnel of the Brigade by nearly a quarter; it was a very severe loss in view of the active operations which were being conducted, but Major Fetherston (A/162) from his own battery position commanded from midnight onwards the rest of the brigade in addition to his own guns, despite the fact that since the 18th he had been suffering from a severe wound in the back which had to be dressed twice a day. It was, indeed, a great feat of endurance and devotion to duty on Major Fetherston's part, for he carried on for a number of days in command of the 162nd Brigade, and took no notice of a wound which, of itself intensely painful, took a long time to heal when ultimately he was forced to go into hospital.

The period 25th/28th was one of much front trench and outpost fighting, bringing many calls for support to the batteries and keeping all guns actively engaged day and night. Pigeon Trench, Targelle Ravine and Honnecourt Wood were frequently bombarded at request of the infantry, while concentrations were continuously fired upon all hostile communications and approaches. On the 25th "A" and C/162 were strengthened by the attaching to them of one gun each from B/162 which owing to casualties on the 23rd was unable to man all its guns, while on the 26th yet another addition, and a strange one at that, was made to the same two batteries. Four captured German 77 mm. guns with a large supply of German "Yellow Cross" gas shells were allotted to them; with grim delight the detachments bombarded the enemy that very evening and far into

N

the night with his own gas, and a particularly deadly form of it at that.

On the 29th the attack broke out afresh in conjunction with the whole of the 3rd, 4th and Debeney's French Armies.   On the previous day battery commanders had reconnoitred the forward areas with a view to a possible advance should the forthcoming operations prove successful, and at 3.30 A.M. the assault was delivered.   Covered by the guns of the 156th and 162nd Brigades, the 98th Infantry Brigade moved forward to capture Villers Guislain, one company working round on the north-west, one from the south-east and one making a frontal attack up the centre.   With each company there went a Tank which latter, however, were all knocked out very early in the day or were blown up in our own minefield, and in front of the whole body an artillery barrage rolled through the village.

Villers Guislain was captured together with two hundred prisoners, but unfortunately the various enemy machine-gun posts, strong points and dug-outs were not mopped up, and the attacking troops found themselves with parties of Germans behind them.   From here onwards the situation became very obscure ; a second attack — a continuation of the first — was launched at 5.50 A.M. when the 100th Infantry Brigade assaulted the trenches east of Villers Guislain, the objective being the line Evett Copse–Crawford Crater, an attack which was accompanied by the advance of the 21st and 12th Divisions on the left and right respectively, but progress by the infantry was very irregular.   Owing to the presence of Germans who had not been mopped up in the rear of the attacking infantry, and as a result of stiff resistance put up by the enemy all along the line, the day developed into one long hard fight, every battery being heavily engaged.   A company of the 1st Middlesex was completely cut off by Germans whose dug-outs had been overlooked in the first assault, and, when our troops ultimately succeeded in capturing this ground next day, the whole of the company which had been surrounded was found lying dead all around.   Whether the Middlesex had been captured and slaughtered in cold blood it was impossible to say, but their general appearance gave grounds for such an idea, and little mercy was shown to the enemy in the succeeding days' operations. By 2.30 P.M. the right infantry brigade was back on its original front line and the enemy had practically regained Villers Guislain, and by evening the whole of the attacking troops had retired once more to their starting point.

Meanwhile, with the success of the earlier part of the day, orders had come for the 162nd Brigade to advance to positions south and south-east of Villers Guislain, and at 2.0 P.M. " A " and C/162 had begun to move forward in accordance with these orders. Hardly had they started, however, than they came under intense fire which continued all along their line of advance, while later, in the intermediate positions which they were compelled to take up owing to the retirement of the infantry, they were heavily bombarded by 4·2 in. and 77 mm. B/156, another battery to move up according to pre-arranged orders—which had been drafted on the assumption that the attack would be a success—went right on to its forward position and stayed there within four hundred yards of the enemy, but it suffered heavily for its temerity.

The night of the 29th/30th passed quietly, and at 10.30 A.M. on the 30th the enemy was reported to be evacuating the ground west of the Canal de l'Escaut. Sunday's attack, although not a success on the batteries' immediate front, had elsewhere pierced the mighty Siegfried line, the effect of which was so great that the enemy was forced to carry out a retirement along the whole front. As soon as information of this withdrawal was received a general advance began, the batteries reconnoitring the ground which covered the crossings of the canal and the zone east thereof, while the infantry reached the line which had been the objective of the 5.50 A.M. attack on the previous day and threw out patrols to the western bank of the canal. Between 11.0 A.M. and 2.0 P.M. the 156th Brigade advanced to positions 2,000 yards east of Peizière, while A/162 came into action just west of Villers Guislain.

During the night 31st/1st the 162nd Brigade brought forward its guns, and by dawn on October 1st was in action 1,000 yards east of Villers Guislain, while the 156th Brigade also advanced its guns to the vicinity of Pigeon and Targelle ravines, 2,000 yards south of the village. From 3.30 A.M. to 7.0 A.M. such guns as had reached the forward position fired a barrage in support of an infantry advance on the right, and for the rest of the day were kept hard at work in engaging the many targets and movement which presented themselves on the far side of the canal. At the same time the batteries were subjected to intense area shoots by the enemy who was trying desperately to cover his retreat.

These area shoots were undoubtedly extremely unpleasant, but just at this time the batteries were given visible proof that counter-battery work was not entirely confined to the German side. During the advance to the Canal, four 5·9 in. enemy howitzers were found deserted, but still in the firing position, along a road. On this road just behind them a German field battery of four 77 mm. guns had apparently been marching—*had*, it should be noticed, for it would never march again. Whether it had been caught in a shell-storm directed upon the 5·9 in. howitzer battery, or whether an aeroplane had seen it and had switched some of our batteries round to catch it will never be known, but whatever had occurred the work was most effectual. The entire battery, personnel and guns, lay dead and smashed upon the ground ; the battery commander at the head of the column, behind him his trumpeter and the whole of the battery staff, all lay dead beneath their horses. Every team of every gun was still in its harness, all three drivers of each team were still in their places, but all were dead, torn and riven by our shells. It was a most uncanny sight, this battery complete in every detail laid out along the road, and swift must have been the storm from our guns which transformed it and its surroundings into a shambles.

October 1st/5th was a period of probing the enemy line and of trying to force the pace of his retreat. Day and night his communications were shelled, his front system bombarded and every sign of movement engaged. Patrols pushed out to the edge of the canal on the 3rd found it still held by machine-gun parties, and as a result certain batteries sent forward sections so as better to engage Honnecourt and the numerous targets which presented themselves in the neighbourhood. On one occasion an aeroplane reported enemy transport to be on the move near Basket Wood, and a storm of shell was immediately directed upon the area involved. During the advance a couple of days later the batteries passed the locality where this transport had been, and the sight of the smashed and broken wagons and the dead drivers and horses who had been killed by the batteries' own fire was most uplifting to the detachments who had done the work. All this time gas concentrations were fired into La Terrière and Basket Wood, and everything was done to render as difficult as possible the retirement which the enemy was clearly carrying out.

At last, on the 5th, the line gave. Further to the right our troops had captured Montbrehain and Beaurevoir, and their loss necessitated a withdrawal by the enemy from the La Terrière Plateau. At dawn the 5th Scottish Rifles, accompanied by forward observing officers from each brigade, pushed patrols across the river and, meeting only slight resistance, advanced to Franque Wood and on through La Terrière, establishing themselves in Aubencheul by 3.0 P.M. As soon as it was known that the enemy had retired to the east of the canal, the 156th and 162nd Brigades began to make rapid preparations for the crossing, the repairing of bridges at Les Tranchées and elsewhere being taken in hand without delay. By 4.0 P.M. the 156th Brigade had completed a rough bridge in the southern end of Honnecourt, and an hour later both brigades were ordered to move across the Canal in support of the infantry. A/156 and a section of C/156 immediately effected a crossing and dropped into action midway between Vendhuille and La Terrière. At dusk D/156 went into action 1,000 yards south of La Terrière, and the remainder of C/156 crossed the canal and took up a position of readiness one thousand yards to the east thereof.

Thus the batteries pushed their way over one of the great barriers which lay across the line of advance, and before night had fallen a proportion of guns was firmly established on the eastern side. Darkness prevented any further work from being done, but with the arrival of dawn on the 6th, B/156 and the remainder of the 156th Brigade crossed over and took up positions covering Aubencheul from south of La Pannerie Wood. The 162nd Brigade, in the meantime, had been seriously held up at the lock south of Honnecourt, as the bridge, although repaired once, had again been broken, but at 4.0 P.M. on the 5th after several hours' delay the crossing was successfully carried out by portions of the batteries ; at dawn on the 6th the remainder came into action in the vicinity of Franque Wood and La Terrière after a perilous march along the east bank of the canal, between the latter and a marsh, with only two inches of clearance on either side of the wheels.

On October 7th the 162nd Brigade again advanced to Basket Wood, while wagon-lines were brought forward to the vicinity of the Canal, and at 1.0 A.M. on October 8th all batteries put down a barrage in support of an attack by the 115th Infantry Brigade of the 38th Division. This Division had relieved the 33rd at 10.0 P.M. on the 5th, and now advanced to the assault of the Beaurevoir Line and Villers Outreaux in conjunction with a general attack on the last of the Siegfried zone by Byng, Rawlinson and Debeney. After much opposition and very severe fighting the final objectives were gained at 10.0 A.M., and three-quarters of an hour later the 162nd Brigade again moved forward—the third advance in three days—to the west of Mortho Wood, while the 156th Brigade guns advanced to the southern edge of Aubencheul. From here another barrage was fired at 11.30 A.M., almost in fact before the guns had dropped their trails—" limber supply " being adopted by certain batteries until the ammunition wagons, arriving at the gallop, came up just in time to prevent a stoppage—and under cover of it the 114th Infantry Brigade assaulted Malincourt and the Malincourt–Serain road beyond.

At about noon it was clear that the enemy was in full retreat, and accordingly the barrage was stopped, the infantry pushing on with little opposition through Malincourt and reaching the final objective at three o'clock in the afternoon. At two o'clock one section of B/156, and shortly afterwards three howitzers of D/156, advanced until they were almost up with the attacking infantry, and by shooting in close support and co-operation with the latter did excellent work in the engaging of hostile movement, machine-guns and strong points. At the same time the whole of 156th Brigade advanced so as to keep touch with the infantry, reaching by 4.0 P.M. the area just south of Malincourt.

At dawn on October 9th the advance was resumed. Tuesday's battle had wiped out the whole of the Siegfried Line, the enemy was now well on the run and the 19th Infantry Brigade (33rd Division) pushed on through the 114th, the C.R.A. 33rd Division taking over control of the guns, which consisted of the 121st and 122nd Brigades in addition to the 156th and 162nd. Little resistance was met with until Clary was reached, but here the infantry were held up by snipers and machine-gun fire. Two guns of A/156 and three of B/156 together with some advanced sections of the 162nd Brigade, which had followed close on the heels of the infantry, came into action immediately on the western outskirts of the village and successfully engaged the enemy machine-guns over open sights. Shortly afterwards the infantry established themselves on the eastern outskirts of Clary, whereupon two of the advanced guns of B/156 were pushed through the village and again came into action, shooting over open sights with extremely good effect at a range of 800 yards. In the meantime the rest of the 156th and 162nd Brigades had been advancing rapidly and, after passing through Villers Outreaux and Malincourt, had dropped into action just west of Clary to help the infantry in the assault on the eastern outskirts. With the fall of Clary the advance quickened and the infantry went right through Bertry unchecked and on to La Fayte and Troisvilles, closely followed by the forward guns of the 156th and 162nd Brigades, which were shooting at very close ranges over open sights all the afternoon and were successfully dealing with every sign of enemy resistance. Keeping pace with the advance came on also the main body of guns of the two brigades, which searched out and broke up every sign of enemy movement and opposition. So rapid was the move forward that the batteries took up three successive positions during the day, night finding them in the vicinity of Bertry with forward guns on the western edge of Troisvilles.

The speed of the advance, indeed, was now beginning to make itself felt; ammunition and food supply became a most serious problem, and on this day (October 9th) tremendous difficulty was met with by the wagon-lines in keeping touch with their firing batteries without either crowding upon or losing all sight of them. The day,

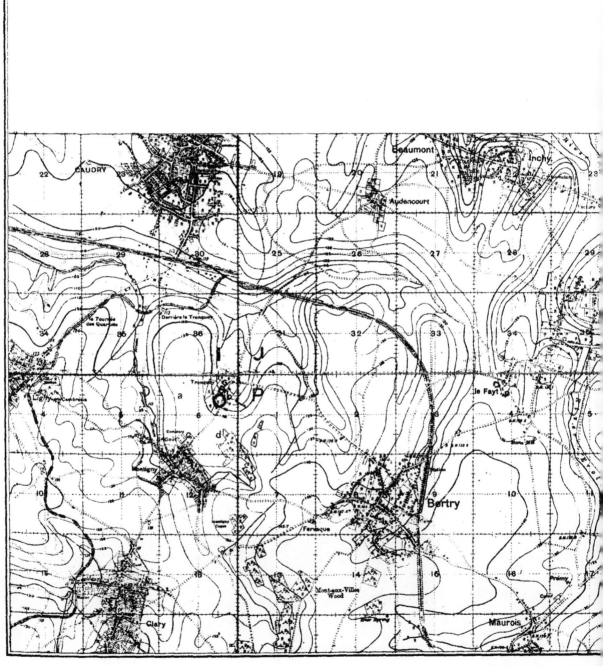

Scale 1: 40,000.

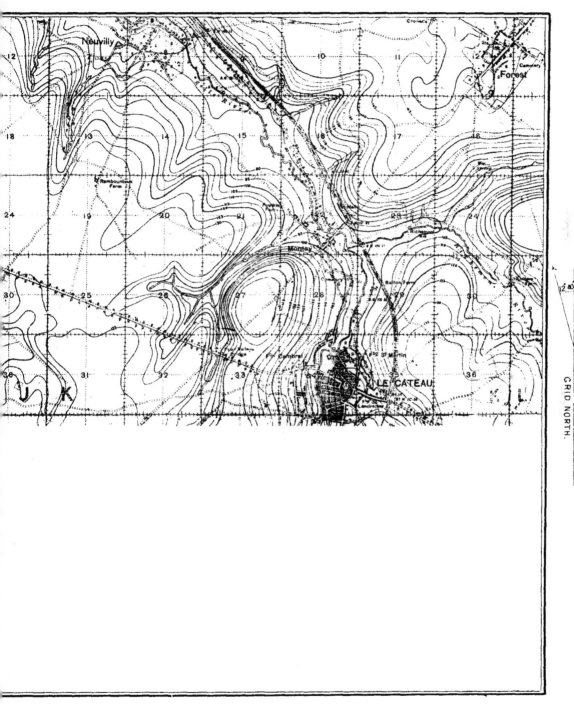

with its eight mile advance and the occupation of three successive positions, laid a heavy strain upon all the wagon-lines which, unable to move in a direct line across country, had to complete a long march before they joined up with their guns at Bertry in the evening; yet throughout this period the guns and detachments were never without ammunition and food, a fact which compares very favourably with the batteries of the United States army which in some cases, being without food, were completely unable to keep up with the advance. There was another and most novel proof of the pace at which the line was pushing forward; on entering Clary and Bertry the infantry and guns were met by cheering French civilians who, in their exultation at the departure of the enemy after so many weary years, rushed to greet our troops with an outburst of joy quite embarrassing! Unable to cope with the rapidity of the attack the Germans had allowed these people to stay behind, and in their excitement at this unexpected relief they vented their delight upon the British troops in the most amazing and wholehearted manner.

Seven o'clock on the morning of the 10th saw all batteries on the move again, supporting an advance by the 98th Infantry Brigade, assisted by cavalry, upon the bridgeheads east of the River Selle between Neuvilly and Montay. This was a great day for the guns and, indeed, for all the troops concerned, for the advance was carried out according to the true style laid down in the drill book for open fighting. Cavalry patrols in front, infantry following on, batteries first in " battery column " and then manœuvring into line, the whole countryside around Troisvilles presented the amazing spectacle of vast masses of troops moving steadily forward exactly as though on an Aldershot field day. The 156th Brigade lay on the right of the 162nd, and together the two brigades manœuvred up to the crest of the hill which commanded the crossing of the Selle. By 8.0 A.M. the infantry were within 800 yards of the river, where they halted until such time as the Divisions on the right and left had come up into line, and by the same hour the batteries had pushed through Troisvilles to a point midway between that village and Le Cateau, from which positions they vigorously shelled hostile batteries and machine guns.

In addition to the delay on the flanks, the enemy on the immediate front was showing clear signs of increased resistance. Several field batteries had come up and were firing over open sights at the infantry, while our own batteries, as they neared the crest of the hill, came under very heavy shell fire. With ammunition wagons detached, however, the guns pressed on under severe fire and reached the crest whence, over open sights, they were able to assist the infantry in no small measure, and throughout the day continued to engage hostile troops and movement of every description. At the same time the German batteries rendered our positions very uncomfortable with 77 mm. and long-range fire, while the teams which went back to Troisvilles to water found the village congested with cavalry, artillery and infantry pack horses, all of whom suffered severe casualties through being spotted by an enemy aeroplane which called down a shell-storm upon the entire village.

The whole of the 10th was spent in registration, harassing fire and counter-battery work, D/156 and D/162 engaging with great success four hostile batteries in action on the forward slopes of the high ground east of the River Selle. Many enemy machine-guns and snipers also demanded the attention of the guns, and so, despite fairly active artillery fire on the part of the enemy, the batteries were kept busy until 5 p.m.; at that hour a barrage was fired to cover the 98th Infantry Brigade in an attempt to cross the river and to form bridgeheads on the crest of the hill to the north-east, in conjunction with the 17th Division on the left.

This attack met with considerable opposition as the River Selle formed a most important part of the enemy defensive line, and nowhere was an advance made beyond the railway. Night fell with the enemy still holding the high ground, and brought with it a most unpleasant time for the batteries. Without cover of any sort or description, lying out in the open and being consistently shelled with 77 mm. and 4·2 in., the detachments awaited the dawn, when it was hoped that this stand on the part of the enemy might be broken down.

Dawn, however, brought no further success, but on the contrary a temporary reverse. The 98th Infantry Brigade at 10.15 A.M. reported that it had been counter-attacked and now only had two posts on the eastern side of the Selle; the 162nd Brigade was accordingly detailed to look after the troops across the river, while the remainder of the artillery covering the infantry were left to fire on observed targets and to engage all movement and all possible hostile batteries. The latter during the morning were quiet, but from 2.0 P.M. until 4.0 P.M. a very considerable bombardment of 5·9 in., 4·2 in. and 77 mm., mainly from the Ovillers direction, descended upon the whole area occupied by the batteries.

No further move was now made until 5.0 A.M. on the 12th when the 100th Infantry Brigade assaulted the high ground east of the river, the objective being the line of the road running from Amerval to the outskirts of Montay. No creeping barrage was utilised in this attack, the batteries firing on selected and observed targets throughout the day. By 8.0 A.M. the left battalion was reported to have gained its objective in spite of strong enemy opposition, but the right battalion was held up by machine-gun fire from the river. An early morning mist rendered observed artillery fire—the only kind of any use at the moment—impossible, and not till the middle of the day could anything be done. Excellent work was then carried out by the batteries but came too late, for by then the left battalion had been forced back to the railway by strong enemy counter-attacks ; evening found our troops, in spite of stubborn fighting and most gallant resistance, back to the west of the river whither they had been driven by superior numbers of the enemy, only a few posts remaining on the eastern bank.

With S.O.S. lines along the railway, both brigades now began a period of continuous harassing fire on all enemy strong points and communications, with synchronised bombardments on areas of especial importance. A lull in the infantry action had set in, but it was essential that the enemy should have no chance of organising his front or improving his defences, and to prevent this the full powers of the batteries were called upon. From October 13th to the 20th under the control of the C.R.A. 38th Division (which had relieved the 33rd on the 13th) the guns bombarded the railway, the hostile trenches and batteries, the ravines east of the Selle and every possible point which might be utilised by the enemy. Gas was fired nightly into the ravines, every hostile effort to put out wire was nullified, and two 6 in. trench mortars were brought into position to help in the bombardment. The result of this firing, although not apparent at the time, was clearly shown later when the batteries, on advancing, found the railway embankment covered with the bodies of dead Germans, all of whom had obviously, from their mangled state, been killed by shell fire. Daily the enemy replied to this activity by shelling the forward and battery areas, but the initiative had passed for ever into the hands of the British Army, and the lull, although of a week's duration, was but a temporary measure. On October 20th Byng struck with seven divisions in an attempt to capture the Selle line north of Le Cateau to Denain, five miles from Valenciennes, and the 38th Division, covered by a barrage from the guns, assaulted and captured by 10.0 A.M. the high ground between Forest and the Selle as its share of the operation ; this, together with victories on other parts of the 3rd Army front, left the way clear for a further general advance.

Next day (21st) the expected orders to resume the advance were received. A general assault by the 3rd and 4th Armies was planned, the objectives of the 33rd Division being Wagnonville and Poix-du-Nord ; the attack was to be on a grandiose scale, tanks assisting the infantry, while in addition to the 156th and 162nd Brigades the whole of the 38th Divisional Artillery and the 223rd Brigade R.F.A. (Naval Division) were to form the creeping barrage behind which the infantry would move forward. Two 6 in. trench mortars were allotted to each infantry brigade, the 6 in. howitzers of the V. Corps Heavy Artillery were detailed to bombard selected targets and engage in counter-battery work, and one 18-pdr. battery of the 162nd Brigade was placed at the disposal of the G.O.C. 19th Infantry Brigade.

In order to cover the Ovillers Slaughter House road for this attack the 156th Brigade moved to within 1,000 yards of the Selle, north-west of Montay. From here all necessary points were registered during the 21st/22nd, and on the 22nd every battery sent forward a reconnoitring party to examine the approaches to and crossings of the River Selle. This was to be no local attack but an operation on the very largest scale with tremendous issues hanging in the balance, for it marked the beginning of the destruction of the new water front, the Scheldt and the Sambre Canal, which the enemy was seeking to hold, and the start of the last of the great conflicts in the west. No precaution was to be overlooked, no step left untaken which in any way might assist in bringing success to this great combined effort further to hurl the enemy back towards his frontiers.

During the night of the 22nd/23rd the infantry of the 33rd Division relieved the 38th, the C.R.A. 33rd Division taking over control of the guns, and at 2.0 A.M. on the 23rd the attack was launched behind a creeping barrage with the 98th Infantry Brigade on the right, the 19th on the left. By 4.30 A.M. the 1st Middlesex were in Forest, and the 4th King's had passed through their lines and were pushing on towards the next objective; an hour later B/156 with one section of D/156 crossed the Selle and followed up the leading battalion of the 98th Infantry Brigade with whom they kept in close touch throughout the day, and by 6.45 A.M. both artillery brigades had crossed the Selle, the 156th shortly afterwards taking up positions 1,000 yards west of Croix, the 162nd dropping into action west of Forest.

Meantime the infantry, in face of strong opposition, were pushing slowly on, and by 10.30 A.M. were lining the Croix–Vendegies road ready for the next advance. Before this took place the guns of the 162nd Brigade again moved up, this time to Richemont, while C/156 pressed on nearly to Croix. So successful was the attack, however, that the batteries found themselves being left too far behind, and accordingly at 12.30 P.M. the 162nd Brigade again advanced

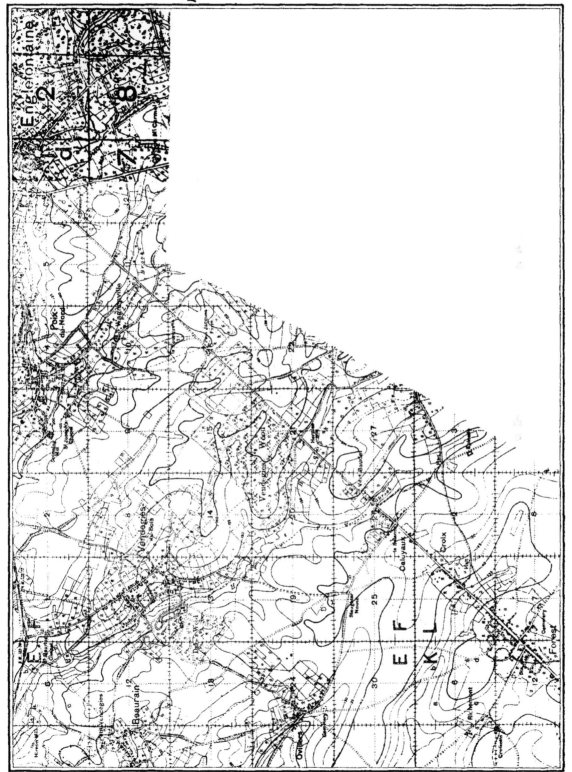

Magnetic

GRID NORTH

2° 40'

Scale 1:40,000.

its guns in close support of the infantry and came into action 1,000 yards north of Croix. Here it remained throughout the rest of the day, neutralizing machine-gun fire and generally assisting in every possible way the infantry who were slowly making their way through Vendegies Wood.

By 5.0 P.M. the British line ran approximately along the northern edge of the wood, and here the advance was stayed for the night, the 156th Brigade, who had occupied the same positions since before midday, pushing up to an area 1,000 yards north of Croix where it remained throughout the hours of darkness. The day had been a complete and overwhelming success all along the line, and the batteries, after sixteen hours of continuous fighting and advancing, were thankful to snatch a short rest. The strain had been great, nor had the victory been won without loss; all batteries had suffered to a more or less marked extent, but in particular must be mentioned the tragic and yet glorious death of Lieut.-Colonel B. A. B. Butler. While riding up from his headquarters at Richemont to visit the batteries he was severely wounded and died the same evening, a loss which the 156th Brigade could ill afford. Elsewhere has been related the story of his gallantry during the enemy offensive, and in the advance of the British line his courage and example were no less marked. His death robbed the Brigade of a friend and a leader than whom a better could not be found, and with victory almost in sight it seemed doubly hard that he should not have survived to share in it.

On the 24th at 4.0 A.M. the advance on Englefontaine was resumed, Major W. G. Sheeres, M.C., taking over command of the 156th Brigade. Heavy bursts of fire were put down in front of the infantry under cover of which they moved forward towards Paul Jacques Farm and Wagnonville, and at dawn, although all ranks were now very exhausted, the batteries began to advance. At 6.0 A.M. the 162nd Brigade had reached the southern outskirts of Vendegies and was directing fire upon the eastern outskirts of Poix-du-Nord, where the enemy was reported to be retreating. By 8.0 A.M. the same brigade had again advanced to a position in observation 1,000 yards further on, the 156th Brigade reaching the edge of the Bois de Vendegies one hour later. From here harassing fire was kept up on the approaches to Englefontaine, while A/156 kept in close touch with the leading battalion of infantry. News was then received that, after the overcoming of strong opposition, Wagnonville had been captured and Englefontaine itself was being rapidly threatened. Upon receipt of this information further battery positions were hastily reconnoitred and all the guns were moved up, the 156th Brigade coming into action between Poix-du-Nord and Wagnonville, the 162nd Brigade in Poix-du-Nord itself.

As events turned out, the infantry were held up between Poix-du-Nord and Englefontaine, and the latter was accordingly kept under the fire of the guns. All through the night of the 24th/25th and during the day of the 25th the exits from the village were continually bombarded, and at 1.0 A.M. on the 26th an attack was carried out by both infantry brigades of the 33rd Division under cover of a thick barrage in which ten per cent. of gas shells were used. The programme for this barrage was worked out almost entirely by Brig.-General G. H. W. Nicholson who, depleted of his staff by "Spanish influenza" and other causes, tackled the work single-handed and with such skill that the operation was a complete success. Five hundred prisoners and many machine-guns were taken, and with the fall of the village one battery of the 162nd Brigade pushed forward to a previously reconnoitred position from which close support of the infantry was possible.

From the 26th until the end of the month the batteries remained in the same positions, and it was well that this was so, for the so-called Spanish influenza was now raging in both brigades. It was believed that this epidemic had been contracted through sleeping in dug-outs and barns recently occupied by the enemy who was known to be suffering from it very badly, but whatever the cause it handicapped the guns to a marked extent. At one time the brigade commander and all four battery commanders of the 162nd Brigade were down with the disease, but despite this counter-preparations were fired morning and evening to break up any would-be counter-attacks by the enemy, while frequent gas concentrations were fired into the hostile lines. On the 29th a successful " mopping-up " of houses on the Englefontaine–Bavai road was carried out by the 17th R.W.F. (the 38th Division had relieved the 33rd on the evening of the 26th), and on the 29th/30th there came to the weary batteries a short relief. On that night the 122nd Brigade R.F.A. " took over " from the 162nd who marched back to Bertry for a 72-hour rest, to be followed two nights later by the 156th Brigade.

For over six long weeks the batteries had been fighting, advancing and fighting again, covering in all a depth of 30 miles and never once enjoying rest of any kind. Upon Brigade and Battery commanders there had been the constant strain of dealing with the ever-arising fresh situations, and of keeping in close touch with the infantry in every stage of the advance ; amongst all the battery personnel there had been no rest, no respite from unending firing, marching and enemy shelling, while the wagon-lines had been hard put to it each day to keep touch with the gun lines in every move and to keep them fully supplied with ammunition. It is scarcely surprising, then, that officers and men were dropping with fatigue when the orders for a 72-hour rest were received, yet so high was the morale of the troops at the time and so inflamed were all with the sense of victory, that grudgingly did they give up their share in the battle and move back to the quieter surroundings of Bertry.

They need not have feared, however, that they would be long left out of the line. The so-called 72-hour rest, although achieved by the 162nd Brigade, was reduced in the case of the 156th to one of twenty-four hours, and November 2nd saw both brigades back into action once more. A great combined attack by the 1st, 3rd and 4th Armies, together with the 1st French Army, was about to be launched upon the formidable defences of the Sambre, the great Mormal Forest and the fortifications of the town of Le Quesnoy, and to take part in this the two brigades were ordered to cover the line due east of Englefontaine from positions in the western outskirts of Poix-du-Nord (156th Brigade) and from Wagnonville (162nd Brigade). These positions they occupied in the afternoon of November 2nd, Lieut.-Colonel C. E. Boyce temporarily commanding the 156th Brigade, and Colonel Pim (who was wounded next day and succeeded by Major Vaughan-Hughes) the 162nd in place of Lieut.-Colonel Warren.

Before any further details of the fighting are entered upon, a word of explanation is called for with regard to this chapter. Hitherto a careful chronicle of the events of each day has been given, the movements of the batteries being followed in detail. As a result, perhaps, of this strict attention to tactics the personal element has found itself excluded, the interest of the chapter being in the main historical. Yet this is unavoidable; in one short chapter must be described the whole of that brilliant advance from September 16th until November 11th, with all its attacks, its changes of position and forward marches. To digress from this and enter upon personal narratives must inevitably destroy the continuity of the story, and moreover, another difficulty has to be faced. In those days no battery had time to think of the doings of any other guns save of its own; no battery had really sufficient time to think and record what it was doing itself, and therefore, were stories of individual exploits narrated in these pages, only a particle could be put down and many as deserving of mention would have to be left untold. On frequent occasions every battery of both brigades performed brilliant exploits in galloping forward guns to a level with the most advanced infantry and in shooting upon the enemy over open sights at almost point-blank range; on frequent occasions batteries had to pass through shell-storms to drop into the positions chosen for them, and had to maintain effective covering fire under the full weight of an enemy bombardment, but each and all did it in turn and the singling out of any one in particular would be invidious. All eight batteries took an equal share in this wonderful advance, and the valour of their work can best be appreciated by an account of the battles in which they were engaged.

On November 2nd the brigades had come back into action; November 3rd was spent in reconnoitring advance positions and in maintaining close co-operation between the infantry and the guns, and on November 4th began the great attack on the Forêt de Mormal. At 6.15 A.M. under a creeping barrage the 38th Division moved forward to the assault, and for two hours the guns continued to maintain a curtain of fire in front of the infantry as they pushed their way on towards the objective. At 8.15 A.M. both the 156th and 162nd Brigades began to advance, one battery at a time, to positions already chosen east of Englefontaine, and by adopting this procedure the continuity of the barrage was in no way interrupted, the rear positions maintaining a brisk rate of fire until a proportion of guns had reached the forward positions and had begun to carry on the work from there. The 162nd Brigade successfully reached the new positions, although heavily shelled on the way, but the 156th was prevented from doing so by intense machine-gun fire, which mere fact alone goes to show how closely the batteries were following up the infantry. Only A/156 was able to get through, the remainder having to drop into action temporarily to the west of the village, but after a time the machine-gun fire slackened and the move was completed, the whole of the 156th Brigade lying 1,000 yards south-east of Englefontaine in the outskirts of the Forêt de Mormal and close alongside the 162nd Brigade.

From here the barrage was continued until 3.0 P.M., when the final objectives were reached. Positions were then reconnoitred 3,000 yards further forward, and at dusk all batteries advanced again. Great difficulty was now experienced as numerous trees had been felled across the roads which had, in addition, been blown up, but by 8.0 P.M. all batteries were in action again in the reconnoitred positions around a *carrefour* or meeting of roads in the forest. The state of the roads, in point of fact, prevented the moving up of any heavy guns except the 60-pounders, the six-inch howitzers being compelled to remain halted far behind until some sort of track had been repaired for them.

During the night of the 4th/5th the batteries again moved forward and were deployed along the Sassegnies–Ribaumet–Sarbaras line, covering the River Sambre, while the infantry of the 33rd Division relieved that of the 38th. At 4.30 A.M. the advance began again, and each battery immediately sent one section forward to keep in touch with the battalion commanders. These sections pushed on through La Grande Pature and took up positions east of Sarbaras which gave easy command of the crossings of and ground beyond the River Sambre, and from which very successful observed fire was carried out, much enemy movement being engaged. In the meantime the remainder of the batteries hurried forward as fast as possible, but great delay was caused by congestion on the roads and by mine craters and felled trees. Not until noon had all the batteries, in extremely wet weather, made their way through the Forêt de Mormal, but by that time they were in action east of Sarbaras and bombarding the ground beyond the Sambre with the utmost vigour.

This day, Tuesday, November 5th, marked the final breaking of the enemy's resistance. With the two wings of his army separated, with the Siegfried and Brynhild zones overrun, he was no longer in retreat but in full flight, and during the afternoon of the 5th a careful reconnaissance of the routes forward and of the crossings over the Sambre was carried out, for the rout of the enemy might enable a crossing to be effected at any moment. During the night of the 5th/6th the enemy retired to the east of the river and the 162nd Brigade was ordered to follow him, the 156th being told to remain in their present positions to the west. Night and day the enemy kept the bridgeheads under the most intense shell and machine-gun fire, and entirely prevented the Sappers and the battery working parties from repairing the bridges sufficiently for the guns to get across. Ultimately, at dawn on the 7th, a rough structure had been thrown up, and the batteries began to move over the river. On the previous evening a reconnaissance of the approach to the bridge had been made by Major Taylor and Captain Heads, and it was found that the proper approach had been hopelessly blocked. The batteries, when they did advance, had to move down a steep, winding and very narrow track, while the only route on the eastern side of the river was a tortuous towing path and necessitated the cutting of gaps in hedges and the manhandling of guns across rivulets and swamps—a very difficult task.

D/162 was the first battery actually to cross the Sambre, but it was so closely followed by A/162 that the latter got into action first, dropping its gun trails just west of Pot de Vin at the moment when the infantry were assembling along a sunken road for the attack on the village. The gratitude of the infantry for this close support by the artillery was very marked, and several of their officers came up to the batteries to express their thanks, for they knew with what difficulty and at what a cost this advance of the guns close under the enemy's nose had been effected. " B " and C/162 were prevented for some time from crossing the river, for an infantry wagon broke down right in the middle of the bridge shortly after " A " battery had got over, but after a delay of about two hours the whole brigade was across the last barrier and, despite severe casualties suffered in the operation, was supporting the infantry to the full extent of its power. November 7th was the last real fighting day of the war on this part of the front, but it was none the less a very nasty day, and in every battery a certain number of casualties were suffered. The enemy was putting up a stiff resistance for he was trying to bar to us the road to Namur, but his was only a forlorn hope and did little more than to slow down slightly our rate of advance.

From this date onwards the only batteries of the 33rd Divisional Artillery to the east of the Sambre were those of the 162nd Brigade, as the 156th Brigade had not been called upon to advance. In fact, the 162nd Brigade shared with the 169th Army Field Artillery Brigade the distinction of being the only guns across the river on this section from the 6th until the conclusion of hostilities.

On the 8th, even while a little group of men were sitting round a table in the Forest of Compiègne discussing the terms of Armistice, the infantry of the 38th Division advanced to the Maubeuge–Avesnes road and later to the Bois de Beugnies, supported as far as possible by the 162nd Brigade which pushed on beyond the cross-roads north-west of Dourlers. On the 9th the enemy retreat became general ; the infantry followed up as far as Wattignies, and " B " and C/162 moved into action 1,000 yards west of the village, " A " and " D " batteries remaining at Dourlers. Saturday, the 9th, was in fact the last day of the war for the 33rd Divisional Artillery. In the early morning of that day the 162nd Brigade fired upon the enemy rear-guards—the 156th were already out of the battle—and reconnoitred forward as far as Wattignies where the infantry had halted. Small patrols of cavalry pushed further on to try and establish contact with the rearguard of the German army, and desultory machine-gun fire could be heard every now and then away in the distance, but to all intents and purposes the enemy had completely vanished and nowhere could our troops get into contact with them.

On November 10th came orders for the wagon-lines to join up with the guns and for all four batteries of the 162nd Brigade to remain in a position of readiness between Dourlers and Ecuelin. To the east all the bridges had been blown up by the retreating enemy, and pursuit by the batteries was utterly impossible. Moreover, it was known by all ranks that German plenipotentiaries had passed through our lines some days before to sue for terms, and the knowledge of that fact, combined with the utter rout of the enemy on the batteries' own front, prepared the men for the news which was shortly to come.

At 9.0 A.M. on Monday, November 11th, 1918, came the news that the war was over.   In the Wattignies sector the order to break off hostilities did not come, as many accounts strove to describe it, in the midst of the battle, with raging gun-fire at one moment and our troops all shouting and waving their helmets at the next.   The orders merely confirmed what already was known and anticipated, and although, when the message from G.H.Q. was read out to the assembled batteries, there was such cheering as comes from deep down in the heart, the occasion was far too great to be grasped in a single moment, and the gunners, as soon as the parade was over, set off to play a football match against the infantry !   Such an attitude of mind must have seemed inexplicable to onlookers of other nationalities who could not understand the temperament of the British soldier, yet in a way the action was only natural.   The Great Pursuit was over ; nay, more, the war, the terrible nightmare of four years, was finished.   How could the realisation of such a mighty event be grasped in a moment by men who for months and years had been hourly awaiting death, and now saw death pass from them ?

CHAPTER XII.

FINALE.

AND so the work is done, the record finished. In all humbleness the pen was taken up to chronicle the deeds of these men; in all humbleness it is laid down again with the closing of the story. In mere bald words it has been impossible to describe the wonderful gallantry, the grand determination and the final success over insuperable difficulties which typified the men of the 33rd Divisional Artillery. The true tale of their heroism, of their suffering and sacrifice can never really be understood by any save those whose privilege it was to be a witness thereof, but the story of the battles in which they took part may perhaps convey a small idea of the glory of their war record.

In December, 1915, they had their first experience of active service; in November, 1918, the last " Cease Firing " sounded and their work was accomplished. In all those ten hundred and fifty days of war the batteries were in the line for over eight hundred days, and these figures offer perhaps the most striking testimonial that can be given of their work. They had been at one time the extreme right-hand unit of the British line, on another occasion at Nieuport they guarded the extreme left. On April 9th, 1917, the guns of one of the brigades were the first of the whole line to follow up the enemy in every successive advance; in November, 1918, they were the first guns to cross the River Sambre. All along the British front they fought, at Nieuport, amid the grim horrors of Passchendaele and Ypres, at Kemmel, Givenchy, Cambrin and Arras; in the ruins of Hebuterne and the wilderness of Gommecourt, High Wood and Delville Wood; in the sea of mud round Bouchavesnes and in the Somme marshes. In the dark days of early 1918 they held with glorious obstinacy and determination the gate of the north; in that wonderful autumn of the same year it was the 33rd Divisional Artillery who took part in that mighty onslaught which flung the enemy back upon his frontiers and ultimately forced him to ask for peace. At this point it would have been gratifying to have been able to record in fuller detail the individual services of various officers and men who were especially connected with the doings of the brigades and batteries during the war, yet to attempt to do such a thing is well-nigh impossible. Each and all contributed their share, each and all played a noble part, and who is to judge as between man and man in the scorching fires of battle? Elsewhere has been described the great work done by Colonel Frederick Hall, whose sheer determination and personal endeavour got all the batteries out to France within eleven months of the date of their first recruitment—a record probably unequalled by any other New Army unit. Already mention has been made of Brig.-General C. F. Blane who took the brigades out to France and initiated them in the rigours of active service; of Lieut.-Colonel Rochfort-Boyd who led the 156th Brigade in the earlier days, and of Lieut.-Colonel O. M. Harris who commanded so gallantly the 162nd; of Colonel A. H. S. Goff and Lieut.-Colonel L. T. Goff, and of Brig.-General C. G. Stewart who succeeded General Blane as C.R.A. of the Division. Already we have spoken of Lieut.-Colonel Butler and Lieut.-Colonel Skinner, the two Brigade Commanders of the latter period of the war, and of Brig.-General G. H. W. Nicholson who controlled the batteries in the final victorious advance in 1918. Yet memory still teems with the names of many others, for who is there from out of all the batteries who is not also worthy of mention? Major Johnston and Major Bennett, both killed on the Somme; Captain Heap and Lieut. Tucker who died at Arras; Majors Studd, Barstow and Fetherston who were never away from the Divisional Artillery for long; Taylor, Sheeres and Heads of the 156th Brigade, Warr the "Mayor of King's Clere"; Benett-Stanford and van Straubenzee of the 162nd Brigade; Cory and Pavitt, Lutyens and Hill, Talbot and Bruce, Turner and Barnes; Gallie who died at Passchendaele, Colonel Johnson and Captain Rhodes of the D.A.C., both killed at Zillebeke. There is no end to the names of those who should be spoken of, since for every name mentioned at least three more immediately present themselves to the mind. One and all did their best, and better than that no man can do.

To follow the movements of the 33rd Divisional Artillery after the Armistice would indeed seem an anti-climax, and yet, just as the story has been told of its first formation, the gradual evolving of a unit of artillery from the original raw mass, so must the final days be recorded until the date when the men cast from them the apparel of war and returned to civilian life once more, men who had for ever deserved from their country the full rights of Citizenship. From November 11th until the 14th the batteries remained in the areas they had been occupying when hostilities ceased, and on the

14th they turned their faces towards the west and began to retrace their steps over the scenes of the late fighting. It was not decreed that they should take part in the occupation of Germany, and accordingly they marched back through Forest, Bertry and Clary to billets in Villers Outreaux (156th) and Lesdain (162nd). Here they remained until December 6th and here, or rather at Crevecoeur near by, was held on November 22nd a thanksgiving service at which officers and men were decorated for gallantry in the fighting now past and done with; here also the men were visited by His Majesty the King who had come over to France to thank in person his victorious troops, and on December 6th began the six-day march to the last rest billets which the men were to occupy in France.

Two routes were followed, one by each brigade, and, as mile after mile rolled by, the batteries turned their backs once and for all upon ground which for them held memories that can never be effaced. Through Tincourt and Manancourt, past Riencourt and Meaulte where they had assembled before moving into the Somme battle of 1916, through Blangy-Tronville and Pont Noyelles, Le Mesge and Picquigny, on beyond Selincourt and St. Maulvis they marched until at last they reached their permanent billets around Brocourt-Liomer, Inval Boiron and Hornoy. Here they stopped and here, for many weeks, they passed the time in educational schemes, in physical training and recreation until such time as authority should permit of their return to civil life once more.

All through the war demobilisation, a return to England, to Peace with no threat of war hanging over their heads, had seemed to these men a wonderful dream which could never come true by any possibility, which was so far removed from the order of things as to be something quite intangible and incredible. It seemed that the war must still be in progress beyond the eastern horizon, that soon they must be flung into the scorching fires of battle again, that this talk of a return to England for ever was fantastic, imaginary —a trick of their brains. Yet even this most wonderful of events did actually occur; in March, 1919, all units were reduced to " Cadre A," the surplus men being sent to the Base for demobilisation, in May a further 25 per cent. of these cadres was dispatched home, and in the second week of June only an equipment guard remained with each battery.

In July these last remnants of the 33rd Divisional Artillery departed from the land of France which owed to them so much. All through the first week of the month the skeletons of the batteries entrained and moved to Havre, and the 9th found them in that port waiting for a ship to carry them home. On Thursday, the

10th, the 156th Brigade embarked for Southampton, on the 12th and 17th the D.A.C. followed, and on Sunday July 27th, 1919, the 162nd Brigade, last remaining unit of the 33rd Divisional Artillery, watched the quays and houses of Havre glide slowly by as the ship gathered way and headed for the coast of England.

Thus the Brigades left France and set foot in England again, their work accomplished, the battle won. Camberwell turned out and gave right royal welcome to its Gunners when, a few days later, they marched as victors through the crowded streets; and well might it be so, for they had returned with such glory as can hardly be believed of mortal man. Several days did the people spend in rejoicing and in welcoming their citizen-soldiers home once more, days in which the pangs and miseries of those dark times of watching and waiting were put aside and forgotten. Yet in all those festivities, beneath all the laughter and song of that week there was for ever present the divine and sacred memory of those whose good fortune it had not been to return from the battle, of those many hundreds who had died in the service of the guns of the 33rd Division and who lay in soldiers' graves along the length and breadth of the far-flung battle line. Their example, their sacrifice must stand for all time as a memorial and a constant reminder to those who come after of the price which has been paid that they may live, and there will ever remain to those who mourn the loss of many whose places can never be filled, the proud memory of their heroism and endurance, the glad knowledge of a man's part nobly played.

" Their seed shall remain for ever and their glory shall not be blotted out. Their bodies are buried in peace; but their name liveth for evermore."

THE END.

APPENDIX I.

CASUALTIES.

33rd Divisional Artillery.

1916.

Officers:
Killed 9
Wounded 43
Missing 1
———
Total 53

Other Ranks:
Killed 117
Wounded 419
Missing 5
———
Total 541

Officer Casualties.

Killed :

Baldwin, 2/Lt. H. D.
Bennett, Major W. P.
Briggs, 2/Lt. H. K.
Fell, 2/Lt. D. M.
Gardner, 2/Lt. F. G. B.

Haylett, 2/Lt. N.
Johnston, Major R. G. M.
Peerless, 2/Lt. C. S.
Prior, 2/Lt. M. S.

Wounded :

Barlow, 2/Lt. C. G.
Barstow, Capt. W. A. T.
Beresford, Lt. F. R.
Body, 2/Lt. M. M. I.
Collins, 2/Lt. G. R.
Cooper, 2/Lt. F. D'A.
Fisher, 2/Lt. L. E.
Forbes, 2/Lt. W. F.
Goff, Col. A. H. S.
Goff, Lt.-Col. L. T.
Greenwood, 2/Lt. T. A.
Hailey, 2/Lt. V.
Hancock, 2/Lt. G. E. L.
Harvey, 2/Lt. W. E.
Henley, 2/Lt. A. W.
Hewitt, 2/Lt. H. H.
Hill, Capt. L. R.
Huddart, 2/Lt. G. H.
Jacobs, 2/Lt. P. A.
Keable, 2/Lt. A. M.
Kernan, Capt. G. E.

Kerr, 2/Lt. J. C.
Macartney-Filgate, 2/Lt. J.
Maxwell, Capt. A.
Milne, 2/Lt. K. W.
Mocatta, 2/Lt. H.
Moore, Lt. C.
Murray, Major A. D.
Ormond, 2/Lt. E. C.
Osborne, 2/Lt. M.
Russell, Capt. R. D.
Shepherd, Lt. T. D.
Swinton, 2/Lt. R. A.
Tait, 2/Lt. J. A.
Thompson, Major R. H.
Turner, 2/Lt. K. F. S.
Vick, Lt. D. M.
Watson, Lt. W. D.
Watson, 2/Lt. J. Irvine.
White, 2/Lt. L. H.
Woodroffe, 2/Lt. F. G.
Wreford, 2/Lt. W. J.

Missing :
Elliott, 2/Lt. F. W.

CASUALTIES 1917.

156th Brigade, R.F.A.				162nd Brigade, R.F.A.			
Officers:		*Other Ranks:*		*Officers:*		*Other Ranks:*	
Killed ..	6	Killed ..	65*	Killed ..	7	Killed ..	62
Wounded	16	Wounded	281*	Wounded	22	Wounded	313
Missing ..	—	Missing ..	—	Missing ..	—	Missing ..	2
Total	22		346	Total	29		377

* Not quite complete.

GRAND TOTAL .. Officer Casualties   51

Other Ranks do.   723

Officer Casualties.

Killed :

Barlow, 2/Lt. C. G. (156th).
Barton, 2/Lt. V. A. (162nd).
Beerbohm, Capt. C. (156th).
Bostock, 2/Lt. N. S. (162nd).
Dean, 2/Lt. G. F. (162nd).
Fitch, 2/Lt. D. (162nd).
Grant, 2/Lt. N. (156th).
Heape, Capt. B. R. (162nd).

Johnson, Lt.-Col. A. G. (D.A.C.).
Lutyens, 2/Lt. C. J. (156th).
Neate, 2/Lt. A. B. (162nd).
Rhodes, Capt. H. (D.A.C.).
Tucker, 2/Lt. A. R. (162nd).
Vickers, 2/Lt. R. (162nd).
Wheatley, 2/Lt. E. R. (156th).
Wimbush, 2/Lt. E. T. (D.A.C.).

Wounded :

Barstow, Major W. A. T. (156th).
Beadle, 2/Lt. F. W. (156th).
Beal, 2/Lt. S. N. (162nd).
Benett-Stanford, Major V. (162nd).
Body, Capt. M. M. I. (162nd).
Bloor, 2/Lt. C. A. (156th).
Bunbury, Capt. T. St. P. (162nd).
Chapman, 2/Lt. J. G. J. (162nd).
Colfox, Major W. P. (162nd).
Cunis, Lt. V. W. (162nd).
Donovan, 2/Lt. E. T. G. (162nd).
Edwards, 2/Lt. H. R. (162nd).
Escott, 2/Lt. H. J. (162nd).
Hanna, 2/Lt. P. R. (156th).
Hannaford, 2/Lt. W. (162nd).
Harrison, 2/Lt. W. E. (162nd).
Howard, 2/Lt. L. M. (162nd).
Kitchin, 2/Lt. E. J. H. (162nd).
Lee, Major F. L. (162nd).

Leigh, 2/Lt. R. (156th).
MacDonald, 2/Lt. A. (156th).
McEwan, 2/Lt. A. (156th).
McLeod, 2/Lt. D. (156th).
Molyneux, 2/Lt. H. P. (156th).
Mousley, 2/Lt. (156th).
Odhams, 2/Lt. R. C. (162nd).
Oxley, Lt. B. L. (156th).
Phipps, 2/Lt. H. E. (156th).
Revels, 2/Lt. D. (156th).
Sall, 2/Lt. B. (156th).
Thompson, 2/Lt. H. A. (162nd).
van Straubenzee, Capt. A. (162nd).
Walker, Major C. H. (162nd).
Whiting, 2/Lt. A. H. (D.A.C.)
Willett, 2/Lt. S. W. (156th).
Wingfield, 2/Lt. R. M. (156th).
Two others—unknown.

CASUALTIES 1918.

156th Brigade, R.F.A.

Officers :		Other Ranks :	
Killed ..	3*	Killed	Lists un-
Wounded	7*	Wounded	obtain-
Missing ..	2	Missing	able.

162nd Brigade, R.F.A.

Officers :		Other Ranks :	
Killed ..	2	Killed ..	49
Wounded	21	Wounded ..	266
Total	23	Total	315

* Lists incomplete.

Officer Casualties.

Killed :

Bruce, Lt. W. G. (156th).
Bruce, 2/Lt. A. P. (156th).
Butler, Lt.-Col. B. A. B. (156th).

Essex, Lt. E. C. (162nd).
Squire, 2/Lt. C. A. (162nd).

Missing :

Blackwell, 2/Lt. K. R. (156th).

Clow, 2/Lt. O. W. (156th).

Wounded :

Barker, Major A. (156th).
Bedford-Pim, Lt.-Col. G. (162nd).
Coleman, Capt. G. (162nd).
Cory, Major H. C. (162nd).
Escott, 2/Lt. H. J. (162nd).
Evans, 2/Lt. A. J. (162nd).
Fetherston, Major G. (162nd).
Garrod, Lt. R. G. (162nd).
Gough, Lt. H. L. R. (162nd).
Greig, 2/Lt. J. G. (156th).
Groves, 2/Lt. F. E. S. (156th).
Hadley, 2/Lt. P. A. S. (162nd).
Herlihy, 2/Lt. W. (162nd).
Lawson, 2/Lt. E. B. (156th).

McNabb, 2/Lt. I. B. (162nd).
Mitcheson, 2/Lt. J. C. (162nd).
Paterson, Lt. B. S. McC. (162nd).
Pavitt, Capt. and Adjt. R. H. (162nd).
Phipps, 2/Lt. H. E. (156th).
Rollason, 2/Lt. M. H. (162nd).
Saunders, 2/Lt. G. (162nd).
Skinner, Lt.-Col. E. J. (162nd).
Tetlow, 2/Lt. (156th).
Warren, Lt. F. D. (162nd).
Williamson, Lt. G. W. (156th).
Wimshurst, 2/Lt. T. E. (162nd).
Two others—unknown.

APPENDIX II.

A LIST OF THE VARIOUS DIVISIONS THE INFANTRY OF WHICH WERE COVERED BY THE GUNS OF THE 33RD DIVISIONAL ARTILLERY IN FRANCE AND FLANDERS.

La Bassée.

February—July, 1916	33rd Division.
	39th Division.

Battle of the Somme.

July—September, 1916	1st Division.
	5th Division.
	7th Division.
	14th Division.
	24th Division.
	33rd Division.
	51st Division.

Dainville, Hebuterne and the Battle of the Ancre.

September—November, 1916	12th Division.
	31st Division.
	33rd Division.
	35th Division.
	49th Division.

The Somme.

November, 1916—March, 1917	4th Division.
	8th Division.
	33rd Division.
	40th Division.

Battle of Arras.

April—June, 1917	Cavalry Division.
	3rd Division.
	4th Division.
	9th Division.
	12th Division.
	15th Division.
	17th Division.
	29th Division.
	37th Division.

Hindenburg Line and the Coast.

June—August, 1917	49th Division.
	50th Division.
	66th Division.

Battles of Ypres and Passchendaele.

September—November, 1917	5th Division.
	7th Division.
	17th Division.
	23rd Division.
	24th Division.
	33rd Division.

Passchendaele.

December, 1917—	33rd Division.
April, 1918	50th Division.

German Flanders Offensive, Kemmel.

April—August, 1918	6th Division.
	9th Division.
	19th Division.
	33rd Division.
	49th Division.
	28th French Division.
	44th French Regiment.
	46th French Regiment.
	30th American Division.

British Final Offensive, 3rd Army.

September—November, 1918	17th Division.
	21st Division.
	33rd Division.
	38th Division.

APPENDIX III.

THE VARIOUS SECTORS OF THE BATTLE-LINE IN FRANCE AND FLANDERS,

Together with the Official Names of the Battles in which the 33rd Divisional Artillery took part.

Period.	Sector.	Battles.
Dec. 1915–July 1916	La Bassée. Givenchy–Cuinchy.	(Holding the line.)
July–Sept. 1916.	The Somme. High Wood–Delville Wood.	The Battles of the Somme 1916 : (i.) Battle of Bazentin Ridge. (ii.) Battle of Delville Wood. (iii.) Attacks on High Wood. (iv.) Battle of Guillemont.
Sept.–Nov. 1916.	Dainville. Hebuterne–Gommecourt.	(Holding the line.) The Battle of the Ancre 1916.
Dec. 1916–Mar. 1917.	Bouchavesnes–Clery-sur-Somme.	(Holding the line.)
April–June 1917.	Arras. Feuchy–Monchy.	The Battles of Arras 1917 : (i.) First Battle of the Scarpe 1917. (ii.) Second Battle of the Scarpe 1917. (iii.) Battle of Arleux. (iv.) Third Battle of the Scarpe 1917. (a) Capture of Roeux.
June–July 1917.	Cherisy–Bullecourt.	(Holding the line.)

Period.	Sector.	Battles.
July–August 1917.	Nieuport.	(Preparation for an offensive.)
Sept.–Nov. 1917.	Ypres Salient.	(i.) Battle of the Menin Road Ridge.
	Reutel–Gheluvelt.	(ii.) Battle of Polygon Wood.
		(iii.) Battle of Broodseinde.
		(iv.) Battle of Poelcappelle.
		(v.) First Battle of Passchendaele.
		(vi.) Second Battle of Passchendaele.
Dec. 1917–April 1918.	Ypres Salient. Passchendaele.	(Holding the line.)
April–August 1918.	Ypres Salient. Mt. Kemmel.	The Battles of the Lys :
		(i.) Battle of Messines 1918.
		(ii.) Battle of Bailleul.
		(iii.) First Battle of Kemmel Ridge.
		(iv.) Second Battle of Kemmel Ridge.
		(v.) Battle of the Scherpenberg
Sept.–Nov. 1918.	Third Army. Peizière–Bertry–Englefontaine–Forêt de Mormal –Wattignies	The Battles of the Hindenburg Line :
		(i.) Battle of Epehy.
		(ii.) Battle of the St. Quentin Canal.
		(iii.) Battle of the Beaurevoir Line.
		(iv.) Battle of Cambrai 1918.
		The Battle of the Selle.
		The Battle of Valenciennes.
		The Battle of the Sambre.

INDEX.

P